[1282z].

First edn.

£25:
cat.

English
Church
Monuments

English Church Monuments

Brian Kemp

B.T. Batsford Ltd London

For my mother and in memory of my father

The illustrations on the endpapers are: *front* the Savage monument (*c.*1631) at Elmley Castle, Worcestershire, and *back* the monument of Lionel 6th Lord Welles (d.1461) at Methley, Yorkshire

First published 1980
© Brian Kemp 1980

ISBN 0 7134 1735 8

Filmset in Monophoto Garamond by
Servis Filmsetting Ltd, Manchester

Printed in Great Britain by
The Anchor Press Ltd, Tiptree, Essex
for the publishers B.T. Batsford Ltd,
4 Fitzhardinge Street,
London W1H 0AH

Contents

List of Illustrations

Acknowledgments

The author is greatly indebted to a number of people in the preparation of this book. In the first place grateful thanks must go to the deans and chapters of cathedrals and to the many clergymen and/or churchwardens of parish churches who have so generously consented to photographs being taken of the monuments in their care and, in several cases, to the reproduction of photographs in this book. Similarly, grateful acknowledgment is extended to the lay owners of private or family chapels for their courtesy in allowing access and photography. The author is indebted to the staff of the Photographic Unit at Reading University for their painstaking concern and skill in the preparation of photographs. Equally, he has benefited from discussions with colleagues at Reading University on a number of points, especially Miss Jane Gardner, Dr Ralph Houlbrooke and the Rev. David Meara, to whom he offers his appreciation. The greatest debts of gratitude are due, however, to Miss Julia Boorman, who patiently read and criticized the text at various stages of composition, and to Mr Simon Eager, who generously gave up a great deal of time to photographing monuments in many parts of the country. Certainly without their ever-ready help and constant encouragement this book could not have been written, and their contribution to its completion is warmly acknowledged.

The author and publishers would like to thank the following for their permission to reproduce the photographs included in this book:

S.T. Eager: 1, 2, 5, 7, 8, 9, 11, 12, 16, 17, 18, 19, 20, 21, 22, 23, 24, 25, 30, 32, 34, 36, 39, 46, 47, 49, 52, 53, 55, 56, 57, 58, 60, 61, 62, 64, 65, 66, 67, 68, 69, 71, 72, 73, 76, 77, 78, 79, 81, 82, 83, 85, 86, 87, 89, 91, 94, 95, 96, 97, 100, 101, 102, 103, 104, 105, 106, 107, 108, 109, 110, 111, 113, 114, 117, 118, 119, 120, 121, 122, 123, 124, 125, 126, 128, 129, 130, 131, 132, 133, 134, 135, 136, 137, 138, 139, 140, 141, 147, 149, 150, 151, 155, 156, 157, 158, 159, 160, 161, 162, 164, 166, 167, 168, 170, 172, 173, 174, 175

The above reproduced by courtesy of the rectors or vicars and/or churchwardens of the churches concerned, and as follows:

5: By permission of the Dean and Chapter of Peterborough
11, 100, 160, 164: Reproduced by courtesy of the Dean and Chapter of Westminster
16: By permission of the Dean and Chapter of Gloucester
17, 67: By permission of the Dean and Chapter of Exeter
18, 132: By permission of the Dean and Chapter of Winchester
30: By permission of the Holland House Estates
58: By courtesy of the Marquess of Salisbury
79: By courtesy of Lord Hazlerigg
124, 138: By courtesy of Lord Brownlow
130: By permission of the Church Corporation, Ottery St Mary
131, 172: By permission of the Dean and chapter of Wells
140: By permission of the Dean and Chapter of Lincoln
147: By permission of the Dean and Chapter of Ely

Note: the churches of Melbury Sampford (Dorset) and Noseley (Leics) are private chapels not normally accessible without permission.

the late H. Felton: 80, 116, 153

B.W. Fisk-Moore: 145

A.F. Kersting: 6, 15, 35, 98, 143

Eric de Maré: 90

L. Maylott: 59

The National Monuments Record: 3, 4, 10, 13, 33, 40, 44, 50, 51, 54, 75, 84, 88, 93, 99, 115, 144, 146, 152, 154, 163, 165, 176

S. Pitcher F.R.P.S.: 70

Canon Ridgeway (for photographs by the late F.H. Crossley): 31, 48, 112

Professor L. Stone: 74

Windsor-Spice Ltd, Reigate: 92

Nos. 14, 45, and 127 are from the publishers' collection

Nos. 26, 27, 28, 29, 37, 38, 41, 42, 43, 63, 142, 148, 169, 171 are from brass rubbings by the author.

Note

All references to county locations in this book are in accordance with county boundaries as they were before the local government re-organization of the 1970s.

1 *Introduction*

Despite the decline of organized religion in this country, old churches have a continuing and increasing appeal. They are visited for a variety of reasons, but among their most appealing features are the memorials to the dead which they contain, for these have an interest peculiarly personal, and the majority of churches, even those whose buildings are not particularly old or rewarding, have one or more of note. Some churches, especially those which have maintained close links with a great house over the centuries, contain large numbers of monuments. The most spectacular case is the church of Bottesford (Leics), dominated by its monuments to the earls of Rutland, but examples can be found throughout the country, the church often standing close alongside the great house, as at Lydiard Tregoze (Wilts), for long the seat of the St John family. The largest single collection of monuments, however, is in Westminster Abbey, which possesses one of the richest and most varied series to be seen anywhere in Europe.

This book has been written to provide a general introduction to the subject of English church monuments, and to indicate some, at least, of the range of interest which they afford. It is concerned solely with funerary monuments erected inside churches and other places of worship – cathedrals, abbeys, chapels, and so on – and not with memorials set up in graveyards or other exterior locations. Moreover, the survey is confined somewhat arbitrarily to England, even though English monument-making originated and developed within a European context and, as we shall see, was subject from time to time to a variety of influences from the Continent. The aim has been primarily not to investigate the social and economic factors affecting the erection of monuments, although these have inevitably been mentioned, but rather to describe, and where possible to explain, the changing forms of monuments and their varying character against a basically chronological framework.

Regrettably the content of monumental inscriptions has had largely to be left out of the account, since, although these are often of great interest and very rewarding to read, they constitute a topic so vast that the merest and most unsatisfactory treatment would have been possible in a work of this size.

We know that the Anglo-Saxons were in the habit of erecting memorial crosses and grave-stones in the open, and indeed considerable numbers of these survive, although many have now been brought indoors, like, for example, the splendid carved stones at Ramsbury (Wilts). There is also slight documentary evidence for the setting up of memorials inside important churches in the late Anglo-Saxon period, but this appears to have been extremely rare and no example has come down to us. The continuous history of English church monument-making begins after the Norman Conquest and, in particular, after the beginning of the twelfth century, from which time the earliest extant examples, in the form of carved coffin lids and grave slabs, have survived. The practice was associated with the burial of persons inside churches, a privilege limited at first to such distinguished people as royalty, high-ranking ecclesiastics and lay founders of churches. Gradually, however, the right was extended to others (though most people could never expect more than a graveyard burial) and monuments slowly became more numerous. Moreover, as the fashion for monuments took root, their character was developed and diversified. The middle ages evolved a range of monumental types in varying degrees of size and magnificence, and later periods added new forms reflecting successive waves of stylistic influence. Perhaps the greatest period of monumental activity was the long span between *c.*1300 and *c.*1800, typified by the erection of enormous monuments comprising effigies and other figures often in elaborate architectural settings, but throughout and beyond this period even larger numbers of less pretentious monuments to suit more slender pockets were produced. In short, for much of the last eight and a half centuries a vast amount of money, materials and artistic effort has been expended on the production of funerary monuments for the dead. In the twentieth century, however, the practice has steadily declined and, particularly since the Second World War, virtually disappeared. Memorials have increasingly taken the form of stained glass windows or the provision of new items of church furniture, such as lecterns, screens and the like; and, apart from plain wall plaques with simple inscriptions, monuments in the tradition of the past have fallen completely out of fashion. The reasons are complex and beyond the scope of this book, but the result has been that the present century has to all intents and purposes brought the long story of church monument-making in England to an end.

The fact that monuments were produced in considerable numbers over so long a period gives the subject an added attraction, since, apart from the interest of individual pieces, it enables comparisons to be drawn at different times between a variety of aspects. The latter are many and diverse. In the first place, there is the personal aspect, which sets monuments apart from all other features found in churches. Monuments, especially those with effigies, give one a link across the centuries with, say, a knight of the thirteenth century, a great lady of the fifteenth century, a lawyer of the sixteenth, a bishop of the seventeenth, a duchess of the eighteenth, or an industrialist of the nineteenth. Many of those commemorated are now forgotten, except in so far as they live on in their monuments, but others are famous figures from the past whose memorials have a special historical appeal. They include kings and queens (mainly in Westminster Abbey, but also at Canterbury, Gloucester, Windsor and Worcester), statesmen (such as Disraeli at Hughenden), ecclesiastics (like William of Wykeham at Winchester), military and naval celebrities (such as Lord Nelson in St Paul's cathedral), literary men (including Shakespeare at Stratford-on-Avon), scientists and inventors (like William Harvey at Hempstead and James Watt at Handsworth), and so on.

Secondly, there is the question of changing forms and the emergence of new types of monuments, and of successive fashions in their embellishment and decorative enrichment. At almost every period monuments had a close affinity with contemporary styles in architecture, which they reflected in their designs. The large canopied monuments developed

in the middle ages, for instance, clearly adopted the same architectural styles as church-building of the period, and in a similar way the classical entablatures and pediments on those of the seventeenth and eighteenth centuries were the equivalent of features on great houses and churches built at that time. Likewise, monumental decoration mirrored contemporary fashions, whether these were in a Gothic, Renaissance, Baroque, Rococo, Neo-classical or Gothic Revival taste. Much of this book is devoted to an examination of these aspects in an attempt to provide a simple kind of 'type series' of developments.

The treatment of effigies of the deceased provides a further point of interest, for, although the earliest depictions were in a rather stiff recumbent (or apparently recumbent) attitude, in the course of our period all manner of alternative postures were evolved, some more common at certain times than others. Moreover, partial depictions of the deceased, such as busts or medallion portraits, enjoyed a wide appeal in the post-medieval centuries. The popularity of particular postures or depictions at particular times was often the result, not of mere chance or whim, but of the ascendancy of certain styles or religious attitudes. These aspects will equally be explored in some detail in the following chapters.

Effigies present other features of interest. They are in particular very valuable in the study of the history of armour and dress, their value becoming proportionally greater the older they are. For much of the medieval period, from which almost no original dress and precious few pieces of armour have survived, effigies are a primary source of the utmost importance, matched only by depictions of dress and armour in paintings and illuminated manuscripts. Accordingly, it has been thought useful to include in the chapter on medieval monuments a substantial section on dress and armour which, while in no way aiming to be comprehensive, indicates the wealth of evidence available and gives some idea of what can be learnt in this respect from medieval effigies. In the chapters on later periods progressively less attention has been paid specifically to dress and armour, since monumental evidence is increasingly supplemented by other material, but effigies continued throughout to provide instructive and often finely detailed examples of contemporary styles and fashions. There is one major qualification to this, however, namely the practice, which grew steadily in the later seventeenth century and was at its height between 1720 and 1750, of depicting men and women in classical Roman dress or armour. It did not affect judges, ecclesiastics and others who were shown in official robes, but for a majority of monumental effigies it meant the disappearance of contemporary dress and in consequence an absence of this type of evidence for the modern student. The same is true, but to a far lesser extent, of relief effigies produced during the heyday of Neo-classicism in the early nineteenth century.

Moreover, monuments in general, and effigies in particular, are of the greatest importance in the history of English sculpture. The great bulk of medieval figure sculpture that has come down to us is monumental sculpture, for, although the middle ages were equally prolific in the production of sculpture for other religious and secular purposes, most of it has been destroyed or damaged by religious iconoclasm or severely weathered by time and the elements. Without the survival of medieval effigies and such ancillary figures as weepers, angels and saints, therefore, our knowledge of sculptural skills in the middle ages would be sadly impoverished. Furthermore, for much of the post-medieval period the main outlet for the figure sculptor's art was the funerary monument. It is true that private patrons from the seventeenth century onward increasingly required statuary, busts and the like in their houses and gardens, and that corporate and public bodies commissioned similar pieces with increasing frequency in the eighteenth and nineteenth centuries. Nevertheless, it is doubtful whether the majority of sculptors could have survived, even in quite modern times, without the continuing demand for monuments with effigies and other figures, and indeed a number of masters devoted their efforts largely or exclusively to this sort of work. Certainly, therefore, no student of English sculpture can afford to ignore monuments. For this reason the present work is full of references to sculptors, and in many cases monuments which have been cited or illustrated have been attributed. The latter task becomes progressively easier from the first half of the seventeenth century onward, since the habit developed and grew of sculptors carving their 'signatures' on monuments.

One cannot fail to be impressed also by the wealth of symbolism and allegory on monuments. In a sense, the very making of a monument was itself a symbolic act, but beyond that a whole range of symbolic and allegorical conventions formed part of monumental designs and iconography from the earliest days. Although the habit rose to its height in the seventeenth and eighteenth centuries, it can be found in operation at all times. Predictably, death and mortality, resurrection and eternity were favourite themes, and were symbolized or represented in an astonishing variety of ways at different periods. In addition, there was the symbolism of the Christian faith and the multiform symbolism of the secular world. The latter included heraldry, which after the early thirteenth century became an almost universal feature of monumental enrichment, for heraldry was essentially a form of symbolic shorthand displaying the family and marriage connections of the deceased. In view of the immense importance and varied nature of symbolism and allegory of all kinds on monuments, a separate chapter has been devoted to the subject at the end of this book.

Finally, a little should be said by way of introduction to the available literature on funerary monuments. This book is thought to be the first to attempt a general survey of the subject over the whole period from the early twelfth to the late nineteenth centuries, but it could not have been written without the assistance of a great deal of earlier work by other scholars, published in the books named in the reading list and in a host of articles and specialized studies not listed. A number of these books are, sadly, now out of print and scarce, more particularly the pioneering works of the late Mrs K.A. Esdaile on post-medieval monuments. Although medieval monuments and effigies had long been objects of interest and serious study, yielding in this century the major works by F.H. Crossley and A. Gardner among others, those of more recent periods (and especially after 1600) had been largely neglected until Mrs Esdaile's tireless and well-informed advocacy of their value and importance in the twentieth century. By her scholarly awakening of interest in these monuments, she provided a sound base on which other scholars could build. Among the most impressive results was the work of the late Dr Margaret Whinney, set out most fully in her masterly study on *English Sculpture 1530–1830*, which, though not concerned only with monuments, contains a mine of information on this aspect of her theme. Another is R. Gunnis's *Dictionary of British Sculptors 1660–1851*, which is an indispensable guide for anyone interested in particular monumental sculptors in that period. In recent years has come the seminal work of Dr Nicholas Penny, whose book on *Church Monuments in Romantic England* provides for the first time a systematic account of monuments between about 1780 and 1840.

In the field of monumental brasses and incised slabs, the past decade has seen the publication of major definitive works, by Malcolm Norris and the late F.A. Greenhill, respectively, which mark the culmination of over a century's devoted study by an army of scholars and dedicated amateurs. The study of Victorian brasses is still in its infancy, but it is well in hand and important contributions to its progress have been made by Richard Busby in *A Companion Guide to Brasses and Brass Rubbing* and

elsewhere.

There is no doubt that both specialized and general public interest in church monuments is on the increase. It is significant, for instance, that as recently as 1978 an 'International Society for the Study of Church Monuments' was founded in London, to complement the activities of the much older and venerable 'Monumental Brass Society'. The present work is offered as a contribution to fostering this interest. If readers are stimulated to pursue the subject in more depth through the detailed works mentioned above and listed in the bibliography, the author's efforts will have been amply justified.

2 The Middle Ages
c.1100-c.1530

Early Coffin Lids and Grave Slabs

Monument-making in the middle ages began very simply with the practice of allowing the carved lids of stone coffins to remain exposed in the floors of churches to provide permanent memorials of those buried beneath. The practice probably developed in the later eleventh century not long after the Norman Conquest, but the oldest surviving coffin lids and grave slabs which clearly served this purpose date from the early twelfth century. Though rare at first, they grew in number in the later twelfth and thirteenth centuries and, despite the emergence of more elaborate memorials, persisted into the fourteenth century. Most of them had a characteristically tapering shape, wider at the head than at the foot, and, although a number in the twelfth century were given coped tops, the majority were flat. Their carving was invariably in low relief, very flat and entirely confined by the dimensions and outline of the slab, its motifs being mainly decorative or symbolic, but, even in the early twelfth century, occasionally taking the form of an effigy of the deceased.

Carving of a largely decorative nature occurred chiefly on slabs of the twelfth century, more especially on those dating from the late Norman period. Such carving had little direct relevance to the context of a funerary monument, but was merely the application to that medium of the standard motifs of twelfth-century craftsmen. Stylized foliage and grotesque animals are cases in point. They occur on two excellent and densely carved slabs in St Peter's, Northampton (*1*), and at Conisbrough (Yorks), both dating from *c.*1150. The former has a prominent foliage trail emerging from the mouth of a human face and inhabited by grotesque beasts, the latter foliage trails and beasts forming part of a crowded scheme which also includes signs of the Zodiac and human figures. Among other examples, grotesque beasts without foliage are the main

features on a Tournai marble slab of approximately the same date in Bridlington priory (Yorks), while on an elegant late twelfth-century slab of the same material at Southover in Lewes (Sussex), inscribed to the memory of Gundreda de Warenne, the principal decoration consists of foliage in the highly stylized form of palmettes.

On other slabs specifically Christian motifs were employed, the most important and frequent of which was the Cross. It appeared in a variety of forms, often alone but sometimes in association with other features, and remained the dominant motif for as long as carved coffin lids were made. Examples of its use in the twelfth century can be seen on slabs at Pamber End (Hants), where the cross is foliated, at Milton Bryan (Beds), an unconventional form accompanied by a pattern of interlace, and at Bishopstone (Sussex), where the cross is combined with the other Christian symbols of the Lamb of God and two doves drinking from a vase. Numerous thirteenth-century crosses of various kinds remain in all parts of the country, often enriched with stylized foliage to form attractive foliated crosses. A simple example occurs on a coffin lid in Blyth priory (Notts), in which the arms of the cross fork into curled leaf buds and the shaft has pairs of leaves sprouting all the way up. In elaborate forms the foliage was more organic and rampant, sometimes spreading out over the entire slab to produce a highly decorative effect. At Studley (Warks) (*2*), for instance, the cross has a foliated head and leafy branches growing from the top of its shaft, while at Middleton Tyas (Yorks) trails of six-lobed leaves emerge from the shaft of an elaborately foliated cross, the edges of the slab being further decorated with rows of leaves. One of the most extreme and beautiful examples, now unfortunately broken, is in Hereford cathedral, where the foliation is so rich as almost to obscure the outline of the cross.

Examples of Christian imagery without the cross

were also produced, particularly in the twelfth century. A Tree of Jesse, for instance, occurs on a Tournai slab in Loncoln cathedral, reputed to be the monument of Bishop Remigius (d.1092) but possibly dating from the mid-twelfth century, while another Tournai slab in Ely cathedral, probably that of Bishop Nigel (d.1169) (*147*), shows a large standing angel holding the diminutive soul of the deceased, a remarkably early use of what was to become a stock symbol on monuments for the salvation of the soul.

Yet other slabs were carved with symbols indicating the calling or profession of the deceased. An early case occurs in Chichester cathedral, where the coped coffin lid of Bishop Ralph Luffa, the builder of the Norman cathedral who died in 1123, displays a mitre and crozier, a precedent followed later by other episcopal monuments there. This kind of symbolism became more common in the thirteenth century. Of that date, for example, the slab of a knight at Stoke Golding (Leics) has a plain sword, another at Butterwick (Yorks) a sword and shield with foliage. In other instances military trophies were combined with the cross, as at Musgrave and Warcop (both Westmorland), where the cross appears with a sword, and in Durham cathedral, where it is accompanied by a sword and a bow. Crafts and trades were likewise represented by appropriate symbols, as can be seen, for example, on two coffin lids in St John's, Chester, which have respectively a hammer and tongs for a blacksmith, and scissors and a glove for a glover.

The Development of Monumental Effigies

By far the most significant of the early coffin slabs, however, were those which showed an effigy of the deceased, for from these momentous developments were to come. In the twelfth century the effigies are exclusively of ecclesiastics, particularly abbots and bishops. Pride of place belongs to Westminster Abbey, for it possesses what is probably the earliest surviving monumental effigy in England, that of Abbot Gilbert Crispin, who died in 1117 or 1118. His tapered coffin lid, preserved in the cloister, shows him carved very primitively in low relief within a panel sunk in the flat surface of the slab. Although very badly worn and devoid of all detail, the full-length figure of an abbot, bareheaded and holding an abbatial staff in his right hand, can clearly be made out. It is a precious object, despite

its poor condition, but more important on account of their better preservation are two slabs of bishops in Salisbury cathedral. They represent Bishop Roger (d.1139) and Bishop Jocelin de Bohun (d.1184). The former (*3*) is of Tournai marble, a costly foreign material fashionable in England in the mid-twelfth century, and may well have been imported as a finished article from the Low Countries a few years after the bishop's death. It is probably not, therefore, a native English work, but it has survived so remarkably unscathed (except for the head of the effigy, which was for some reason replaced in the fourteenth century) that it must be regarded as the earliest well-preserved effigy still extant in England. It is an excellent example of the shallow carving which characterizes these early representations. The treatment of the figure is in very general terms akin to that of Abbot Gilbert's at Westminster, for the bishop is, as it were, sunk in the slab and does not, apart from the later high-relief head, rise at all above its level surface. The portrayal is flat, stiff and diagrammatic.

Bishop Jocelin's slab (*4*) provides an instructive comparison, for by 1184 the figure and other features, rather than being carved into the slab in sunken fashion, are carved out of the slab and made to appear in raised low relief by cutting back the slab around them. The monument conveys an altogether more rounded and three-dimensional impression, with a more developed awareness of the contours of the bishop's body beneath his vestments. Moreover, the head appears slightly raised, an effect enhanced by allowing the front peak of the bishop's mitre to lie over the shallow surround of his head. Thus, although the figure remains a predominantly flat representation, it has begun to free itself, so to speak, from the constraints of a primarily two-dimensional medium.

Roughly contemporary with Bishop Jocelin's monument are two important slabs at other places in south-west England. Exeter cathedral has the full-length effigy of Bishop Bartholomew (d.1184), but in spite of its date its modelling is cruder and less advanced than that of Jocelin, and in its flat sunken carving is more reminiscent of Bishop Roger's memorial. In Sherborne abbey (Dorset) there survives a fragment (head and shoulders only) of a memorial slab of Abbot Clement, who died between 1175 and 1189 (and not, as is often stated, in *c.*1160) and who is identified by the inscription incised on the surround of his head. This surround is somewhat similar to that of Bishop Jocelin's at Salisbury

1 St Peter's, Northampton: coffin slab (*c*.1150)

2 Studley (Warks): coffin lid (thirteenth century)

3 Salisbury cathedral: Bishop Roger (d.1139)

4 Salisbury cathedral: Bishop Jocelin de Bohun (d.1184)

5 Peterborough cathedral: Abbot Benedict (d.1193)

and both monuments are of Purbeck marble, the English material which among others superseded Tournai marble for high-quality work in the second half of the twelfth century. In so far as one can judge from the Sherborne fragment, the relief and treatment of the figure might also have been similar to Jocelin's, while the close relations existing between Sherborne abbey and Salisbury cathedral at this time would make a common workshop not unlikely. All this fits very well with a date in the 1180s for Abbot Clement's monument.

The next stage of development can best be illustrated at Peterborough cathedral (a Benedictine abbey until the Reformation), for it contains five slabs of abbots, identified as such by the abbatial staffs held by the effigies and dating on stylistic grounds from the late twelfth and early thirteenth centuries. All are of Alwalton marble and all save one show the effigy in a kind of shafted niche. One of the best preserved is possibly also the earliest, to judge from the simple water-leaf capitals of the side-shafts, and may represent Abbot Benedict (d. 1193) (5), while another cannot be much later in view of the bearded face of the effigy, even though the figure is housed in a cinquefoil-headed niche. The major point for the present purpose, however, is that all present the effigy in higher relief than has yet been seen, with a more undulating treatment of the figure, more rounded modelling of the head and more care in portraying the folds of vestments.

Slightly higher in relief than the Peterborough effigies is the fine effigy of Bishop Henry Marshal (d. 1206) in Exeter cathedral. The mitred head, the left hand holding a crozier and the feet are especially prominent, the carving of the face is more deliberate and the bishop's torso rises noticeably higher than the lower part of his figure, creating a pronounced 'slope' of the effigy from head to foot. However, although the figure appears in quite high relief, particularly in relation to the arched niche which surrounds him, the detail on the vestments is in very low relief, rather stiff and unrealistic, quite unlike the very competent rendering of folds which was later to be achieved in, for instance, the effigy of Archbishop Walter de Gray (d. 1255) in York Minster. A distinct move in this direction is apparent in a remarkable series of episcopal figures of stone in Wells cathedral, which represent Saxon bishops of Wells and of which most, judging by the close similarity of their carving and stiff-leaf decoration, were made at the same time, probably in the 1220s. They are all in high relief, with their vestments hanging in many deeply-cut folds and their hands placed in varying relaxed positions.

At this point the monopoly of ecclesiastical effigies is broken by the first appearance of effigies of laymen, particularly knights. It has been claimed that some effigies of knights, notably certain of those in the Temple Church in London, belong to the twelfth century, but in truth none can be dated definitely earlier than the 1220s. In fact the dating of most thirteenth-century military effigies is highly problematical, and in many instances dates and identifications attributed long ago on flimsy or insecure evidence continue to be repeated without serious re-examination. There is an additional difficulty, which is common to all early monuments and to many later ones as well, of not knowing precisely when an effigy was made (even if one can be sure of its personal identification), since several years may have separated the dates of death and manufacture of the memorial. Much further study is needed before a more accurate sequence of military effigies can be established, and for the moment individual dates must remain approximate. Nevertheless, enough is known to enable a picture of very general outline to be drawn. The thirteenth century also saw the first of the English royal effigies, that of King John in Worcester cathedral, and the earliest figures of ladies and laymen in civilian dress. Moreover, the range of materials was extended with the production of wooden and metal effigies, the first of the latter being the gilt bronze figure of King Henry III in Westminster Abbey. There is thus an altogether larger and more varied corpus of effigies available for study.

In its intrinsic quality and almost perfect preservation the effigy of King John (d. 1216) (6), made of Purbeck marble in about 1230, is one of the finest pieces yet encountered. It is of superb draughtsmanship and execution. The king is carved in the highest relief on a slab bare except for two small figures of bishops censing his head and a lion at his feet, and lies in quiet nobility, his face finely modelled and his robes falling round his body in natural and carefully observed folds whose verisimilitude is enhanced by varying the depth of carving. When first made, with its original painted colouring and insets of semi-precious stones, it must have presented a most realistic image of a recumbent monarch and set a new standard for monument-making in England. Despite this, however, the effigy is integral with the slab from which it is carved and, in the absence of undercutting in the sculpture, particularly evident when viewed from the side, remains a figure in relief rather than a free effigy.

Among the earliest effigies of knights are those of (supposedly) William Marshal, earl of Pembroke (d.1219) in the Temple Church and William Longsword, earl of Salisbury (d.1226) in Salisbury cathedral. The former may be a little earlier than King John's monument, the latter possibly contemporary with it. Effigies of knights provided greater scope for freeing the effigy from the slab in that the arms and legs, not being clothed in loose robes, tended to encourage a more articulated form and the beginnings of undercutting. William Marshal (if such he be), although restored in the nineteenth century and damaged in a Second World War air-raid, shows this very clearly, for, while his head and upper body lie closely to the slab, his mailed legs are undercut and rise quite free of it, returning to contact at the feet. The splendid figure of William Longsword is not undercut in this way, but on the other hand the treatment of the effigy is so rounded, with the head perfectly formed and the folds of the surcoat handled in the competent manner of King John's robes, that, coupled with the relaxed attitude, the impression is approaching that of an effigy lying upon the slab. Like King John the earl rests his head on a pillow and there is no ornamental surround on the surface of the slab. These features are common to all the earliest lay effigies and provide a notable contrast with those of ecclesiastics. Whereas the latter, despite the fact that their slabs were laid flat, were almost always before the fourteenth century shown standing in canopied niches, the early lay effigies were represented as (apparently) recumbent, with pillows for their heads and without niches. However, a monument to an unknown knight in St Bartholomew's hospital at Sandwich (Kent), dated *c.*1240–50, shows the high-relief figure in a niche and may be the first surviving example of a military effigy depicted in this way.

All the knightly effigies so far discussed have the legs straight, but round about the middle of the thirteenth century the fashion began, and lasted for roughly a hundred years, of showing the legs crossed. Excellent early examples occur in Salisbury cathedral (possibly William Longsword the Younger, who died in 1250) and in the churches of Walkern (Herts) and Stowe-Nine-Churches (Northants) (7), all dating probably from the third quarter of the century. The old myth that crossed legs indicate a crusader is widespread and persistent, but although William Longsword the Younger was killed on crusade, there is no truth in it as a principle of general application. Rather, crossed legs were a new artistic device, whose first appearance chimed very nicely with the development we have been observing, for it inevitably contributed further to the emancipation of the effigy. Indeed, the figure at Stowe-Nine-Churches has to all intents and purposes reached the stage of complete freedom from the slab.

Although less marked the same trend can be observed in effigies of ecclesiastics and ladies. From shortly after 1250 come the three excellent and well-preserved episcopal effigies of Bishop Silvester Everdon of Carlisle (d.1254) in the Temple Church, Archbishop Walter de Gray (d.1255) in York Minster and Bishop William Kilkenny (d.1256) in Ely cathedral. Moreover, although they are still depicted in niches, the side-shafts of these niches now tend themselves to become free of the slab. Those of Archbishop de Gray and Bishop Kilkenny, for example, are deeply undercut and connected with the slab at regular intervals by crockets of stiff-leaf. In the late thirteenth century side-shafts became much less obtrusive, allowing the full relief of the figure to be more readily apparent, and virtually disappeared altogether in the next century. The effigy of Bishop Walter Bronescombe (d.1280) in Exeter cathedral is shown in a markedly reticent niche, in no way detracting from the relief of the figure, and exhibits another tendency gathering momentum in the second half of the century, to move away from the portrayal of bishops as standing figures towards a suggestion of the truly recumbent attitude, for, although the bishop remains in the act of blessing, his head rests on pillows and his vestments are permitted to fall in overlapping folds on to the slab.

Effigies of ladies are *mutatis mutandis* similar, save that they are from the start shown recumbent with their heads supported on pillows. The earliest are already in the highest relief, and the most telling indication of further development is to be found in the treatment of their garments. Among the first is an unknown lady at Wolferlow (Herefs) (*32*), whose rigid pose and garments, clinging to her in stylized folds which make virtually no concession to the recumbent attitude, indicate a mid thirteenth-century date. A slightly later female figure in Romsey abbey (Hants) lies in a more relaxed attitude with garments falling on to the slab in a distinctly

6 Worcester cathedral: King John (d.1216)

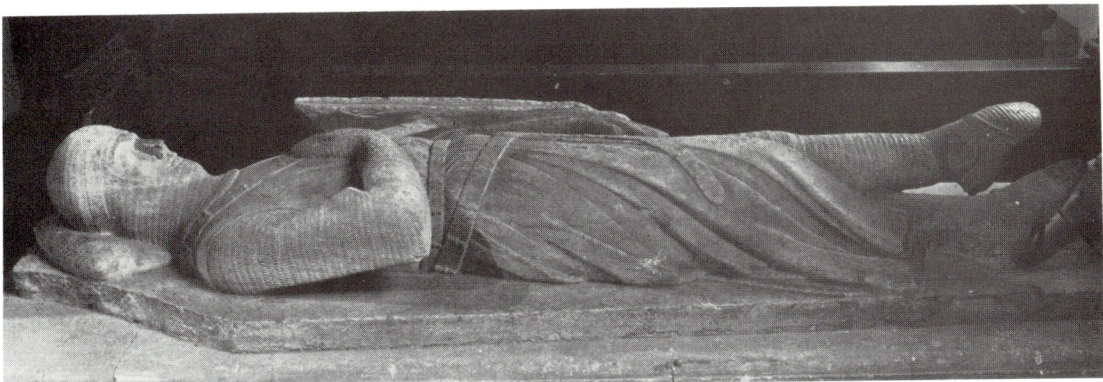

7 Stowe-Nine-Churches (Northants): knight (*c*.1250–75)

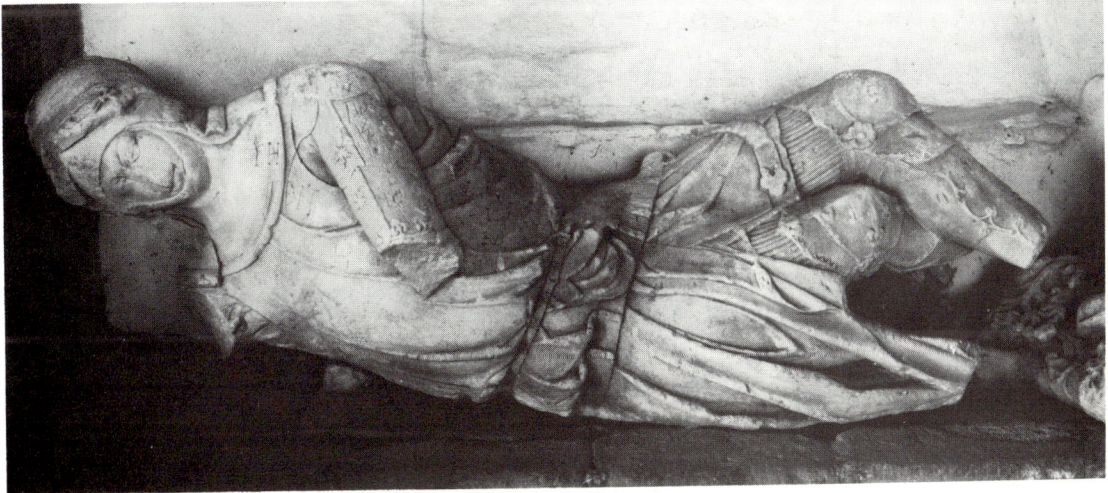

8 Aldworth (Berks): knight of the De la Beche family (*c*.1350)

realistic manner, but without doubt the finest thirteenth-century examples are the effigies of Eleanor of Castile (d.1290), queen of Edward I, and Aveline countess of Lancaster (d.1273, monument *c*.1290), both in Westminster Abbey. The latter in particular displays remarkable virtuosity and realism in its treatment of the recumbent female figure – the lady's head is supported at a comfortable angle on pillows, her body lies in an easy restful posture and her garments drape on to the slab in naturalistic folds.

It was, however, effigies of knights that achieved the most spectacular feats. Later versions of the cross-legged military figure are numerous, though often poorly preserved, and most are shown in a relaxed state, as in Pershore abbey (Worcs), *c*.1280, and at Dodford (Northants), perhaps Sir Robert de Keynes (d.1305). Others appear in a state of suspended animation, either drawing or about to draw their swords, as at Hanbury (Staffs), or more rarely sheathing them, as in Southwark cathedral, where the knight's sword is still three inches out of its scabbard. At Great Haseley (Oxon) the knight has apparently just drawn his sword, which rests upon his right leg, the empty scabbard being still grasped in his left hand. Most dramatic, however, is the famous late thirteenth-century knight in Dorchester abbey (Oxon), for not only are his hands vigorously engaged in drawing his sword, but his legs, although crossed, hardly touch one another and are placed in so restless an attitude as to convey a vivid impression of movement. Indeed, the whole conception of this figure is packed with energy, the very antithesis of calm repose. Although it has some features in common with the much restored contemporary wooden effigy of Robert Curthose duke of Normandy (d.1134) in Gloucester cathedral, the Dorchester knight remains a virtuoso and highly individual achievement by an unknown sculptor.

This kind of approach did not last much beyond the middle of the fourteenth century, but until then other arresting touches of originality can be found. In Norfolk, for example, two knightly figures, those of Sir Roger de Kerdiston (d.1337) at Reepham and Sir Oliver de Ingham (d.1344) at Ingham, are portrayed on beds of pebbles in uncomfortably strained positions, and a related anonymous figure occurs at Burrough Green in the neighbouring county of Cambridgeshire, all three being no doubt the products of a regional workshop or individual craftsman. At Bedale (Yorks) the roughly contemporary wife of Sir Brian Fitzalan appears in an extraordinarily restless state, with her body slightly bent in alternate directions at neck, waist and knees, and her ample dress lying in disturbed folds about her legs, as though blown from one side. A calmer local peculiarity is to be seen in Herefordshire on the monuments of Blanche Lady Grandison (d.1347) at Much Marcle and a lady of the Paunce-foot family (*c*.1350) at Ledbury, in both of which the long trains of the ladies' garments hang down realistically over the ends of their slabs. But perhaps the most striking example of experiment in the attitude of the effigy is provided by a knight in the much mutilated series of De la Beche figures at Aldworth (Berks) (*8*), which, though variously dated in the past, seem on the latest evidence to belong to *c*.1350. The knight in question is uniquely not lying on his back, but semi-reclining in an attitude half-turned towards the viewer, his torso raised on his right elbow (now missing) and his crossed legs drawn up towards his waist, creating an undulating outline from head to foot.

Moreover, apart from figures engaged in some action, such as knights drawing their swords or bishops in the act of blessing, the position of the hands on effigies in general was far from standard. On effigies recumbent and at rest the closing of hands in prayer became increasingly common, but some ladies, for example, were shown clutching at their garments and other figures appeared holding symbolic or devotional objects. The most frequent of the latter was a heart held between the hands, as in the case of a lady of the Heriz family (*c*.1300) at Gonalston (Notts) (*33*), but more rarely, and by charming variation, a later thirteenth-century lady of the Mohun family at Axminster (Devon) has between her hands a tiny Virgin and Child. Again, the contemporary effigy of an abbot in Gloucester cathedral holds a model of a church, establishing almost beyond doubt that he represents Abbot Serlo (d.1104), who rebuilt the abbey church (now the cathedral) after the Norman Conquest.

In the later middle ages, however, a rigid formalism descended. The normal attitude of effigies of all types came to be that of the hands closed in prayer with the body straight and at rest, the only significant exception being in the treatment of the hands in a number of representations of married couples. It was at the beginning of the fourteenth century that the practice began of showing ladies alongside their husbands, early cases being the two unknown couples at Bere Ferrers and Landkey (Devon), members of the Reynes family at Clifton

Reynes (Bucks), all of *c*.1300, and Sir Lambert and Lady de Threkingham, *c*.1310, at Threkingham (Lincs). Although normally such pairs of effigies were depicted at prayer and without physical contact between them, occasionally they appeared holding hands, as do, for example, Thomas Beauchamp earl of Warwick (d.1369) and wife in St Mary's, Warwick, and Sir Ralph Greene (d.1417) and wife at Lowick (Northants). This fashion was never very widespread, however, and in the later fifteenth century died out altogether.

The vast majority of later medieval effigies were shown in the highly formal posture described above, the representations being conventional and in all but a small minority of cases lacking in any attempt at portraiture. At the same time, however, a generally high standard of craftsmanship, with very competent figure modelling and meticulous depiction of detail, was achieved in their execution. The skills of later medieval carvers were most effectively displayed on monuments in alabaster, a substance first employed for funerary purposes in the early fourteenth century, and nowhere better than on alabaster monuments of knights and their ladies. Among the best of these is the splendid pair of effigies of Sir Richard Vernon (d.1451) and Lady Vernon at Tong (Salop) (*9*). They are carved entirely in the round, recumbent in a formal attitude of prayer, Sir Richard in full armour with his head resting upon a helm and his feet supported by a couchant lion, Lady Vernon in elegant dress with her head resting on pillows held by small angels and with two lap-dogs frolicking in the hems of her garments. The scheme is conventional enough, but carried into effect by excellent, if rather stiff, modelling of the figures and exquisite attention to details of dress and armour, especially the lady's sumptuous head-dress and the ornamental orle of Sir Richard's helmet. Fine as all this is, it must not be forgotten that the original achievement was even more striking, for the effigies were finished with paint and gilding which served further to highlight the finer points of the carver's art. Accomplished works of this kind, ranging in date from the later fourteenth to the sixteenth centuries and differing chronologically in details of dress and armour, were provided all over England. The finest and best preserved include the following: Sir Thomas Arderne (d.1391) at Elford (Staffs), Sir Sampson de Strelley (*c*.1400) at Strelley (Notts), Sir William Wilcote (d.1410) at Northleigh (Oxon), Thomas 5th earl of Arundel (d.1415) at Arundel (Sussex), Sir

William Gascoine (a judge, d.1419) and (?) Edward Redman (d.1510) at Harewood (Yorks), Lord Bardolph (d.1441) at Dennington (Suffolk), Sir Reginald Cobham (d.1446) at Lingfield (Surrey), Sir Humphrey Blount (d.1477) at Kinlet (Salop), Sir Ralph Fitzherbert (d.1483) at Norbury (Derbs), Sir John Mordaunt (d.1506) at Turvey (Beds), Lord Roos (d.1513) in St George's Chapel, Windsor (Berks), and Sir George Forster (d.1526) at Aldermaston (Berks), all with their wives. Individual effigies remained common as well, notably Bishop William of Wykeham (d.1404) in Winchester cathedral, William Canynge, priest (d.1474), in St Mary Redcliffe, Bristol, and Alice duchess of Suffolk (d.1475) at Ewelme (Oxon) (*39*). Canterbury cathedral contains two alabaster effigies of special interest, namely, that of Archbishop Henry Chichele (d.1443) which, in its restored paint and gilding, gives some idea of the bright colours which all once shared, and that of King Henry IV (d.1413) which, unlike most, is undoubtedly a portrait.

Fine effigies were also produced in a variety of local stones and in other materials. Purbeck marble was abandoned for this purpose after the early fourteenth century and the use of wood became uncommon thereafter. Gilt bronze effigies, however, continued to be made in the later middle ages, including in particular those of the Black Prince (d.1376) in Canterbury cathedral, King Edward III (d.1377) and King Richard II (d.1400) and wife, both in Westminster Abbey, and (possibly the finest) Richard Beauchamp earl of Warwick (d.1439) in St Mary's Warwick. In exceptional cases wooden effigies were encased in metal to produce a similar effect. That of Henry V (d.1422) in Westminster Abbey was originally covered in gilt silver plates which bore the king's likeness, but these have long since disappeared. From the end of the thirteenth century, however, there survives the now unique effigy of William de Valence (d.1296), also at Westminster, which miraculously still retains its splendid casing of copper plates partly engraved and partly inlaid with enamel.

In the later middle ages delightful additional features commonly appeared with the effigy on the slab. Although the shafted niche of earlier days virtually disappeared, a sizeable and intricately carved tabernacle was sometimes placed on the slab above the effigy's head, especially in the fifteenth century, good examples being the monuments of Sir Ralph Greene (d.1417) at Lowick (Northants) and Alice duchess of Suffolk at Ewelme. From the

9 Tong (Salop): Sir Richard Vernon (d.1451) and wife

10 Canterbury cathedral: Archbishop Hubert Walters (d.1205)

surviving contract for the Greene monument we know that they were called 'gablettes', no doubt in order to avoid confusion with superior architectural canopies. The heads of effigies usually lie either on pillows which are supported by small angels or, in the case of military figures, often on a helmet bearing the family crest. The feet of men rest against an animal, most frequently a lion, but otherwise an heraldic beast pertaining to the family. Occasionally a charming variation occurs in which tiny figures of weepers or possibly bedesmen sit on the back of the lion against the soles of the effigy's feet, as can be seen on the monuments of Sir Sampson de Strelley at Strelley (Notts) and Sir Ralph Fitzherbert at Norbury (Derbs) among others; Bishop Wykeham in Winchester cathedral rests his feet against three small seated figures. On female effigies the feet are not normally visible, but commonly puppies or lap-dogs with bell-collars play in the hems of their garments.

Tomb-chests

Having surveyed the development of the fully three-dimensional effigy, it will be necessary in due course to consider the survival of low-relief effigies beyond the twelfth century and the appearance of strictly two-dimensional figures. For the moment, however, we leave the effigy and turn our attention to the other major features of monumental design which emerged in the thirteenth century, namely, the tomb-chest and the canopy.

In the later middle ages effigies were almost invariably placed upon raised tomb-chests, the origins of which practice can be traced back to the beginning of the thirteenth century. A major early monument in this respect, though one which never had an effigy, is that of Archbishop Hubert Walter (d.1205) in Canterbury cathedral (*10*), the monument being completed probably a few years after his death. Rectangular in plan, it consists of an arcaded tomb-chest rising from a finely moulded base and surmounted by a coped roof-like top decorated with geometrical patterns and high-relief heads in quatrefoils. Closely related and similarly lacking an effigy is the near-contemporary but unfortunately damaged monument of Bishop Gilbert Glanvill (d.1214) in Rochester cathedral, which also has an arcaded tomb-chest and coped top, with half-length figures instead of heads. These monuments are quite different from the other early ones discussed above, for in contrast with an interment leaving only the grave-slab exposed, they suggest the apparent (but not actual) enclosing of the coffin within a raised tomb-chest standing entirely above the floor level of the church. This type of monument probably arose by imitation of twelfth-century shrines of saints. None of these have survived from so early a date, but we know that the bodies of saints were enclosed in raised shrines in whose sides embrasures were hollowed out to enable the sick and lame to get as close as possible to the healing powers of the saint within. Later examples showing these salubrious openings remain from the thirteenth century onward, notably those of St Osmund in Salisbury cathedral, St Edward the Confessor in Westminster Abbey, St Alban in St Albans cathedral and St Wite at Whitechurch Canonicorum (Dorset). It is possible, therefore, that the arcading on the sides of Hubert Walter's tomb-chest may represent an artistic adaptation of similar arcaded embrasures, perhaps like those on the long-vanished twelfth-century shrine of St Thomas Becket in the cathedral. The coped top of the tomb-chest may likewise reflect the roofs of such shrines, as it finds a parallel in the lids of smaller reliquaries of the period, but is also related to the coped coffin lids surviving from the twelfth century.

The tomb-chest with coped top devoid of effigy was no more than a passing fashion, but it was of importance in encouraging the concept of the standing tomb-chest. It was apparently at about this time that the momentous step was taken of raising the flat slab with effigy on to a tomb-chest. Precisely when it first happened is impossible now to tell, but there was a definite and increasing movement in this direction during the first half of the thirteenth century. At first tomb-chests were low and on some the slab continued for a time to be coffin-like in shape. Discounting the present form of Bishop Marshal's monument at Exeter as being of doubtful authenticity, among the earliest tomb-chests with effigies must be that of a deacon, *c.*1210, at Avon Dassett (Warks), which is of very modest height and decorated with shafts. A little later is the tomb-chest at Peterborough supporting the latest of the series of abbots discussed earlier, namely that supposed to be Abbot Alexander of Holderness (d.1226), similarly low and decorated with shafts and quatrefoils. The effigy of William Longsword earl of Salisbury (d.1226) in Salisbury cathedral is carried on a low wooden tomb-chest enriched with trefoiled arcading, while tomb-chests of a generation or so later can be seen in the monuments of Bishop Giles of

Bridport (d.1262) at Salisbury and Bishop Peter d'Aigueblanche (d.1268) in Hereford cathedral. By the last quarter of the century the placing of effigies on at least moderately high tomb-chests of rectangular plan had become quite normal, very fine instances being provided by the monuments of Archbishop John Pecham (d.1292) in Canterbury cathedral and those of Edmund Crouchback earl of Lancaster (d.1296) and Aveline his countess, of about the same date, both in Westminster Abbey. Each of these has a canopy rising from the tomb-chest, but equally impressive examples without canopies were also erected. Ths most spectacular and self-assertive case is the exceptionally high tomb-chest and effigy of King Henry III (d.1272) in Westminster Abbey, which, partly of foreign workmanship and completed only in 1291, cannot but have encouraged the growing fashion for tomb-chests. Examples multiply from 1300 onwards and, although there continued to be exceptions, it is clear that by then the standard type of later medieval tomb-chest with effigy had been established.

In general tomb-chests are either free-standing, that is, clear of all adjacent walls and capable of being viewed from all sides, or set back into a wall under a canopied recess. Less commonly a tomb-chest might be placed under an existing arch, such as one of those dividing a chancel from its side chapel, or set in an aperture specially made for it in a wall between two parts of a church, in each of which cases the two long sides only of the tomb-chest are visible. A number of tomb-chests survive today standing against a wall (not recessed under a canopy), but, although such placing was not unknown in the middle ages, most instances are undoubtedly the result of subsequent moving of an originally free-standing chest. Evidence that this is what has happened is sometimes present. At Warkworth (Northants), for instance, the monument which may be that of Sir John Lyons (c.1350) is placed endwise against a wall, but the decoration of the tomb-chest at the point where it touches the wall is broken in so inept a manner as to suggest that it was not originally in this position. Again, at Clifton (Beds) the early sixteenth-century tomb-chest of an unknown knight has one of its long sides against a wall, upon which is fixed above the monument a rectangular panel of carved enrichment identical in every respect with the front of the tomb-chest and clearly belonging originally to the now invisible side of the chest.

The Enrichment of Tomb-chests

Tomb-chests, whether free-standing or otherwise, provided an excellent opportunity for the carver's art which was readily taken up. Although a tiny minority of chests were left plain in the thirteenth and early fourteenth centuries, the rest were enriched on their sides and ends with carved decoration of various kinds. The two most popular basic forms were blind arcading and quatrefoils, both of which appeared with the earliest tomb-chests, notably those of Hubert Walter at Canterbury and Abbot Alexander of Holderness at Peterborough. Each remained common throughout the later middle ages, changing in detail to reflect successive architectural and decorative fashions, but more importantly each acquired additional ornamental features as time passed.

Simple thirteenth-century, or 'Early English', arcading can be seen on William Longsword's chest at Salisbury (c.1230), on the strange coffin-like tomb-chest at Albrighton near Shifnal (Salop), possibly dating from c.1260–70, and, fragmentarily, on the monument of William de Valence (d.1296) in Westminster Abbey. The first two have trefoiled heads to the arcading, the last simple pointed arches, but on all three the arcading is empty. In later versions the arcading developed into shallow arched panels, as, for example, on the chests of Bartholomew Lord Burghersh (d.1355) in Lincoln cathedral and Miles Salley bishop of Llandaff (d.1516–7) in St Mark's, Bristol, but after about 1250 empty arcading was very much the exception. Additional motifs were in turn introduced below the arches, firstly shields of arms, followed toward the end of the thirteenth century by small figures of 'weepers', and about a century later by figures of angels and saints.

Shields of arms appear in this position on the wooden monument ascribed to John of Pitchford (d.1285) at Pitchford (Salop) and on the beautiful tomb-chest of Eleanor of Castile (d.1290) in Westminster Abbey. Later instances occur on the monuments of Lady Grandison (d.1347) at Much Marcle (Herefs) and Margaret countess of Devon (d.1449) at Colyton (Devon). In the earlier cases the shields were often depicted as hanging by straps from nails or knots of foliage, but later on as fixed in an unspecified fashion against the chest.

In the later thirteenth century tomb-chest arcading began to be adapted to serve as niches for miniature standing figures known as 'weepers', that is, men and women associated with the deceased and usually including members of his family. Among the earliest extant examples is the tomb-chest base of the shrine of St Thomas Cantilupe bishop of Hereford (d. 1282) in Hereford cathedral, which has small figures of knights placed in bold cinquefoiled niches. The idea was taken up with relish in a superb group of monuments of the late thirteenth and early fourteenth centuries, namely, those in Westminster Abbey of Edmund Crouchback earl of Lancaster (d. 1296), his wife Aveline, and Aymer de Valence earl of Pembroke (d. 1324), and in Canterbury cathedral that of Archbishop Pecham (d. 1292), on each of which the weepers stand in trefoil-headed niches under steep gables separated by pinnacled shafts. The fine alabaster tomb-chest with effigy of Edward II's second son, John of Eltham earl of Cornwall (d. 1336), also at Westminster, has rows of weepers under cinquefoiled arches with a shield of arms below each. That the fashion was being adopted in the country at large is apparent from the simple tomb-chest of an unknown knight of the early fourteenth century at Castle Combe (Wilts), the more ambitious monument of Sir Roger de Kerdiston (d. 1337) at Reepham (Norfolk) and the once even grander but now sadly mutilated monument of Bishop Henry Burghersh (d. 1340) in Lincoln cathedral, where, however, the weepers are canons of the cathedral and appear in pairs in the exceptional seated posture. The tradition was continued on later royal monuments in Westminster Abbey, especially those of Queen Philippa (d. 1369) and her husband, King Edward III (d. 1377), whose tomb-chests were once adorned with rows of weepers in niches with noticeably projecting canopies, but all but one have been lost from Queen Philippa's and those of the king's survive only on the south side. The latter monument is of Purbeck marble, but the weepers, like the king's effigy above, are cast in bronze and gilt (*11*). They are of particular interest, since we know that they were intended to depict members of his family and were identified by enamelled bronze shields of arms, some of which still exist below the weepers. A very instructive comparison can be made between the attitude adopted by the weepers on these two royal monuments and those on all the earlier cases mentioned, for it illustrates one area of contrast between the 'Decorated' and 'Perpendicular' periods, and parallels the transition from the fairly free treatment of the principal effigy, which typified the first half of the fourteenth century, to the more conventional and rather stiff treatment of the later

middle ages. Weepers on earlier monuments were shown in various elegant poses, often swaying and sometimes almost in motion, but by the time of Edward III's monument they normally stood upright and rather static, a portrayal which was to remain typical for the next century and a half. It can be seen, for example, on the fifteenth-century alabaster tomb-chests of Thomas 5th earl of Arundel (d. 1415) at Arundel (Sussex) and Sir Humphrey Blount (d. 1477) at Kinlet (Salop). Nevertheless, the carving varied in detail, especially as weepers of different dates reflected current fashions in dress, and in the late fifteenth and early sixteenth centuries the figures were occasionally grouped in pairs under a single arch, as on the chest of Henry Foljambe (d. 1510) at Chesterfield (Derbs), or even threes, as on that of Thomas Babington (d. 1518) at Ashover in the same county. Moreover, in the late fifteenth century weepers began to hold shields, sometimes beside them, as can be seen on the chest of Sir Ralph Fitzherbert (d. 1483) at Norbury (Derbs), and their rigidity tended to loosen again into a more relaxed stance. At Stanford-on-Teme (Worcs) the tomb-chest of Sir Humphrey Salway (d. 1493) represents the weepers kneeling sideways at prayer, a pose exceptional for the middle ages but one which was to become conventional in the later sixteenth century, while on a late fifteenth-century tomb-chest at Prestwold (Leics) they are seated. Also worthy of note in passing are three extremely unusual, if not unique, positions for weepers on medieval monuments: on that of Lord Harrington (d. 1347) in Cartmel priory (Lancs) they stand upon the tomb-chest, leaning diminutively against the effigies and carved with them from the same blocks of stone; on the tomb-chest of Cardinal John Morton (d. 1500) in the crypt of Canterbury cathedral three weepers kneel on each side of the effigy; and at Hingham (Norfolk) the canopied wall monument of Thomas Lord Morley (d. 1435) has the weepers kneeling frontally on the backplate above the tomb-chest. The last two examples are further interesting anticipations of later practices.

In the late fourteenth century the motif of standing angels was introduced, particularly on monuments of alabaster, among the first being that of Sir Thomas Arderne (d. 1391) at Elford (Staffs), where angels appear with weepers in alternate shallow niches on the tomb-chest. In the first half of the fifteenth century tomb-chests were often given over entirely to angels, as on the monument probably of Sir Edmund Thorpe (d. 1417) at Ash-

11 Westminster Abbey: King Edward III (d. 1377). Tomb-chest showing weepers

12 Ewelme (Oxon): Alice duchess of Suffolk (d. 1475). Detail of tomb-chest showing angels

wellthorpe (Norfolk) and those of Sir Ralph Greene (d.1417) at Lowick (Northants) and the rather later unknown knight at Lutterworth (Leics). For the later fifteenth century good examples are provided by the monument of Sir Thomas Fettiplace (c.1442) at East Shefford (Berks) and, very spectacularly, by that of Alice duchess of Suffolk (d.1475) at Ewelme (Oxon) (12). Almost invariably angels hold armorial bearings – at Elford and elsewhere these are in the form of large rectangular plates of arms covering their bodies, but more commonly they are shields of appropriate size. Angels were normally shown bare-headed and wearing alb-like vestments, but at Ewelme, for instance, they are mitred and some are dressed in feathered costumes, a motif familiar in minor decorative sculpture of the later middle ages and possibly deriving from imitation of costumes worn in mystery plays. The standard pose was erect and frontal with the wings spread out behind the head, but occasionally a kneeling posture was adopted, as, for example, on certain fifteenth-century chests at Harewood, Swine and elsewhere in Yorkshire.

It should not be thought, from what has been said above, that the introduction of new motifs under the niched arcading led to the disappearance of older motifs, for in truth many later medieval tomb-chests exhibited any or all of them in various combinations. So, for example, shields and weepers appear together on the chest perhaps of Sir John de Lyons (c.1350) at Warkworth (Northants), and weepers with angels on that of Sir Thomas Arderne (d.1391) at Elford (Staffs). In the fifteenth century figures of saints, identifiable by their emblems, were added to the repertoire, appearing in combination with angels on the tomb-chests of Sir Ralph Grey (d.1443) at Chillingham (Northumb.), Sir Richard Vernon (d.1451) at Tong (Salop) and Sir David Phillips (d.1506) in St Mary's, Stamford (Lincs); and in combination with weepers on those of a Lord Lovell (c.1450) at Minster Lovell (Oxon) (170), Sir John Neville (d.1482) at Harewood (Yorks) and members of the Kirkham family (c.1500) at Paignton (Devon). Only in rare cases were saints shown on their own, as, for example, on the tomb-chest of Bishop Richard Mayeu (d.1516) in Hereford cathedral. They were normally depicted in a standing posture, but occasionally seated, the latter being so, for example, on the chest of Sir John Curzon (c.1480) at Kedleston (Derbs), where seated saints alternate with standing angels.

In general these arrays of little figures have come down to us devoid of colour, but, although as such they form a most attractive feature of later medieval monuments, particularly those of alabaster, when first made they shone with paint and gilding like the effigies above and presented a totally different spectacle from the restrained effect conveyed today. Moreover, the zeal of religious iconoclasts and the carelessness of church-users over the centuries have resulted in broken and incomplete sets of figures on many tomb-chests and denuded others altogether of their weepers, angels or saints, whose former existence is now betrayed only by the miniature brackets which once supported them. This is true, for example, of the monuments of King Edward II (d.1327), in Gloucester cathedral, Sir Hugh Calverley (d.1394) at Bunbury (Cheshire) and many others. Clearly, then, in order to recapture the pristine splendours of some tomb-chests a leap of imagination is necessary to re-people the empty rows of niches with figures from the secular and spiritual worlds of the middle ages.

The other basic motif employed on tomb-chests from the start was the quatrefoil, which like arcading soon received additional decorative features. The earliest were heads and figures, which appeared on the early thirteenth-century monuments in Canterbury and Rochester cathedrals noted above. However, although later examples of quatrefoils containing figures occur on the tomb-chests of Maud countess of Arundel (d.1270) in Chichester cathedral and Bishop Godfrey Giffard (d.1302) in Worcester cathedral, the quatrefoil generally lost these human associations after the early thirteenth century and was pre-eminently adapted to contain shields of arms. Numerous instances witness to the popularity of this device from the later thirteenth century onward, including the chests of an unknown knight (c.1300) at Whatton (Notts), Sir John Wingfield (d.1361) at Wingfield (Suffolk), Sir Ralph Cheney (c.1401) at Edington (Wilts) and John de la Pole 2nd duke of Suffolk (d.1491–2) also at Wingfield. On earlier examples quatrefoils were simple and touched one another in an uninterrupted sequence, but from about 1350 they became increasingly cusped and were invariably enclosed each within a square panel. The south-west particularly favoured elaborate cusping, as can be seen on the chests of Sir Giles Daubeny (d.1445) at South Petherton and Sir Richard Choke (d.1486) at Long Ashton (both in Somerset), the latter being especially fine and dainty in its cusping and subsidiary carving. Another monument in the same county, that of Sir John Newton (d. 1488) at Yatton, exhibits a less common variation in which stylized flowers or foliage replace shields of arms in the quatrefoils. Numerous other variations occur, of which mention can be made only of some of the more important and interesting. Quatrefoils are placed in circles, for example, on the chest of an unknown ecclesiastic (*c.* 1400) at Edington (Wilts), and in lozenges on that of Sir John Mordaunt (d. 1506) at Turvey (Beds). Cusped octofoils with shields are found on several chests, including that of the Black Prince (d. 1376) in Canterbury cathedral, and, more rarely, hexafoils appear on that of Bishop William Edington (d. 1366) in Winchester cathedral. The exceptional case of shields in encircled trefoils occurs on the tomb-chest of Sir John Swinford (d. 1371) at Spratton (Northants). The placing of shields against panels of cusped diaper design was a late innovation, which can be seen, for instance, on the chest perhaps of Sir William Martyn (d. 1503) at Puddletown (Dorset) and, very late, on that of Sir John Clerke (d. 1539) at Thame (Oxon). Moreover, quatrefoils and the like might alternate with panelling, weepers, angels and saints in any of numerous combinations.

The enrichment of some late medieval tomb-chests, especially those made of alabaster, occasionally included carvings of religious scenes and representations of central tenets of the Christian faith. Among the most common were the Annunciation, the Virgin and Child and the Holy Trinity, and it is particularly appropriate to find them on monuments of alabaster, since they related closely to the extensive output of the northern alabaster workshops in altar-reredoses, religious panels and images of saints. They will be discussed more fully, however, in a later chapter.

Finally, the top edges of the tomb-chest must be mentioned, since their decoration varied subtly through the middle ages. In the fourteenth century they normally carried a fairly pronounced chamfer, often plain, but sometimes enriched with small stylized flowers or leaves, known as fleurons, examples of which include the monuments of an unknown lady (*c.* 1310) at Aldborough (Yorks) and Sir Humphrey Littlebury (*c.* 1360) at Holbeach (Lincs). A somewhat similar treatment occurs on the fifteenth-century tomb-chest of Bishop John Stanbury (d. 1474) in Hereford cathedral, but here the decoration is not fleurons but regularly spaced sprigs of foliage. However, in the fifteenth century the chamfer began to be used for an inscription

carved in relief and running all round the top of the chest, an early instance of which is Bishop William of Wykeham's monument (d. 1404) in Winchester cathedral. The practice did not become popular until the late fifteenth and early sixteenth centuries, and then chiefly on alabaster monuments, such as, for example, those of Edmund Stafford earl of Wiltshire (d. 1499) at Lowick (Northants), John de Strelley (d. 1501) at Strelley (Notts) and Sir George Forster (d. 1526) at Aldermaston (Berks). However, since the inclusion of an inscription round the edges of effigy-bearing slabs had been in use from as early as Bishop Jocelin de Bohun's grave slab of 1184 in Salisbury cathedral, it is likely that many now plain chamfers on late medieval tomb-chests originally carried either painted inscriptions, which have since mostly worn away but of which a fragment survives, for example, on Aymer de Valence's monument in Westminster Abbey, or strips of engraved brass inscriptions, such as have been restored on the monument of Alice duchess of Suffolk at Ewelme. Another feature of some later medieval tomb-chests, especially the free-standing type, was a shallow crenellation topping the chest on all sides like a miniature embattled parapet. It first appeared in the fourteenth century, occurring as early as the monument of Prior Henry Eastry (d. 1322) in Canterbury cathedral, but remained uncommon until the second half of the century, after which it was a feature of numerous tomb-chests until the beginning of the sixteenth century. It can be seen on the chests, among others, of Bishop Ralph Shrewsbury (d. 1363) in Wells cathedral, John Lord Neville (d. 1388) in Durham cathedral, William Lord Roos (d. 1414) at Bottesford (Leics), Sir Reginald Cobham (d. 1446) at Lingfield (Surrey) and Sir Nicholas and Sir Ralph Fitzherbert (d. 1473, 1483) at Norbury (Derbs).

Monumental Canopies

In many later medieval monuments the ensemble was completed by the provision of a canopy over the tomb-chest. Canopies fall basically into two categories: those covering tomb-chests which are wholly or nearly free-standing, and those covering tomb-chests set in recesses in the wall. Both types appeared at about the same time, the mid-thirteenth century, but wall canopies, although foreshadowed earlier in the simple decoration of arched recesses, did not become prominent until the late thirteenth century. It is notable that the earliest free-standing canopies relate to monuments of bishops and that in general they resemble contemporary saints' shrines. It may be, therefore, that the inspiration came partly from the latter source, but it has also been supposed that stone canopies represent a translation into more permanent form of the temporary canopies of wood and cloth which were customarily placed over the coffin and burial place. Since canopies, particularly in free-standing form, have a distinct architectural character, they mirror contemporary building styles and decorative fashions. Examples survive for all later medieval building periods – Early English, Geometrical, Decorated and Perpendicular – and their distinguishing features assist in the dating of monuments where an effigy is anonymous or has disappeared.

The earliest extant canopy is that over the low free-standing tomb-chest with effigy of Archbishop Walter de Gray (d. 1255) in York Minster (*13*). The most shrine-like of all, it is also a fine example of Early English design and decoration. It consists of an open lower storey made up of nine tall slender shafts (four on each side with an extra one at the west end) carrying an arcade of deeply moulded trefoiled divisions, the whole surmounted by a solid, steeply-pitched 'roof' with blind trefoiled arcading under crocketed gables. The carved decoration is predominantly of the stiff-leaf type, typical of thirteenth-century Early English work, and the canopy as a whole is a notably restrained and noble piece.

The next in time is that of Bishop Giles Bridport (d. 1262) in Salisbury cathedral, filling the lower part of an arch so that only its long sides are visible. It is a grander and more sumptuous conception which marks an advance on the Gray monument both in its architecture and in its enrichment. The canopy is similarly topped by a pitched shrine-like roof, but the elevation of each side introduces an early form of traceried opening, very like the bays of contemporary cloisters, notably those at Salisbury itself. The façade consists of two main arches, below each of which is inserted an open design of two trefoiled divisions surmounted by an encircled quatrefoil. These are simple and early forms of geometrical plate tracery, which was at this time beginning to be employed in church windows. The carved decoration is very rich, including advanced forms of stiff-leaf, quatrefoils, animals, human heads and, in the spandrels over the main arches, scenes from the bishop's life.

More restrained in decoration, but with con-siderably more prominent tracery, is the latest of the early episcopal canopies, that of Bishop Peter d'Aigueblanche (d. 1268) in Hereford cathedral (*14*). Here the echoes of a saint's shrine are fainter and the superstructure is lighter and far more open. Both long sides exhibit a design vertically divided into three sections, each consisting of a main arch surmounted by a circle, originally containing an open-work trefoil, and a steep gable; below each main arch is a scheme of two trefoiled divisions with an encircled quatrefoil in the spandrel between them. All main and subsidiary arches rest on tall thin shafts and the three-part division is accentuated by rising shafted pinnacles. This show conceals, however, an unobtrusive roof to the canopy, whose underside takes the form of a miniature vault with ribs and bosses.

The next major group of canopies dates from the late thirteenth and early fourteenth centuries and extends to monuments of lay men and women. It comprises those of Edmund Crouchback earl of Lancaster (d. 1296) in Westminster Abbey, Bishop William of Louth (d. 1298) in Ely cathedral and Archbishop William Greenfield (d. 1315) in York Minster, but with these should also be considered the simpler monument of Aveline countess of Lancaster in Westminster Abbey and the wall monument of Archbishop John Pecham (d. 1292) in Canterbury cathedral. The first is the most splendid and best preserved of the group, but that of Bishop Louth, now lacking its tomb-chest, is so closely similar that it must once have been as fine. All display a richly carved version of the Geometrical style which in some respects heralds the dawn of the Decorated period. The basic design is derived ultimately from that of Bishop d. Aigueblanche's canopy at Hereford, with its emphasis on lightness in the upper part and on sharply articulated vertical divisions. Detailed descriptions cannot be attempted here, but the most prominent feature common to all is a steep gable above an arch with a blind trefoil or similar motif in the space between. In each case the arch assumes a cinquefoiled form, except for that of Aveline of Lancaster, which is trefoiled. The canopies of Edmund Crouchback and Bishop Louth are made more impressive by the addition, on either side of the central gabled arch, of a narrower and extremely steeply gabled section of the same general design, the three divisions being separated by buttress-like shafts terminating in crocketed pinnacles. The blind trefoil under the main gable of Crouchback's monument has a relief carving of a

13 York Minster: Archbishop Walter de Gray (d. 1255)

14 Hereford cathedral: Bishop Peter D'Aigueblanche (d. 1268)

15 Beverley Minster: the Percy Tomb (c. 1340)

16 Gloucester cathedral: King Edward II (d. 1327)

knight on horseback, that of Bishop Louth a seated figure, perhaps of Christ. In every case carved enrichment which can definitely be called Decorated appears, notably the knobbly-leaved crockets and finials of the gables and, on Crouchback's canopy, the exclusively Decorated motif of the ballflower and the ogee-arch, used as a surface decoration on the smaller side-gables.

The ogee-arch belonged pre-eminently to the Decorated style of the first half of the fourteenth century, but it never quite disappeared thereafter and returned to enjoy a new lease of life toward the end of the middle ages. It has been described as a 'concave-convex' arch, beginning from below like an ordinary pointed arch, but as it approaches the apex turning outward so that its sides meet in a far sharper point. It could take a variety of forms, from the thin and tall to the wide and depressed, but all shared the characteristic change in direction of the curves. A more wilful refinement was the 'nodding' ogee-arch, which was made to rise three-dimensionally, leaning forward as the curves ascended to the apex. Although never used as a structural feature of buildings, the ogee-arch was frequently employed in the Decorated period for smaller structures, such as monumental canopies, and as an applied decorative motif.

The monument of Aymer de Valence earl of Pembroke (d.1324) in Westminster Abbey illustrates the highly decorative and exciting effect which the ogee could create. Like those just discussed, the canopy comprises a crocketed and finialed gable above a cinquefoiled arch, but the crucial difference is that the lobes of the cinquefoil assume an ogee form. Its use here is somewhat tentative, since the main arch is pointed simply, but in the celebrated canopy known as the Percy Tomb in Beverley Minster (Yorks) (15) the ogee-arch is employed without any trace of diffidence. The monument presents problems, since it lacks any tomb-chest it may have had, but, although the heraldry on the canopy indicates a date of completion not earlier than 1340, the most likely person to whom it relates is Lady Eleanor Percy, who died in 1328. Apart from its positively encrusting carved enrichment, the most pronounced feature is the use of the ogival form. The familiar gable is there, but below it there appears a great nodding ogee-arch, its head projecting forward of the vertical plane of the monument and its cinquefoiled design being realised in ogival lobes, while in the spaces between gable and arch blank tracery in the form of

mouchettes with ogival lines is employed. The same scheme is used on both north and south façades of the canopy, and the gables are flanked on each side by tall, buttress-like shafts with pinnacles. The canopy is one of the high-points of Decorated funerary work in England, and no description can do justice to its richly varied carving or to the excellent quality of the craftsmanship. Virtually no space on the main gables and arches is left uncarved, and the decoration continues on the inside of the arches and on the vaulted underside of the roof. Trails of vine with lumpy Decorated leaves at intervals in the manner of crockets line gable and arch, and the gables are topped by luscious fruiting vine finials. From the gables project pairs of brackets supported by little men and carrying statuettes of angels, and the apex of each nodding ogee-arch terminates in a seated figure of Christ, that on the south receiving the soul of the deceased from a napkin held by two tiny angels. The cinquefoils of these main arches are deeply cusped and sub-cusped, the cusps taking the form of small angels, and the spandrels of the cusping are crowded with diminutive figures. No-one contemplating this magnificent piece can doubt the appropriateness of the name 'Decorated' for this style of architecture and adornment.

Equally splendid, though quite different in form, is the monument of King Edward II (d.1327) in Gloucester cathedral (16), another masterpiece of the Decorated period. Dating from c.1330, its canopy relies for effect not so much on lavish carving as on the decorative use of cusped and crocketed ogee-arches in combination with richly pinnacled and crocketed shafts. The ensemble is very light and airy. From the tomb-chest there rise two tiers of three ogee-arches, cinquefoiled with ogival lobes, the horizontal division between the tiers being marked by the barely visible roof of the lower storey, and each vertical pair of arches being separated from the next by upright pinnacled buttresses, each with two smaller attached buttresses placed diagonally. The upper level terminates in a complex system of crocketed gables and pinnacles, the total effect being that of a fantastic and impossibly delicate edifice, not unlike those imagined by some late medieval illuminators and painters.

The example set by Edward II's canopy was clearly followed in the rather later monument of Hugh Baron Despenser (d.1348) in Tewkesbury abbey (Glos), but in this case the canopy rises more daringly in four tiers and there are two roofs, topping the first and second stages. Moreover, since the tomb-chest is proportionally wider in order to accommodate the effigies of Hugh and his wife, the canopy is enabled markedly to recede as it rises, tapering on all four sides to a single arch at the top. The arches themselves are not ogees but two-centred, with cusped and sub-cusped open-work cinquefoils, and it is the gables over the arches which assume the ogee form. This canopy was in turn imitated for the adjacent monument of Guy de Brien, probably set up some years before his death in 1390.

The Decorated period also saw the first widespread use of the wall canopy. In part this had been adumbrated, initially by the plain arches of early tomb recesses and then by the occasional addition of carving to the arches, as can be seen for the mid-thirteenth century in Carlisle cathedral, but the fashion for wall canopies proper developed in the later thirteenth century. Strictly speaking, the term is still something of a misnomer, for in most cases the canopy was little more than an honorific decoration applied to the wall above and around the recess. However, for the viewer prepared to disregard the existence of the wall, the effect is like that of one side of a free-standing monument, of which it is, of course, a cheaper version. As a general rule, therefore, and in so far as was practical, the designs of wall canopies paralleled those of contemporary free-standing canopies.

A primitive version, dating perhaps from as early as 1250, occurs in Tewkesbury abbey (Glos) over the rather earlier grave slab of Abbot Alan (d. 1202), in which the recess takes the form of a moulded trefoil-headed opening with tiny side-shafts, contained under a moulded straight-sided gable. It is a singularly plain and unostentatious Early English piece. For the late thirteenth century the far richer canopy of Archbishop Pecham's wall monument in Canterbury cathedral has already been mentioned. Its single crocketed gable containing a single cusped arch and flanked by ascendant shafts was a standard type in the early fourteenth century, appearing in numerous variations and often, after about 1310, adopting an ogival form for the arch. Early versions without ogee can be seen, for example, at Bere Ferrers (Devon), Halsall (Lancs) and Wickhampton (Norfolk), all of *c*.1300, and more splendidly on the monument probably of Stephen Alard admiral of the Cinque Ports (d.1300, monument *c*.1312) at Winchelsea (Sussex); while examples with the ogee-

arch include the canopy of Sir Edmund de Mauley (d.1314) at Bainton (Yorks), whose design is closely related to that of the Percy Tomb at Beverley, and three anonymous monuments of *c*.1310–20 at Winchelsea. Alternatively and as a later Decorated fashion, the gable rather than the arch assumed the ogee line, as happens, for instance, on the monument perhaps of Sir Robert Fitzelys (d.1343–6) at Waterperry (Oxon) and that of Sir John Wingfield (d.1361) at Wingfield (Suffolk). The same idea occurs in a twin-gabled version over the monument of Sir Roger de Kerdiston (d.1337) at Reepham (Norfolk).

In other cases the gable was dispensed with altogether and the canopy comprised simply an arch between shafts, the arch being often ogival and normally carrying the crockets which otherwise would have appeared on the gable. Examples include the monuments of Sir Richard de Stapledon (*c*.1320) in Exeter cathedral (*17*), which has a cinquefoiled ogee-arch with cusps terminating in heads, and three anonymous figures at Shipton Moyne (Glos), who lie under similarly shaped canopies with very pointed cusps and much enrichment of the typically Decorated ball-flower motif. An attractive variant occurs at Ducklington (Oxon), where two canopied recesses of *c*.1340 have each a steeply pointed trefoiled arch with, instead of crockets, the unusual feature of a vine trail occupied by heads at intervals. These examples are all quite modest in size, but an impressive though much restored series of lofty canopies of similar type is to be seen at Aldworth (Berks). They are part of a scheme undertaken in *c*.1350 to commemorate several members of the De la Beche family and are distinguished, apart from their height, by a deeper than normal projection from the wall and by an original form of bifurcated cusping on their cinquefoiled arches.

Apart from these variations on common themes, the creative vitality and resourcefulness of the Decorated period produced other highly individual results, none more so than a series of canopied wall-monuments in Bristol cathedral of strikingly idiosyncratic character. Each has a cusped recess of semi-octagonal shape, surrounded by a star-like design achieved by placing a number of arcs convex-wise around the recess with a leafy finial wherever two adjacent arcs meet. The inventiveness and disregard of standard models which these monuments display was a feature of the age and can be found in large-scale architecture as well, notably elsewhere in Bristol cathedral, in the porch of St Mary Redcliffe church in Bristol, the central lantern of Ely cathedral and the unique Jesse Window in Dorchester abbey (Oxon).

Before leaving canopied recesses of the Decorated period, mention must be made of a feature that most probably once possessed but which has now almost totally disappeared. Although their back-plates now appear plain, it is beyond doubt that in many cases they were originally painted with appropriate scenes or religious imagery. On a mere handful of examples such painted schemes have survived, mostly in a fragmentary state, and others now destroyed are known to have existed. The Last Judgement appears on a recess of *c.*1300 at East Bedfont (Middx), and until recently a painting of a soul borne up by angels survived on the arch of an early fourteenth-century recess at Dodford (Northants); at Ingham (Norfolk) in the nineteenth century a hunting scene could still be made out on the back of the recess of Sir Oliver de Ingham (d.1344). On later canopied recesses carving was more commonly employed, but the technique of painting continued, as is clear from the monument of John Wotton (d.1417) at Maidstone (Kent), which has a painted representation of the deceased being presented by a group of saints to the Virgin Mary.

By the second half of the fourteenth century canopies of all types were affected by the arrival of the Perpendicular style. Enduring thereafter until the end of the middle ages, the Perpendicular style was peculiar to England and stood in marked contrast to the Flamboyant development from Decorated which characterized much of Europe in the later fourteenth and fifteenth centuries. It was opulent, but altogether less soaring and more 'earthbound' than earlier Gothic, having as a typical, though by no means universal, feature the 'four-centred' arch, wide in relation to height and depressed in pitch. Instead of the sinuous and upward-thrusting tendencies of the Decorated, the Perpendicular style preferred vertical and horizontal lines and square or oblong outlines. Tracery, whether in windows or as blind decoration on wall spaces, was more uniform and consisted frequently of identical arched panels with trefoiled or cinquefoiled heads repeated many times over. Nonetheless, certain features introduced or much developed in the Decorated period survived, more especially the ogee-arch and ogee-gable, particularly favoured in the later fifteenth and early sixteenth centuries, and the crocketed pinnacle,

ubiquitously employed to enliven roof-lines and the like.

A second major development took place around the middle of the fourteenth century, when the chantry chapel made its appearance and soon superseded the standing canopied monument as the most magnificent form of funerary display. In essence a chantry was the provision of a regular and perpetual intercession for the souls of those named in the foundation, usually a person immediately deceased and his or her family. It was set up and maintained by a special endowment whose income enabled chantry priests to be retained to celebrate the required masses. In simple cases an existing altar in a church would be used for this purpose, but the most elaborate forms of chantry involved the building on to the church of a separate chapel with its own altar or even the transformation of an entire parish church into a collegiate establishment of chantry priests.

We are not concerned with either of these extremes, however, but rather with an intermediate category, found particularly in cathedral and monastic churches, in which a miniature self-contained chapel was erected wholly inside the larger building. Such a chantry chapel usually contained the tomb-chest of the deceased along with an altar for perpetual intercession, and its walls were commonly pierced with arches, tracery and a doorway for access. The majority were given flat roofs with delicate lierne-vaults or fan-vaults on their undersides, and the interiors were enriched with panelling, blind tracery and canopied saints and other religious imagery. The best place to visit for chantry chapels such as this is Winchester cathedral, which has no fewer than six ranging in date from the fourteenth to the sixteenth centuries, but good collections can also be seen in the cathedrals of Ely, Exeter, St Albans and Wells, the abbeys of Tewkesbury and Westminster, Christchurch priory (Hants), St George's Chapel, Windsor, and (exceptional among parish churches) the church of Newark-on-Trent (Notts).

Among the earliest is that of Bishop William Edington (d.1366) in Winchester cathedral (*18*). Although faint traces of the Decorated period remain, it is unquestionably Perpendicular in style and character, its façade being an oblong filled with panel-like tracery and surmounted by a horizontal crested top. There is everywhere an emphasis on vertical and horizontal lines, there are no crocketed pinnacles and carved decoration is completely

17 Exeter cathedral: Sir Richard de Stapledon (c1320)

18 Winchester cathedral: Bishop William Edington (d.1366). Chantry chapel

lacking, except for the cornice. A more severe reaction to the elaborate canopies of the Decorated period would be difficult to imagine.

This cage-like elevation with crested horizontal top was repeated in several later chantry chapels, differing in details of tracery and the like, and generally acquiring more carved enrichment the nearer they approached the end of the middle ages. Good examples are provided by the chantries of Edward Lord Despenser (d.1375) in Tewkesbury abbey (Glos), Bishop Nicholas Bubwith (d.1424) in Wells cathedral, William Lord Hastings (d.1483) in St George's Chapel, Windsor, Precentor William Sylke (d.1508) in Exeter cathedral, Bishop Edmund Audley (d.1524) in Salisbury cathedral and Bishop Richard Fox (d.1528) in Winchester cathedral. Of these, the Bubwith chantry at Wells is distinguished by its hexagonal plan. A closely connected and rather late group was similar up to the cornice, at which point a further more solid stage was added, usually containing heraldic designs or niches for saints. Such, for example, are the chantries of Sir John Speke (d.1518) in Exeter cathedral, Abbot John Islip (d.1532) in Westminster Abbey and, in a lighter and more pierced version, Abbot Thomas Ramryge (d.1519) in St Albans cathedral.

A second major category of chantry chapels comprised those in which the top erupted into a riot of pinnacles and canopied niches around the vaulted roof. The sides of this type did not assume the form of traceried stone screens, but were either opened up with large four-centred arches or left largely as solid walls minimally pierced and encrusted with decoration. The open form can be seen in the chantries of Cardinal Henry Beaufort (d.1447) and Bishop William Waynflete (d.1486), both at Winchester, and, with variations, in those of William 9th earl of Arundel (d.1487) at Arundel (Sussex) and Richard Beauchamp earl of Worcester (d.1422) in Tewkesbury abbey (Glos), the last being unusually two-storeyed. The solid-wall form is best seen in Ely cathedral in the chantries of Bishops John Alcock (d.1500) and Nicholas West (d.1533). Here the chapels are veritably surrounded by large canopied niches which once contained sacred images, and the roof-line of Bishop Alcock's chantry is nothing short of an extravaganza of pinnacles and open-work spirelets. It is probably the most sumptuously decorated of all chantry chapels and certainly ensured that, architecturally speaking, the middle ages went out in a blaze of glory at Ely.

Three royal chantry chapels deserve special consideration, since each is in different ways highly individual. The first is that of King Henry V (d.1422) in Westminster Abbey, which is ingeniously fitted in at mezzanine level to the east of St Edward the Confessor's shrine and extends by means of a bridge over the eastern ambulatory of the abbey. Its plan and elevation are unique and its decoration includes one of the largest assemblies of carved figures surviving from the period. In addition to conventional images of saints, heraldic beasts and angels holding shields of arms, there are scenes of the king royally seated at his coronation and fully armed on horseback. In St Albans cathedral the chantry of the king's youngest son, Duke Humphrey of Gloucester (d.1447), stands near the shrine of St Alban, for whom he had a special veneration. The canopy stage is a composition of traceried openings and tiers of canopied niches, but the centre of the lower stage is left entirely open in order not to impede the passage of pilgrims to the saint's shrine. Finally, the chantry in Worcester cathedral of Prince Arthur, the elder son of Henry VII whose death in 1502 left the way to the throne open for the future Henry VIII, looks fancifully like a filigree castle of stone. Its sides are filled with the most refined and delicate Perpendicular tracery surmounted, in place of a crested cornice, by open-work pinnacled battlements, such as were favoured for the crowns of church towers in the west of England in the late middle ages.

The canopies of other monuments of the Perpendicular period, though simpler, made use of the same architectural features as chantry chapels, the façades of free-standing and wall canopies alike sharing a preference for a basically rectangular frame containing the various elements of the composition. This is shown at a very early date on the unique wall monument of Peter de Grandison (d.1352) in Hereford cathedral, where the effigy lies in a rectangular recess, above which appears a row of six gabled arches occupied by figures, topped by a horizontal crested frieze; the base, vertical side-shafts and straight top establish the rectangle as the basis of the design. The monument is, moreover, a further illustration of the tendency (noted above in connection with the Edington chantry at Winchester) for early Perpendicular vigorously to assert its credentials against departing Decorated. But the trend was already apparent in some late Decorated wall canopies in which, although the main feature continued to be a large gabled arch, its upward thrust was counteracted by a horizontal crested or embattled band placed behind it and below the peak of the gable, as, for instance, on the monument of Sir John Wingfield (d.1361) at Wingfield (Suffolk). In fully developed Perpendicular this band commonly rose to enclose the arch or gable entirely, the spandrels in the upper corners of the rectangle being filled with panelling or tracery.

This can be seen on numerous canopied wall monuments of the later fourteenth and fifteenth centuries. On some there is a single arch, on others more than one; some have the ogee-arch, others the four-centred type; variations abound, but the important common element is the containing rectangular frame. Examples with a single ogee-arch include those of Sir William Mainwaring (d.1399) at Acton (Cheshire) and Sir Thomas Berkeley (d.1464) in St Mark's, Bristol, while the canopies of the poet, John Gower (d.1408), in Southwark cathedral and Sir Richard Choke (d.1486) and wife at Long Ashton (Somerset) have, respectively, three and five ogees under the straight top. By contrast, the four-centred arch under a horizontal crested frieze can be seen on the canopies of John de la Pole 2nd duke of Suffolk (d.1491–2) at Wingfield (Suffolk) and Bishop Miles Salley of Llandaff (d.1516–17) in St Mark's, Bristol.

Emphasis on the rectangle is equally apparent in the façades of free-standing or nearly free-standing canopies of the period. For example, the scheme of a wide four-centred arch in a rectangular frame surmounted by a row of quatrefoils appears on those of Bishop Edmund Stafford (d.1419) in Exeter cathedral and William Browning (d.1467) at Melbury Sampford (Dorset), the former topped by cresting, the latter by crenellation, and a grander and loftier version, with side-shafts standing clear of the tomb-chest, occurs on the monument of Sir John Spencer (d.1522) at Great Brington (Northants). Yet more ambitious, the canopy of John Tiptoft earl of Worcester (d.1470) in Ely cathedral has a design of three arches under ogee-gables set against blind and open tracery, which is finished off with a straight crested top.

The horizontal element is asserted uncompromisingly on the monument of Archbishop Henry Chichele (d.1443) in Canterbury cathedral, for here there is no arch at all, the canopy consisting merely of a high straight top between two massive octagonal supports. The canopy of Alice duchess of Suffolk at Ewelme has the same basic shape, but differs in being not an independent canopy, but

rather carved enrichment applied to the top and sides of a rectangular opening made to house the tomb-chest in the wall between chancel and side chapel. It is instructive to note, too, that in the later middle ages royal tomb-chests with effigies in Westminster Abbey were provided with horizontal wooden canopies in the form of testers slung, as it were, between the piers of the abbey's arcade under which the monuments stand. This was first done for Edward III (d.1377), but the feature was added to the earlier monuments of Henry III (d.1272), Queen Eleanor of Castile (d.1290) and Queen Philippa (d.1369), and supplied for the later monument of Richard II (d.1400). In Canterbury cathedral, moreover, the royal monuments of the Black Prince (d.1376) and Henry IV (d.1413) also have flat wooden canopies.

It would be wrong, however, to assume that Perpendicular canopies never departed from this restricting 'sky-line', for, like chantry chapels, some examples of the late fifteenth and early sixteenth centuries indulged in highly decorative and even playful displays. The so-called Wakeman Cenotaph in Tewkesbury abbey, for instance, although fundamentally rectangular in elevation, has a system of intricately cusped and traceried arches surmounted by an impressive band of tabernacle work. It probably dates from the second half of the fifteenth century. Among the most unconventional, however, is the canopy of Bishop Richard Mayeu (d.1516) in Hereford cathedral, for, apart from the tell-tale Perpendicular tracery in its upper stage, its design is so original and its spatial rhythms so unsettling that one might be forgiven for supposing it to be a work of the Decorated period.

Low-relief Effigies, Incised Slabs and Monumental Brasses

Although the more grandiose monuments of the later middle ages comprised most or all of the elements so far discussed, that is, effigies recumbent upon tomb-chests with or without superior canopies, much simpler monuments were produced throughout the period.

In particular, despite the general trend toward the free and fully rounded effigy, slabs with low-relief or sunken effigies continued to be made, especially down to the late fourteenth century. Examples include a late thirteenth-century married couple holding hands at Winterbourne Bassett (Wilts), a priest of the first half of the fourteenth century at Welwick (Yorks) and a man and wife, perhaps of *c.*1350, at Offord Darcy (Hunts). As often as not, however, only part or parts of the low-relief figure were shown. Particularly in the north and north-east midlands, but also occurring elsewhere, there was a strange tradition of showing only the sunken head and shoulders and the feet of the effigy; in these cases the rest of the figure appears either to be concealed by a block across the middle of the slab, as at East Markham and Staunton-in-the-Vale (both Notts), or to be covered by a stone 'blanket', as at South Stoke (*19*) and Careby (Lincs), at both of which places married couples are depicted as though at prayer in bed, especially those at Careby where the feet are also covered. In other variations the head and feet appear in the head and base of a cross whose stem is carved in relief down the centre of the slab, examples of which can be seen at Kingerby (Lincs) and at Gilling and Melsonby (both Yorks). Alternatively, just the head and shoulders or the head alone might be shown in this way, as on the slabs of priests at Garmston, Tuxford and Gedling (all Notts) and on those of a man at Preston Gubbals (Salop) and a lady holding her heart at East Tisted (Hants). All of these date from the early fourteenth century, as does possibly the most beautiful and interesting example at Bredon (Worcs) (*20*), which is carved with a cross bearing the crucified Christ and, above the arms of the cross, the heads and shoulders of a man and his wife, each under a crocketed and finialed gable.

By the early fourteenth century, however, other alternatives to the free effigy were becoming increasingly popular and would in time virtually oust the low-relief effigy. These were the strictly two-dimensional portrayals which appeared on incised slabs and monumental brasses.

The incised slab in particular was cheap and relatively easy to make, the effigy and other features being merely incised in the flat surface of the slab. The earliest surviving examples date from the thirteenth century (one or two possibly earlier) and are coffin-shaped, including the fragment of a naked figure (*c.*1200) at Shillingstone (Dorset), a knight (*c.*1225) at Sollers Hope (Herefs), Bishop William of Bitton II (d.1274) in Wells cathedral and Prior William de Malton (d.1279) at Watton (Yorks), but the incised slab appears not to have been widely employed until the later middle ages, when it was invariably rectangular. From that period some hundreds survive, especially from the fifteenth and sixteenth centuries, some intact but many only as broken pieces. Most were laid in the floor of the church, but others were set upon tomb-chests which, though in many cases since destroyed, survive for the slabs of Sir John Wydevyl (*c.*1415) at Grafton Regis (Northants) and an anonymous figure (late fifteenth century) at Prestwold (Leics) among others. Incised slabs might be made from almost any serviceable stone, but the majority of those produced in England were of alabaster, following the first use of that substance for monumental work in the early fourteenth century, and occur most densely in the north and midlands. At first the standard of design and craftsmanship on alabaster slabs was high, notably, for example, on the excellent specimen for Sir William de St Quintin and wife (d.1384) at Harpham (Yorks), but in the late middle ages the general level fell considerably, figures being often crudely and naively drawn with little creative originality. Among the best are the slabs of Peter de la Pole (d.1432) at Radburne (Derbs), Sir Thomas Boughton (d.1454) at Newbold-on-Avon (Warks), Robert Barley (d.1467) at Barlow (Derbs), Robert Downes (d.1495) at Prestbury (Cheshire) (*21*), Nicholas Graviner, rector (d.1520), at Haughton (Staffs) and Abbot John Barwick (d.1526) in Selby abbey (Yorks), all these being in the north or in the midlands; and, further south, those of John Sprot, priest (d.1466), at Crundale (Kent), John Doggett (d.1480) at Pusey (Berks) and John Stone, priest (*c.*1510), at Aldbourne (Wilts). Late medieval incised slabs of other materials are commonly of foreign manufacture and display on the whole greater attention to detail and higher standards of craftsmanship. Boston church (Lincs), for example, has, among others, a splendid slab in Tournai marble for Wissel Smalenberg, a Hanseatic merchant who died in 1340, while a magnificent specimen in limestone for Lady Alice Tyrell (d.1422), French in origin and dated by Greenhill to *c.*1440, can be seen at Layer Marney (Essex), recently removed there from East Horndon in the same county. For special effect slabs were occasionally enriched by the partial inlay of brass or a form of cement, often plaster of Paris. These inlays have in most cases disappeared, but their empty matrices are clear on a number of examples, notably on the fine French slab of John de Cherewin (d.1441) at Brading (Isle of Wight) and on a number of other foreign slabs at Boston (Lincs). Exceptionally, inlays of cement remain, whole or in part, on a group in Herefordshire, most remarkably on that of Sir Andrew

19 *Above* South Stoke (Lincs): knight and lady under 'blanket' (early fourteenth century)

20 *Far left* Bredon (Worcs): coffin lid with Crucifixion and busts of a man and woman (early fourteenth century)

21 *Left* Prestbury (Cheshire): Robert Downes (d.1495) and wife. Incised slab

Herl and wife (*c.*1390) at Allensmore.

Monumental brasses, the other popular two-dimensional medium, were closely related to incised slabs and may have originated by extension of the inlay technique employed on some of them. A great deal has been written about monumental brasses, particularly in recent years, largely in response to an increasing public interest in the subject stimulated by the ease with which attractive reproductions can be made in the form of brass-rubbings. Indeed, there has emerged what amounts almost to an industry to satisfy the demand, but in all this one essential fact must not be lost sight of, namely, that brasses, like incised slabs, were but one form of late medieval funerary monument which in many respects, and as far as was possible in a two-dimensional medium, paralleled their three-dimensional counterparts.

The most characteristic type of medieval English brass consisted of an engraving on flat plates of brass cut to shape and set flush in a stone slab whose surface had been indented with matrices to receive them (*22*). The majority were in the form of a representation of the deceased, the figure being typically cut out and set in the slab, and invariably accompanied by one or more other elements, such as an inscription, shields of arms, religious symbolism, canopies and so on, which were similarly engraved, cut out and set separately into the slab. In contrast, a number of imported Flemish brasses took the form of rectangular plates entirely covered with engraving of the effigy and other details, as can be seen for the fourteenth century at King's Lynn (Norfolk), Topcliffe (Yorks) and in St Albans cathedral. The slab containing the brass was most commonly placed in the floor of the church, but it might be raised upon a tomb-chest, decorated in the same manner as for effigies in the round, and at the close of the middle ages brasses were frequently inserted not into a horizontal slab but into the backplate of a canopied wall monument. Throughout the medieval period the metal plates for brasses made in England were imported from Flanders, the Rhineland and, to a lesser extent, northern France. The metal is usually described as brass, and that usage is followed here, but it is better called latten, since its consistency differed considerably from most modern brass. It was an extremely hard substance, admirably suited to the engraving alike of bold figures and intricate detail, as is evidenced by the survival of hundreds of brasses little affected by the dust, neglect and feet of several centuries.

Like incised slabs, brass features might themselves be inlaid with other substances, sometimes enamel but chiefly painted lead, and were commonly so treated in the fifteenth and sixteenth centuries to enable heraldic colours to be supplied or to indicate such materials as fur on garments. Often the inlay has gone, but lead survives surprisingly frequently, in many cases still with traces of its painted colouring.

Effigies in brass began to appear in England in the late thirteenth century, increased rapidly in numbers in the fourteenth century and acquired enormous popularity in the fifteenth and early sixteenth centuries. They are most densely concentrated in the south-east of England, East Anglia and Yorkshire, becoming in general less frequent as one moves north-westward or westward. Although this distribution is partly to be explained by varying densities of population in medieval England, there is a rough correlation with the distribution of incised slabs, for on the whole where the latter are most numerous brasses are fewer. The point cannot be pressed, of course, but the easier availability of brass plates or, in particular, alabaster in certain areas seems to have led to a preference for either monumental brasses or incised slabs when cheaper two-dimensional effigies were required.

Chief among the earliest surviving English brasses is an impressive group commemorating knights, all of which display military figures in complete suits of mail, the most famous being that at Stoke D'Abernon (Surrey) traditionally assigned to Sir John D'Abernon (d.1277) and for long honoured as the oldest surviving figured brass in this country. However, the dating of these and all early brasses is beset with the same problems as the dating of effigies in the round, and modern research has rightly called in question the traditional dates both as to their period and as to their precision. From documentary and other evidence it now seems likely that no existing figured brass dates earlier than the fourteenth century and that the famous series of military brasses should be dated after 1310 and probably to the years *c.*1320–1330.

Be that as it may (and the question is far from finally resolved), the Stoke D'Abernon brass is certainly one of the finest English brasses and displays in exceptional degree the high quality of craftsmanship which all early brasses share. The life-size figure of the knight is engraved with clean, decisive lines, both for the detail of his sword and suit of mail and for the folds of his linen surcoat. He is shown alone except for a small shield of arms and a lion at his feet, but he was originally surrounded by an inscription composed of individual letters of 'Lombardic' character set separately into the border of the slab, where indents for them still remain. The depiction has, however, a number of features unique to it (the uncrossed legs of the effigy, the inclusion of a lance bitten by the lion at its foot and the lavish inlay of enamel in the shield) which may argue a primacy of date among the rest of the group, placing it possibly at *c*.1320.

Of the other early military brasses the more important are those at Trumpington (Cambs), traditionally Sir Roger de Trumpington (d.1289); Chartham (Kent), traditionally Sir Robert de Septvans (d.1306); Acton (Suffolk), Sir Robert de Bures (*26*), certainly after 1310 and possibly dating from *c*.1325; and, with slightly more advanced armour, that of Sir William FitzRalph (*c*.1325–35) at Pebmarsh (Essex). The knightly class was not alone, however, in adopting the new fashion for monumental brasses, for at about the same time figures of ladies and ecclesiastics began to be made. Ladies appeared initially alone, including Lady Margaret Camoys (d.1310) at Trotton (Sussex) and Lady Joan de Cobham (*c*.1320) at Cobham (Kent), slightly later with their husbands, such as Lady Creke (*c*.1340) at Westley Waterless (Cambs) (*27*), Lady Wantone (1347) at Wimbish (Essex) and Margaret Torrington (1356) at Berkhamsted (Herts). Notable among the earliest brasses of ecclesiastics are those of Archbishop William Greenfield (d.1315) in York Minster and Laurence de St Maur, priest (d.1337), at Higham Ferrers (Northants). By the middle of the fourteenth century came brasses of men in civilian dress, including Nicholas de Aumberdene at Taplow (Bucks) and John Pecock in St Michael's church, St Albans (Herts), both of *c*.1350. Eventually members of all classes of 'monument-conscious' folk, apart from kings and queens, adopted the monumental brass and in the later middle ages it became a favourite form of monument for lesser clergy and civilians.

Several important developments occurred, however, in the design of brasses after the earliest examples. Firstly, there was an overall reduction in the size of figures, becoming quite marked in the fifteenth century, when, with some notable exceptions, the majority of effigies were half or less the size of the early ones. The standard pose was throughout recumbent and at prayer, but this was often made ambiguous in the later middle ages by showing figures apparently also standing on grassy mounds or on brackets, an early example of the latter being the famous brass of Sir John de Foxley (d.1378) at Bray (Berks). Some married couples were depicted holding hands, and in the fifteenth century the kneeling attitude was introduced, becoming common in sixteenth-century brasses on wall monuments.

Secondly, the practice grew, clearly by analogy with the low-relief half-effigies on some slabs noted above, of showing at times only the upper part of figures, perhaps the earliest surviving instances being two brasses of knights in Lincolnshire, at Croft and Buslingthorpe, dating from the first half of the fourteenth century. The form was particularly favoured by priests and men and women in civil dress, such as a priest of *c*.1340 at Great Brington (Northants), Benedict English (*c*.1360) at Nuffield (Oxon), John de Kyggesfold and wife (*c*.1370) at Rusper (Sussex) and numerous fifteenth-century cases; but it was occasionally still used for knights, as is clear from the late fourteenth-century brass of Sir Edmund and Lady Malyns at Chinnor (Oxon) and that of Ralph de Cobham (d.1402) at Cobham (Kent), the latter being probably unique in that the demi-figure is shown holding the inscription plate.

Thirdly, in addition to depicting married couples or other relations (such as father and son or brother and sister) together, it became increasingly common in the fifteenth century to portray children as well. This might be done by including them as small figures alongside their parents, as on the brasses of Sir Reginald Braybrook (d.1405) and Sir Nicholas Hawberk (d.1407), both at Cobham (Kent), and those of Thomas Lord Camoys (d.1419) at Trotton (Sussex) and Thomas Roose (d.1441) at Salle (Norfolk); a variation on this method occurs at Stoke D'Abernon, where the brass of Anne Norbury (d.1464), a widow, shows her children standing about her feet and sheltered by her ample cloak. Much more frequently, however, the children appeared as small figures standing or kneeling in groups below their parents or (in wall brasses) kneeling behind them. Examples include the brasses of Sir John Cottusmore (d.1439) at Brightwell Baldwin (Oxon), Sir Thomas Urswick (d.1479) at Dagenham (Essex) and Sir Robert Eyre (*c*.1500) at Hathersage (Derbs).

Fourthly, from the early fourteenth century there was a growing tendency to house the figure under a two-dimensional shafted canopy of brass set into the slab. Such canopies followed as far as possible the designs of architectural canopies studied above, particularly wall canopies, and like them reflected changes of building styles, with the difference that late Decorated forms tended to survive well into the Perpendicular period. An early Decorated canopy honours the figure of Lady Joan de Cobham (*c.*1320) at Cobham (Kent) and a late Decorated version that of Sir Robert de Grey (d.1387) at Rotherfield Greys (Oxon) (*28*), while the straight-topped form of Perpendicular canopies appears over the figures of Archbishop Thomas Cranley of Dublin (d.1417) in New College, Oxford, and Nicholas Carew (d.1432) and wife at Beddington (Surrey) (*37*). Some fifteenth-century canopies were particularly elaborate, such as that of Prior Thomas Nelond of Lewes (d.1433) at Cowfold (Sussex), which has double side-shafts supporting a triple arch topped by several rising pinnacled shafts and figures of the Virgin and Child, St Pancras and St Thomas of Canterbury. The treatment of the inscription also underwent a change, for the early method of inserting separate letters into the slab gave way by the 1330s to the carving of the inscription on strips of brass or, later, on plates of brass. Most commonly the words were incised, but on occasions they were more expensively carved in relief, as on the brasses of Sir John Wilcotes (d.1410) at Great Tew (Oxon) and John Estbury (*c.*1485) at Lambourne (Berks).

A number of brasses, originally much larger but drastically reduced by religious iconoclasm in the sixteenth and seventeenth centuries, portrayed the deceased kneeling in devotion to the Holy Trinity or to various saints. The sacred subject might be represented either in the head of a cross, as in the beautiful brasses of Robert Paris and wife (*c.*1400) at Hildersham (Cambs) (*171*) and John Mulsho (d.1400) and wife, formerly at Newton-in-the-Willows and now at Geddington (Northants), or on a bracket, as in the uniquely complete example of John Strete, rector (d.1406), at Upper Hardres (Kent).

Some brasses did not include an effigy at all, but consisted simply of religious imagery, especially the cross, or of some object identifying the profession of the deceased. Excellent examples of crosses alone can be seen on the brasses of Thomas Chichele (d.1401) at Higham Ferrers (Northants) and Richard Pendilton (d.1502) at Eversley (Hants), but, as we have seen, the cross might also be present with effigies and other features. The heart, seat of the

emotions and also symbolic of the Sacred Heart, occurs occasionally: on the brass of Thomas Smyth, vicar (d.1433), at Margate (Kent) it is accompanied by statements of pious belief, while on that of John Merstun, rector (d.1466), at Lillingstone Lovell (Bucks) it is held by two hands. The most frequent professional symbol was the chalice and wafer, indicating a priest's memorial, which occurs chiefly in Yorkshire and East Anglia, including the brasses of Peter Johnson, vicar (d.1460), at Bishop Burton (Yorks) and Thomas Hoont, rector (d.1510), at Bintree (Norfolk). By way of variation, the trade of a glover is suggested by a pair of gloves on the brass of Peter Denot (*c.*1440) at Fletching (Sussex).

Although a great many brasses have been lost or destroyed, their former existence can often be deduced from the survival of the slabs which once held them, retaining matrices for their inlay. Ely cathedral, for example, contains a remarkable number and many parish churches will yield one or more examples. However, in spite of the losses, England retains an immense number of medieval monumental brasses, probably more than the rest of Europe put together, and some churches have impressive collections, notably Cirencester and Northleach (Glos) and, best of all, Cobham (Kent).

Miscellaneous Types of Monument

The vast majority of medieval monuments fall into one or other of the above categories, but there remain a few exceptional pieces to be considered.

Firstly, although effigies in the round were almost always full-length recumbent figures, a tiny minority broke this rule and in a remarkable way anticipated fashions of the late sixteenth and seventeenth centuries. In Tewkesbury abbey (Glos) the chantry chapel of Edward Lord Despenser (d.1375) has the deceased kneeling at prayer in a small canopied housing on the roof. As we have seen, the kneeling posture is found on medieval monumental brasses and occasionally among weepers and angels on tomb-chests, but this is probably its only surviving use in a free effigy of the deceased in the middle ages. Another foreshadowing of later practice occurs at Bakewell (Derbs), where the wall monument of Sir Geoffrey Foljambe (d.1377) and wife depicts them as fully rounded half-effigies at prayer in a curiously arched recess. The portrayal is clearly adapted from the fashion for demi-figures on monumental brasses, but for some reason it had virtually no appeal in the middle ages, the only other known example being the early sixteenth-century half-effigy of Arthur Vernon (d. 1517) resting on a canopied wall-bracket at Tong (Salop).

A small number of heart monuments survive, relating to the custom, particularly when a person of note died overseas or far away, of burying his body in one place and removing the heart and perhaps the viscera for burial at home. Heart monuments are correspondingly small in size and commonly include a heart in their carving. A fine thirteenth-century example in Winchester cathedral commemorates Bishop Aymer de Valence (d. 1260), where, within a rich mandorla decorated with stiff-leaf, the half-effigy of the bishop is shown in relief, holding his heart in his hands. Simpler versions of the late thirteenth century, with low-relief half-effigies of knights holding hearts, occur at Coberley (Glos) and Hampton-in-Arden (Warks). In a wall of the north transept at Yaxley (Hunts) is a different type of heart monument carved with two hands holding a heart aloft, probably for William of Yaxley, abbot of Thorney (d. 1293) (*23*); in this case a wooden box containing remains of the heart was found in 1842 in a cavity behind the carved stone and is now displayed in an alcove nearby. Similar heart monuments exist also at Bredon (Worcs) and Careby (Lincs). A third type of heart monument consisted of a full but miniature effigy recumbent and holding a heart in its hands, as is found, for example, at Adwell (Oxon), Letchworth (Herts) and Mappowder (Dorset), all of the early fourteenth century.

Finally, some medieval monuments were designed so that they could also be used for certain liturgical or ceremonial purposes. There is no doubt, for instance, that an unusual piscina of *c.*1275 at Long Wittenham (Berks) is also a memorial, perhaps a heart monument, for in front of its drain lies the tiny figure of a knight and at the top of its recess two small angels fly upward, originally bearing in a napkin the soul of the deceased, his head alone now remaining under the arch (*24*). Other monuments were adapted for use as an Easter Sepulchre, the feature which played so prominent a part in the ceremonial of Holy Week in the later middle ages. In such cases the monument comprised a tomb-chest without effigy set in a canopied wall recess. An early fourteenth-century example survives at Cockfield (Suffolk) and another of *c.*1526 at Woodleigh (Devon), the latter having on the back of the recess appropriate carvings of the Deposition

from the Cross, the Resurrection and the Visit of the Three Maries to the Sepulchre. But the most remarkable instance of dual function occurs in Durham cathedral, where the monument and chantry chapel of Bishop Thomas Hatfield (d. 1381) includes the provision of a new episcopal throne raised high on an arched platform above the bishop's tomb-chest.

Dress and Armour in the Middle Ages

One of the most interesting aspects of effigies throughout this period is the dress or armour in which they are depicted, for, whether in two or three dimensions, it is frequently shown in great detail. Moreover, since for many classes of effigy it varies from period to period with changing fashions, it is important in the dating of those effigies which are anonymous and have survived without other dateable features. More especially is this true of effigies of knights and ladies.

The earliest armour found on monumental effigies is basically of the type that had been in use since at least the time of the Norman Conquest. It consisted of a complete suit of mail, made up of small interlinked metal rings, covering the body from head to foot. Over this was worn a linen surcoat reaching to below the knees and open in front and back below the waist. Slung in front was a great sword suspended from a leather belt, while on the left arm was worn a shield and on the heels prick spurs. This armour is well illustrated by a number of thirteenth-century effigies, including that of a knight of *c.*1250–75 at Stowe-Nine-Churches (Northants) (*7*). Most effigies do not show, however, the great helm that was worn over the mailed head, since to do so would have prevented the face from being seen, although it does appear, for instance, on an incised slab of *c.*1225 at Sollers Hope (Herefs) and on effigies in the round of *c.*1250 at Walkern (Herts) (*25*) and Kirkstead (Lincs).

The earliest brasses of knights depict this mail armour extraordinarily well, and none better than that of Sir Robert de Bures at Acton (Suffolk), arguably the finest military brass in England (*26*). It is clear, however, from this and other examples that by the early fourteenth century reinforcements of boiled leather (or possibly steel) were strapped over the knees for additional protection. The contemporary brass of Sir John D'Abernon at Stoke D'Abernon (Surrey) is unique in showing a pictorially shortened lance in the crook of his right arm,

22 Northleach (Glos): William Lander (d.1530). Brass. Note the empty 'matrices' formerly containing representations of the Trinity and the Virgin and Child

23 Yaxley (Hunts): Abbot William Yaxley of Thorney (d.1293). Heart monument

24 Long Wittenham (Berks): Piscina monument (*c.*1275). Note small figure of a knight

25 Walkern (Herts): Knight (*c.*1250). Detail showing the great helm

while that at Trumpington (Cambs) displays, exceptionally, the great helm behind the knight's head and attached by means of a chain to his waist.

In the 1320s a process began by which, gradually over succeeding generations, additional defences of plate armour were worn over the suit of mail, until eventually, by about 1410, the body came to be entirely encased in plate armour. During the same period the linen surcoat was progressively shortened and tightened and ultimately replaced in the later fourteenth century by a boiled leather jupon covering the knight's torso. Equally, prick spurs were succeeded by rowel spurs and the shield ceased to be shown after about 1350.

The first additions of plate can be seen on the brass of Sir William FitzRalph (c.1325–35) at Pebmarsh (Essex), whose basic suit of mail is supplemented by metal plates strapped on the front of his legs and feet and on the sides of his arms, while extra plates or leather reinforcements protect the elbow-joints and shoulders. The next stage is apparent on the brasses of Sir John D'Abernon the Younger at Stoke D'Abernon and Sir John de Creke at Westley Waterless (Cambs) (27), both of c.1340, and on the alabaster effigy of John de Eltham (d.1336) in Westminster Abbey. On these the most important aspect, apart from the shortening of the surcoat, is the introduction of the 'bascinet', a close-fitting pointed helmet, from which hangs a mail defence for the sides of the face and the neck, called a 'camail' or 'aventail'. This type of helmet was to remain standard into the early fifteenth century. A further stage in the shortening of the surcoat is illustrated by the famous but sadly mutilated brass of Sir Hugh Hastings (d.1347) at Elsing (Norfolk).

By about 1360–70 a certain stability in defensive armour was achieved which was to endure until the early fifteenth century. It was supremely characteristic of the reign of Richard II (1377–99), from whose time numerous two- and three-dimensional effigies survive in good preservation to give a clear idea of its form. The brasses of Sir John Harsick (d.1384) at South Acre (Norfolk) and Sir Robert de Grey (d.1387) at Rotherfield Greys (Oxon) (28) may be taken as typical examples. The body is by now entirely encased in plate, except for the lower face and neck, which continue to be protected by the aventail dependent from the bascinet, and the torso, which is protected by a mail shirt (usually visible at its hem and at the armpits) and, over it, a tight boiled-leather jupon. Moreover, the sword-belt has been simplified and shortened, allowing the sword

to hang on the knight's left side. In many other examples, a small dagger is attached to the right side of the figure.

A curious detail occurs on some three-dimensional effigies, which have, upon the bascinet immediately above the knight's forehead, a carving of the Latin abbreviation for the words, 'Jesus of Nazareth'. Amongst others, it can be seen on the effigies of early fifteenth-century knights at Hornby and Swine (Yorks), Sir William Wilcote (d.1410) at Northleigh (Oxon) and Sir William Marney (d.1414) at Layer Marney (Essex). The practice referred to a superstition, dating back to the twelfth century, that the inscribing of these sacred words on one's forehead constituted a protection against danger, but it is odd that it is not found on effigies earlier than the late fourteenth century and did not survive long in the fifteenth.

By about 1410 the knight's body was wholly encased in plate armour of a type that was to retain a standard appearance for approximately thirty years. It is superbly illustrated by the figure of Sir Thomas Swynborne (d.1412) at Little Horkesley (Essex) (29), part of a double brass which also depicts his father (d.1391) in the typical armour of the preceding generation. The main differences are that the mail defence for the neck has been replaced by a plate metal gorget and that the jupon has been discarded in favour of a cuirass and short skirt of plate armour. Fairly frequently in this phase an ornamental circlet of padded material, known as an 'orle', is worn round the helmet, as can be seen, for example, on the brass of the 5th Lord Willoughby (d.1410) at Spilsby (Lincs) and the alabaster effigy of Sir Richard Vernon (d.1451) at Tong (Salop) (9). Equally, it was not uncommon for effigies of knights (and some others) to be shown wearing an 'S-collar', composed of a chain of S's and associated originally with adherence to the House of Lancaster.

Further developments in armour followed in the mid-fifteenth century, mainly in the form of additional plate defences for the shoulders and arms, extra plates suspended from the 'skirt' and enlargements of the knee protections. A typical example of the mid-fifteenth century is provided by the brass of Sir Thomas Shernborne (d.1458) at Shernborne (Norfolk), and of a generation later by that of Thomas Peyton (d.1484) at Isleham (Cambs) (38).

Later medieval military effigies, and particularly those dating after 1450, were commonly shown bare-headed. Partly this was due to changing

26 Acton (Suffolk): Sir Robert de Bures (*c.*1320–30). Rubbing of brass

27 Westley Waterless (Cambs): Sir John and Lady de Creke (*c.*1340). Rubbing of brass

28 Rotherfield Greys (Oxon): Sir Robert de Grey (d.1387).
Rubbing of brass

29 Little Horkesley (Essex): Sir Thomas Swynborne (d.1412).
Rubbing of part of a brass which also shows Sir Thomas's
father

fashions in the presentation of the deceased, but partly also to the difficulty of accurately depicting a new form of helmet, known as a 'sallet' or 'salade', which formed part of the typical knight's defences by the middle of the century. It is, however, worn by the alabaster effigy of William Browning (d.1467) at Melbury Sampford (Dorset) (*30*) and by the brass figure of John Teringham (d.1484) at Tyringham (Bucks) among others, in each of which, although the beavered and visored defences for the face are omitted, its characteristic shape, with a broad outward-curving base extending down to protect the back of the neck, is clearly apparent.

In the early sixteenth century, when the use of guns and cannon was beginning to undermine its importance, armour was simplified. It took on an altogether more rounded and less spiky appearance, the excessive growth of some additional pieces in the preceding period was reversed and a mail skirt became prominent beneath and below the plate armour. This type of armour is in many cases better portrayed on three-dimensional effigies than on brasses, a good example being provided by the figure of Sir Randle Brereton (dating 1522) at Malpas (Cheshire) (*31*).

The dress of ladies was far more variable than that of knights, especially in the later middle ages, but, despite this, certain basic fashions can be discerned. The earliest female effigies date from the thirteenth century and wear costume which, though differing from individual to individual, was to remain fundamentally the same until the mid-fourteenth century. It consisted essentially of a kirtle with tight-fitting sleeves, over which was worn a loose, waistless gown, while the head, with the hair gathered into bunches at the sides, was covered by a veil and the sides of the face and chin by a wimple which hung down over the neck. This type of dress is shown to good effect, for example, on the effigies of a mid-thirteenth-century lady at Wolferlow (Herefs) (*32*) and a lady of the Heriz family (*c*.1300) at Gonalston (Notts) (*33*), and rather later on the brass of Lady Creke (*c*.1340) at Westley Waterless (Cambs) (*27*).

From the mid-fourteenth century changes came with increasing momentum, affecting in particular the head-dresses of ladies, as the veil and wimple were discarded allowing greater scope for a variety of fashions in the dressing of the hair. In the later fourteenth century a favourite form was the so-called 'reticulated' or 'nebulé' head-dress, easy enough to recognize but rather difficult to interpret.

In all versions the hair partly or largely encircles the face as viewed from the front, but it is not always clear whether the hair is visible through a net or enclosed within an ornamental or frilly band. The brass figure of Lady Harsick (*c*.1384) at South Acre (Norfolk) appears to wear her hair in plaited bands at the sides of her face, while the wife of Thomas Beauchamp earl of Warwick (d.1369) in St Mary's, Warwick, clearly has hers within a stiff, crinkled band surrounding the face. The most extraordinary version of the fashion occurs on the monument of Thomas 8th Lord Berkeley (d.1361) at Berkeley (Glos) (*34*), where his wife's hair appears to be gathered into enormously long crimped tresses on either side of her face, reaching down almost to her breast.

These fashions passed away in the early fifteenth century, giving way to a practice of gathering the hair into bunches or blocks at the sides of the face and enclosing them in jewelled nets or cauls. The habit was extremely variable, almost every example being slightly different from any other, but its various manifestations have been loosely lumped together under the umbrella term, 'crespine' head-dress. A fine example of one version is provided by the wife of Sir Sampson de Strelley (*c*.1400) at Strelley (Notts) (*35*), where the hair is clearly enclosed in ornamental cauls and a veil is worn over the back of the head, held in place by a fillet. In other examples, the hair is gathered into cauls and surmounted by a highly decorative circlet of padded material and a jewelled net. The richness of some of these creations is usually only apparent on well-preserved effigies in the round, such as, for example, that of the wife of Sir William Wilcote (d.1410) at Northleigh (Oxon) (*36*).

A very characteristic form of a generation later involved the enclosing of the hair in great blocks of netting on either side of the head, with a loose veil thrown over all and hanging down in great length behind. Among the most famous examples is that worn by the wife of Sir Ralph Greene (d.1417) at Lowick (Northants), but many less elaborate versions are to be seen on brasses of the period, including that of Nicholas Carew (d.1432) and wife at Beddington (Surrey) (*37*). A much rarer, but basically similar, head-dress is worn by the brass effigy of Lady Peryent (*c*.1415) at Digswell (Herts), where the face is framed by hair gathered into a triangular-shaped netted block rising high above the head, the veil being pinned up at the top.

As the decades passed, the netted blocks of hair

were progressively turned up at their ends to form the so-called 'horned' head-dress, a veil continuing in most cases to be worn over all. This form is very commonly shown on brasses, an extreme example being that of Jane Keriell (d. 1455) at Ash (Kent), in which the veil is absent and the pointing of the 'horns' is emphasized by a padded horned centre-piece. But perhaps the best-known method of dressing the hair in the later middle ages came in the 1470s and 1480s with the butterfly head-dress. This involved the drawing of the hair back into a tightly netted and jewelled bun behind the head, on which was erected a system of wires to support an extravagant flimsy veil or stiffer calico structure fancifully resembling a butterfly's wings. A splendid example is worn by Lady Fitzherbert (c. 1483) at Norbury (Derbs), but the head-dress was difficult to portray accurately on recumbent effigies in the round and is more commonly found on brass figures, including, for instance, the two wives of Thomas Peyton (d. 1484) at Isleham (Cambs) (*38*).

At the end of the fifteenth century a quite new type of head-dress was introduced which in various forms remained fashionable well into the next century. It abandoned the elaborate netting of the hair, enclosing it instead in a cap, to the front of which was attached an ornamental band of material framing the face and extending down on to the shoulders. At first the band simply followed the curve of the head, but in the sixteenth century it developed a pointed, gable-like outline, producing the so-called 'pedimented' or 'kennel' head-dress so familiar from the well-known portrait of Catherine of Aragon. The head-dress is nicely illustrated by the effigy of Lady Brereton (1522) at Malpas (Cheshire) (*31*) among many others.

The rest of the costume of ladies after the mid-fourteenth century underwent parallel, if less variable, developments. The most remarkable phenomenon was the adoption of the sideless cote-hardie, the upper part of which was entirely cut away at the sides from above the arms to well below the waist. In some cases the bodice was made of a material different from that of the skirt, but in others the whole was of the same material. In general it pulled the waist low, but, although it survived into the 1470s, as is clear from the effigy of Alice duchess of Suffolk (d. 1475) at Ewelme (Oxon), other alternative fashions in the fifteenth century emphasized an excessively high waist. Typical, for example, is the brass figure of Nicholas Carew's wife (c. 1432) at Beddington (*37*), who wears

a very full dress with ample sleeves and a waist set just below her bust. In the late fifteenth century, as is apparent on the Peyton brass of c. 1484 at Isleham (*38*), the dress above the waist was uniformly tight-fitting, while the skirt was usually wide and voluminous.

In contrast with these successive fashions in clothes and head-dress, an appreciable number of female effigies of the later middle ages were depicted in the characteristic attire of widows, which remained remarkably unchanged throughout the period. These 'widow's weeds', as they are called, consisted essentially of a large veil for the head and a 'barbe', somewhat resembling a wimple, which fitted over the chin and hung down in front over the neck. They were typically worn with a simple kirtle and mantle, as on the brass of Eleanor de Bohun, duchess of Gloucester (d. 1399), in Westminster Abbey, but toward the end of the middle ages they increasingly appear in conjunction with ordinary dress of the period. So, for example, the alabaster effigy of Duchess Alice at Ewelme wears widow's weeds with a sideless cote-hardie and mantle, and a duchess's coronet is placed upon her veiled head (*39*).

Effigies of men in civilian dress similarly reflected changing fashions. Among the earliest surviving is an excellent stone effigy of an unknown man (c. 1240) in St James's, Bristol, but civilian effigies, either in two or three dimensions, do not become at all common before the mid-fourteenth century. We may take two examples which will serve to illustrate fashionable male attire at different points in the later middle ages, although it must be remembered that numerous variations in dress occurred both at these and other times. At Much Marcle (Herefs) a fine wooden effigy of c. 1360 (*40*) depicts a male figure in one form of tunic typical of the fourteenth century, reaching to just above the knees and buttoned down the front, a short tippet being worn over the shoulders and tight hose and pointed shoes on the legs and feet. In other depictions of the period the details of this type of costume are frequently obscured by the addition of a cloak over all. The second example comes from the fifteenth century and occurs on the brass of Nicholas Carew (d. 1432) at Beddington (*37*). Here the belted tunic is longer, extending to below the knees, and much fuller, with exceedingly voluminous sleeves which narrow to fairly close-fitting cuffs at the wrists. The tunic is partially open in front at the neck and above the hem, and the ensemble is completed by leg-hose and

30 Melbury Sampford (Dorset): William Browning (d.1467). Detail showing the sallet

31 Malpas (Cheshire): Sir Randle and Lady Brereton (1522)

32 Wolferlow (Herefs): lady (*c.*1250)

33 Gonalston (Notts): lady of the Heriz family (*c.*1300)

34 *Top left* Berkeley (Glos): Lady Berkeley, wife of Thomas 8th Lord Berkeley (d. 1361)
35 *Above* Strelley (Notts): Sir Sampson and Lady Strelley (*c.* 1400)
36 *Top right* Northleigh (Oxon): Lady Wilcote, wife of Sir William Wilcote (d. 1410). Detail of head-dress

37 *Above* Beddington (Surrey): Nicholas Carew (d. 1432) and wife. Rubbing of brass

38 *Top right* Isleham (Cambs): Thomas Peyton (d. 1484) and wives. Rubbing of brass

39 *Right* Ewelme (Oxon): Alice duchess of Suffolk (d. 1475). Detail showing widow's weeds

pointed shoes. Similar male attire in various forms was worn for much of the fifteenth century and can be paralleled on numerous effigies of the period.

On the other hand, male effigies were often depicted in the official dress of their respective professions, which in most cases underwent little or no change. Such effigies provide valuable evidence of the appearance of professional men in the middle ages. At Skegby (Notts), for instance, an early fourteenth-century figure is clad in the costume and accoutrements of a forest official, while in a number of places effigies of judges in their legal robes are to be seen. Examples include the alabaster figure of Sir William Gascoine (d.1419) at Harewood (Yorks) and the brasses of Sir John Cassy (d.1400) at Deerhurst (Glos) and Sir John Cottusmore (d.1439) at Brightwell Baldwin (Oxon), all of which show the long gown, the fur-lined mantle fastened at the right shoulder and held up over the left arm, the hood and the distinctive close-fitting cap (or 'coif'). Academic dress is also found, although it occurs almost exclusively on brasses and is largely confined to memorials in the chapels of Oxford and Cambridge colleges. Among them New College, Oxford, has a particularly good selection of fifteenth-century academic brasses, including that of Thomas Hylle (d.1468), who appears in his robes as a Doctor of Divinity (*43*).

The most numerous professional group of all, however, was that of the clergy, large numbers of whose effigies survive, extending in date back to the twelfth century and ranging in rank from archbishops to chantry priests. Especially frequent were depictions of priests, particularly on monumental brasses. In the majority of cases they were shown in eucharistic vestments, robed for the celebration of Mass and wearing the distinctive priestly vestment, the chasuble. Such vestments are illustrated, for example, on the brasses of Laurence de St Maur, rector (d.1337), at Higham Ferrers (Northants) and Nicholas de Caerwent, rector (d.1381), at Crondall (Hants) (*42*). Rather less commonly priests were depicted in processional vestments, the most notable elements of which were the almuce (a fur-lined cape with long fur ends hanging down in front) and, over it, a rich cope fastened by an elaborate clasp at the neck and enriched on its front edges with embroidered

borders, known as 'orphreys' and commonly adorned with figures of saints. Processional vestments of this kind are to be seen, for instance, on two fine brasses of rectors (d.1401 and 1462) at Balsham (Cambs). Occasionally, one encounters priests robed in processional vestments without the cope, in which cases the form of the almuce is more readily apparent, as, for example, on the brass of Richard Adams, vicar (d.1522), at East Malling (Kent).

At the top of the ecclesiastical hierarchy, surviving effigies of archbishops and bishops are mostly in three dimensions, the majority showing the deceased in full pontificals with crozier or cross. Several have been cited earlier in this chapter, but the splendour of an archbishop vested in pontificals is made especially clear on a fifteenth-century brass, that of Archbishop Cranley of Dublin (d.1417) in New College, Oxford (*41*). In addition to the vestments of a bishop, it displays also the 'pallium', a woollen vestment conferred by the pope and worn over the shoulders as a symbol of metropolitan authority.

Other clerical ranks were also depicted in their characteristic vestments, and, apart from the secular clergy, members of religious orders were equally commemorated by monumental effigies which displayed their respective habits. The vast majority of these have not survived, for they were placed in monastic churches which were subsequently destroyed or pillaged at the Dissolution of the Monasteries in the sixteenth century. Nonetheless, a sample has come down to us, including effigies of abbots and priors in places like Gloucester and Peterborough, where a medieval abbey was transformed into a cathedral at the Reformation, and a handful of others and of brasses and incised slabs elsewhere. At St Albans, for instance, there is one of the finest Flemish brasses in England, depicting Abbot Thomas de la Mare (d.1396), and a smaller brass for a monk, Thomas Beauner, dating from c.1450. These were Benedictines, and a brass for a Benedictine abbess, Elizabeth Herwy (d.1527), is to be seen at Elstow (Beds). Brasses depicting members of other orders include those of a Cluniac, Prior Nelond of Lewes at Cowfold (Sussex), and an Augustinian, Abbot Richard Beauforest (c.1510) at Dorchester (Oxon).

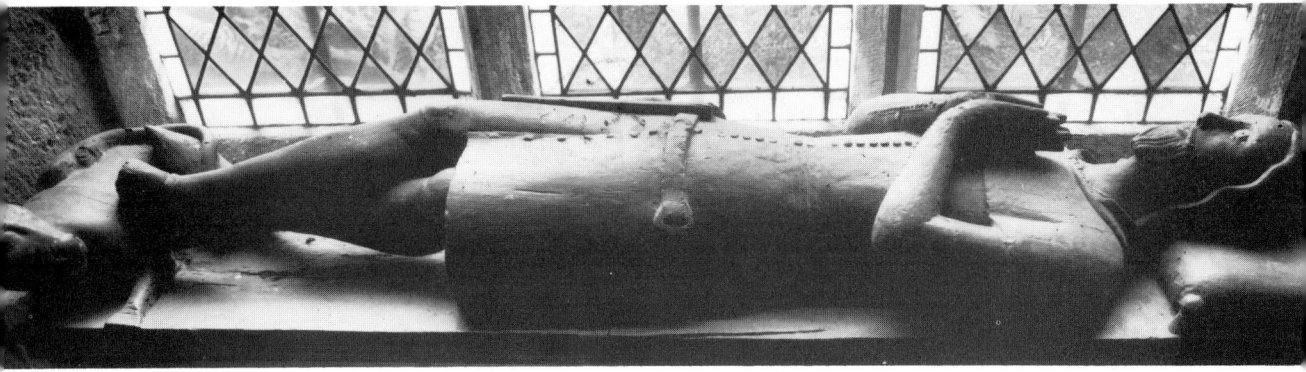

40 Much Marcle (Herefs): civilian (*c*.1360). Wooden effigy

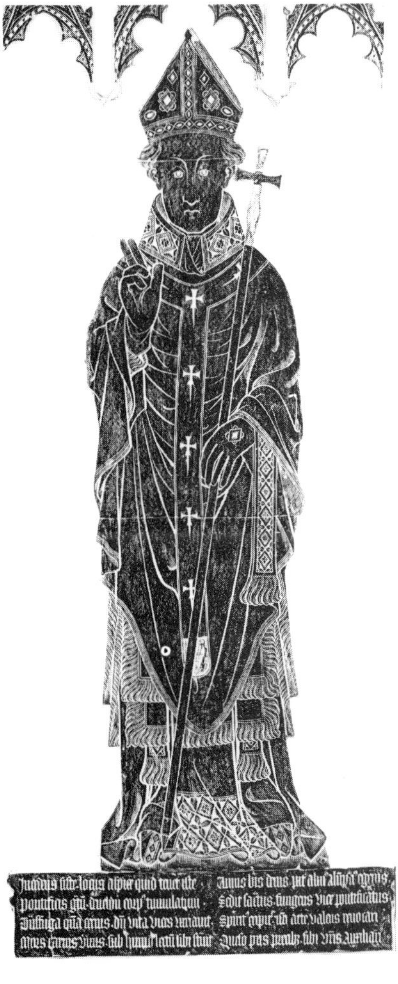

41 *Left* New College chapel, Oxford: Thomas Cranley, archbishop of Dublin (d.1417). Rubbing of brass (detail)
42 *Centre* Crondall (Hants): Nicholas of Caerwent, rector (d.1381). Rubbing of brass
43 *Right* New College chapel, Oxford: Thomas Hylle, Doctor of Divinity (d.1468). Rubbing of brass

3 Renaissance Monuments of the Sixteenth & early Seventeenth Centuries c.1530-c.1620

At the beginning of the sixteenth century England's church monuments were still wholly Gothic in character, and the late medieval Perpendicular style continued everywhere to flourish, whether in courtly circles or in remoter and more conservative centres. But in the course of the sixteenth century the situation was to be utterly changed by the arrival of the Renaissance style from the continent of Europe. At first its adoption was halting and hesitant, yet within a period of little over fifty years the Renaissance had come to predominate over late medieval Gothic in the design of monuments and by the end of the century had completely supplanted it.

Renaissance art was in origin Italian, the Renaissance having begun in the later middle ages in Italy and especially in Florence, where it came to an early maturity in the first half of the fifteenth century. It was a complex and fundamental revolution in art and culture whose mainspring, certainly as far as the plastic arts were concerned, was the desire to return for inspiration and example to ancient Rome and thereby to bring about a rebirth of classical values in sculpture, painting and architecture after what was regarded as the debased and impure civilization of the Gothic middle ages. Although in the course of time, and particularly when the Renaissance spread outside Italy into northern Europe, its creative spirit liberated it from slavish dependence on classical models and enabled it to experiment with new forms and motifs, it remained essentially and avowedly un-Gothic. It set its face not only against the techniques and idioms of Gothic art, but also (one might even say) against its very soul.

The Introduction of Renaissance Embellishment

The new style first appeared on English church monuments shortly after the accession of Henry VIII in 1509. In that year both King Henry VII and his mother, the Lady Margaret Beaufort, died, and within a few years contracts for their monuments, to be erected in Henry VII's new chapel in Westminster Abbey, were awarded to an Italian Renaissance craftsman, Pietro Torrigiani, who signed agreements for Lady Margaret's in 1511 and for the king's in 1512. The former monument was probably completed in essentials in 1513, the latter in 1518. While both works were traditionally English and medieval in form, comprising recumbent effigies on rectangular tomb-chests, their great significance lay in the fact that their embellishment and the combination of materials used were entirely new and Renaissance in character.

Henry VII's tomb-chest is particularly unequivocal in its use of Renaissance motifs (44). Instead of rows of niched Gothic figures or shields of arms, its sides are adorned with roundels in circular wreaths enclosing pairs of saints in relief, their bodies not elongated and static but rounded and posed in rhetorical gestures. The roundels are separated by shallow pilasters having antique Corinthian bases and capitals and enriched on their surface with characteristic early Renaissance candelabra designs. One end of the tomb-chest has the royal arms flanked by naked winged cherubs (or 'putti'), while on top at the four corners sit youthful angels dressed in loose classical garments. To complete the scheme the base and top of the chest are decorated with Renaissance foliage scrolls and the corners of the plinth consist of antique masks. The monument is constructed of white marble and black marble (or touch) and most of the ornamental features, like the effigies of the king and queen above, are of gilt bronze, the use of this material on such a scale being hitherto unprecedented in England. Lady Margaret's monument is more modest, but the tomb-chest is only slightly less emphatic in its Renaissance character. Made entirely of touch, it is decorated with heraldic shields enclosed in circular wreaths and separated by fluted pilasters of a Composite order. In contrast, however, the gilt-bronze effigy is provided with a recumbent shafted niche of Gothic type, also of gilt bronze, after the fashion of earlier royal effigies in the abbey.

The decision to entrust such important commissions to an Italian artist reflects the increasingly cosmopolitan outlook of the Tudor court and its desire to emulate the patronage of Renaissance rulers in Italy, France, the Low Countries and elsewhere. Renaissance influences were not, of course, unknown in England before Torrigiani's arrival (indeed, in Henry VII's own lifetime plans for his monument even more novel than the one finally adopted were being discussed with other Italian masters), but no noticeable effect on English monuments had been felt. It was Torrigiani's achievement to set before native makers of monuments and their clients new models of design and execution, and to point the way for the introduction into England of a range of decorative and symbolic enrichment, and ultimately of structural form, quite alien to the country's deep-rooted and rather insular Gothic traditions.

The impact of Torrigiani's work was, however, neither immediate nor direct. Although he was responsible for at least one other monument, the small bronze portrait medallion of Sir Thomas Lovell in Westminster Abbey, and probably for the standing wall monument of Dr Yonge (d.1516) in the Public Record Office, he left England in 1520 without founding a permanent school here. Two other Italians followed him for a brief time to England in the 1520s, but their commissions were mainly architectural and, apart from an uncompleted tomb for Cardinal Wolsey and plans for Henry VIII's monument, they were not concerned with funerary works. Moreover, Torrigiani's works were all in London. There was thus no continuous flow of Italian monuments, disseminated widely throughout the country, to stimulate an immediate English response. Conversely, the strength of native tradition militated against any sudden and spontaneous abandonment of Gothic concepts. It was not in fact until the 1530s that major changes in the embellishment of monuments began to gather momentum, and by then the immediate sources of Renaissance influence on English tomb design were not Italian, but north European, especially French and to a lesser extent North German and Flemish. Despite the religious upheavals of the English Reformation, which began in the 1530s, French influence remained the primary channel of foreign

Renaissance ideas until the early years of Elizabeth I's reign. Indeed, it is possible that a number of more progressive monuments of the period 1530–60 were either the work of French artists invited over by individual patrons or at least made under French inspiration.

Despite the more widespread adoption of the Renaissance style after 1530, it was confined initially to surface decoration. The types and architectural forms of late medieval monuments persisted unchallenged until the mid-sixteenth century. In particular, the rectangular tomb-chest with one or more recumbent effigies continued in popularity throughout and beyond the sixteenth century, and the same is largely true of two-dimensional memorials in brass and incised slab. Similarly the canopied wall monument endured, though radically altered by Renaissance considerations after 1550, and the chantry chapel survived intermittently until the end of Mary I's reign. Moreover, despite some important exceptions, there was a marked reluctance to change to new materials, stone and alabaster remaining the standard media throughout the sixteenth century.

The novel substance of terra-cotta was employed, however, for a remarkable group of East Anglian monuments, notoriously difficult to date precisely but usually assigned to c.1530, which display a thoroughgoing, if not entirely felicitous, scheme of Renaissance decoration and are among those which may be the result of French influence. The most important are the two Bedingfield monuments at Oxborough (Norfolk) and those of the 1st and 2nd Lords Marney (d.1523 and 1525) at Layer Marney (Essex) (45). The scheme is the late medieval one of tomb-chest under a low-pitched canopy (except for the 2nd Lord Marney's, which lacks a canopy), but all uprights are rendered as balusters or pilasters, the frieze and cresting of the canopies are wholly Renaissance in shape and enrichment, and the tomb-chests are decorated with square or oblong panels separated by balusters or pilasters. The panels of the Bedingfield chests are carved with candelabra designs and surmounted by semi-circular arched heads, those of the Marney tombs having egg-and-dart borders and containing heraldic shields in roundels.

These exuberantly Renaissance monuments are followed in date by a series of effigy-bearing tomb-chests, without canopies and executed in familiar materials, which show an equivalent commitment to the new style, though differing widely in the

44 *Above* Westminster Abbey: King Henry VII (d.1509) and Queen Elizabeth. By Pietro Torrigiani

45 *Right* Layer Marney (Essex): Henry 1st Lord Marney (d.1523)

46 *Below* Cobham (Kent): George Brooke, 9th Lord Cobham (d.1558)

combination of motifs and the precise source of their inspiration. Their sides and ends are articulated in the earliest examples by balusters or pilasters, slightly later by colonnettes, and the square or oblong panels thus created are commonly carved with circular wreaths, shields of arms or exceptionally with other devices, while in some cases the panels are surmounted by shell-heads, that is, attractive semi-circular arches fluted radially to resemble shells. The group includes the monuments of Prior Thomas Vyvyan (d.1533) at Bodmin (Cornwall), Sir Thomas Unton (d.1533) at Faringdon (Berks), Sir Anthony Browne (d.1548) at Battle (Sussex), the royal and Howard tombs at Framlingham (Suffolk) and that of the 9th Lord Cobham (d.1558) at Cobham (Kent).

The Framlingham series comprises the monuments of Henry FitzRoy duke of Richmond, Henry VIII's illegitimate son who died in 1536; Thomas Howard 3rd duke of Norfolk, who died in 1554; and the two wives of the 4th duke (d.1557 and 1564). The first is the least impressive of the three and lacks an effigy; the tomb-chest is articulated by fluted pilasters creating oblong panels filled with shields or lozenges of arms, above which is a frieze of narrative biblical scenes (not of Renaissance style) separated by miniature caryatids. By contrast, the other two Framlingham monuments are of exceptionally high quality: the 3rd duke of Norfolk's chest is adorned with deep shell-headed niches occupied by very competently carved figures of saints and divided by elegantly formed balusters, while that of the 4th duke's two wives has panels with egg-and-dart borders containing heraldic shields or lozenges and divided by colonnettes. Colonnettes also articulate the splendid tomb-chest of Lord Cobham at Cobham (*46*), which, though unique in composition, is closely related to the Framlingham monuments: here the colonnettes appear between shell-headed niches, similar to the 3rd duke of Norfolk's, but occupied by kneeling children instead of saints. The use of colonnettes on the latest of this series is of significance in that, as a High Renaissance feature, they came into fashion later than balusters and pilasters, around the middle of the sixteenth century. They were much employed thereafter and, though the types favoured on different monuments varied, together they represented all the major Roman orders of columns. At Framlingham they are Corinthian, at Cobham Ionic, while, to anticipate a little, the tomb-chest of Frances duchess of Suffolk (d.1559, monument

1563) in Westminster Abbey has Roman Doric and that of Sir William Petre (d.1572) at Ingatestone (Essex) Tuscan Doric.

The tomb-chests discussed so far may be described as Renaissance in that their enrichment is composed wholly or mainly of Renaissance elements, but the total of such monuments is not large and they cannot be regarded as typical of the English output in these years. Most monuments were produced by native craftsmen working under less immediate Renaissance influences, especially in the continuing alabaster workshops of the north and midlands, but these too, although their understanding of the new style was limited, began in the 1530s to show an increasing receptivity to Renaissance motifs, more particularly some of those employed by Torrigiani.

Until the 1530s 'English' tomb-chests remained basically late medieval in enrichment, with standard rows of figures or shields in Gothic contexts, the only concessions to Renaissance influence being the more rounded and relaxed treatment of weepers on some monuments and the occasional inclusion of a Renaissance motif in an otherwise Gothic scheme. Good examples of this latest Gothic phase can be seen in the monuments of Sir William Smythe (d.1525) at Elford (Staffs), Sir Richard Knightley (d.1534) at Fawsley (Northants) and Sir Roger Mynors (d.1536) at Duffield (Derbs). At the same time, however, other monuments reveal a willingness to adapt traditional schemes to the new, and as yet incompletely digested, designs. The tomb-chests of Sir John Blount (d.1531) at Kinlet (Salop) and Sir Walter Devereux (d.1537) at Stowe-by-Chartley (Staffs) are cases in point, for, while each is adorned with weepers under arches, the whole is dressed up in a Renaissance guise. The small figures in twos and threes adopt more rhetorical poses, the 'arches' consist of Renaissance-inspired scrolls resting on balusters or colonnettes, and the decoration is completed by pilasters enriched with candelabra. These tomb-chests are no longer Gothic, but they are not truly Renaissance either; they are hybrids. Equally hybrid, though in different ways, are the chests of Nicholas Purefoy (d.1545) at Fenny Drayton (Leics) and Thomas Manners 1st earl of Rutland (d.1543) at Bottesford (Leics) among others.

This kind of approach might well have led in time to a fuller appreciation of the Renaissance style and to a wider and more imaginative adoption of its principles, but the English schools appear to have suffered from the drying up of direct foreign influence and from the disruption in monument-making caused by the iconoclasm of the mid-sixteenth century. In these circumstances English monumental craftsmanship and the standard apparently acceptable to patrons declined. The decline was gradual, however, as is evidenced by the still fairly high standard of the monuments of Chief Justice Bromley (d.1555) at Wroxeter (Salop) (*66*) and Sir Thomas Andrew (d.1564) at Charwelton (Northants), and it did not affect all workers to the same degree: the monument of Archbishop Edwin Sandys of York (d.1588) in Southwell Minster (Notts), for example, indicates that for a major commission competent work could be produced by the northern alabaster school at that date. But this was exceptional and the rot had long set in, reaching a nadir in the prolific output of the Royleys of Burton-on-Trent, Thomas and his son Gabriel, who were active from the 1560s to *c*.1590. In their hands effigies became stiff, ignoble parodies of the human figure and tomb-chests displayed increasingly coarse designs often poorly executed and with what Renaissance elements they contained misunderstood or inexpertly handled. Numerous tomb-chests with effigies produced by these schools in the later sixteenth century have survived, especially in the midlands, and, while they cannot be regarded as among the best funerary art, some are better than others and all have undeniably a naive charm of their own. The standard ingredients of their enrichment include small stiffly standing figures, heraldic shields (sometimes in the plainest of surrounds), balusters, colonnettes plain or twisted, and pilasters decorated with debased candelabra designs.

A few examples will suffice to indicate the range. At Ratcliffe-on-Soar (Notts) the chest of Sir Henry Sacheverell (d.1558) has a scheme of standing children holding shields and corner pilasters with the candelabra motif, a Royley version of the same occurring on that of Thomas Fermor (d.1580) at Somerton (Oxon). The monuments of Sir Fulke Greville (d.1559) at Alcester (Warks) (*47*) and Sir Thomas Giffard (d.1560) at Brewood (Staffs) have standing children and primitive twisted colonnettes, that of Sir Richard Newport (d.1570) at Wroxeter (Salop) being similar save that the children hold shields. At Ashby-de-la-Zouch (Leics) the chest of Francis Hastings 2nd earl of Huntingdon (d.1560) has an ungainly composition of standing figures under polygonal canopies interspersed with large shields resting on small pedestals, and the usual corner pilasters with candelabra. On that of John Shirley (*c*.1585) at Breedon-on-the-Hill (Leics), another Royley work, the decoration consists of shields and balusters, while balusters of the crudest kind appear with standing children on that of Kenelm Digby (d.1590) at Stoke Dry (Rutland). Among these monuments and their many fellows the Renaissance feature which undergoes the gravest degeneration and shows most vividly how English craftsmen could misinterpret the unfamiliar is the candelabra motif. The progressive decline in its carving is so marked that in some late examples, such as that of Humphrey Peyto (d.1585) at Chesterton (Warks), it is almost unrecognizable.

The contrast between many of these Elizabethan tomb-chests and those made at the same time in what may be called the mainstream of Renaissance development in England is striking. From early in Elizabeth's reign a group, especially in the southeast of the country, shows the continuing vitality of the Renaissance style and the introduction of new motifs. Although French influence remained, it had for some time been supplemented from other north European sources coming in in the form of imported pattern books and engravings, and was soon to be superseded by a powerful influx of ideas and craftsmen from the Netherlands. Among the new decorative features whose introduction owed as much to the Low Countries as to France, the most important were strapwork and ribbonwork.

Strapwork consisted initially of thin, flowing and sometimes intertwining bands, frequently curling at their ends, the resemblance of which to leather straps has given the motif its name. It first appeared on tomb-chests as a discreet surround for shields of arms. A very early instance has been noted on that of Sir Thomas Cheyne (d.1558) at Minster-in-Sheppey (Kent), followed soon after by the monuments of Frances duchess of Suffolk (1563) in Westminster Abbey and Elizabeth countess of Shrewsbury (d.1568) at Erith (Kent). On more ambitious canopied monuments, however, it occurred soon after 1550 and in a wider variety of uses. Its development was rapid and prodigious. Not only did the bands tend to increase in width and in the complexity of their patterns, but strapwork quickly spread throughout the country to become one of the most typical forms of later Renaissance decoration in England. An excellent example of the richer version is provided by the tomb-chest of Sir Christopher Hildyard (d.1602) at Winestead

47 Alcester (Warks): Sir Fulke Greville (d.1559). The brass railing is Victorian

48 Winestead (Yorks): Sir Christopher Hildyard (d.1602)

(Yorks) (*48*), on which shields of arms are set into strapwork frames with prominently curled projections, while that of George Slee (d.1613) at Tiverton (Devon) has panels entirely covered with strapwork.

Ribbonwork is the term applied to a particular type of regularly waving and commonly crinkled ribbon decoration fashionable in the late sixteenth and early seventeenth centuries. On tomb-chests it was associated especially with the apparent hanging of shields of arms along the sides, a highly decorative example of which can be seen at Great Bedwyn (Wilts) on the tomb-chest newly supplied in 1590 for the effigy of Sir John Seymour (d.1536). Like strapwork, ribbonwork served as a major ingredient of larger-scale monumental enrichment, and it will be necessary to return to both later.

Consideration of these later tomb-chests has taken us well into the Elizabethan period. By then, however, changes of great moment were affecting the whole range of monument-making, including other types which had survived from the middle ages, in particular the canopied wall monument. The development of canopied monuments, and also of chantry chapels, in the first half of the sixteenth century was similar to that of tomb-chests, a story of persisting late medieval forms coupled with the gradual application of Renaissance decoration.

Throughout the reign of Henry VIII (1509–47) the canopied wall monument remained essentially as it had been in the fifteenth century, that is, comprising a rectangular tomb-chest under a more or less recessed canopy with a depressed four-centred or Tudor arch and horizontal top. There were differences, however, for on occasions the arch was dispensed with, leaving the canopy's aperture virtually straight-topped with the merest curves at the sides, and in some cases the tomb-chest projected far in front of the canopy. There were commonly no recumbent effigies, the representation of the deceased, if included at all, usually appearing as a brass on the backplate. Such monuments frequently retained purely Perpendicular enrichment both on chest and canopy well into the century, as in the comparatively late instance of Sir John Clerke (d.1539) at Thame (Oxon). Others began in the 1520s to introduce a greater or lesser amount of Renaissance decoration alongside Gothic elements, producing genuinely hybrid schemes. Notably is this true of a group in Sussex, including the monuments of Thomas 5th Lord Delaware (d.1524) at Broadwater, Sir John Dawtry

(1527) at Petworth, Sir William Shelley (d.1548) at Clapham and two Ernley memorials of *c*.1545 at West Wittering. They vary in their individual combinations of the two styles. Renaissance decoration may be applied to the cresting, frieze or spandrels of the canopy and to the panels or dividers of the tomb-chest, and its motifs range between acanthus scrolls, cherubs, mermaids, circular medallions, balusters and oddly diagonal pilasters with candelabra, everything being in low relief, small-scale and rather roughly carved. Their hybrid character is further emphasized by the retention of late medieval types of religious sculpture in the ensemble (scenes of the Trinity, Annunciation, etc.), particularly striking on those dating from and after the 1540s. Where effigies are present, they appear as small relief figures kneeling in association with the religious imagery. Somewhat similar, though not of the same series, is the monument of Richard Norton (*c*.1540) at East Tisted (Hants) (*49*), which has, under a surprisingly plain Perpendicular canopy, a tomb-chest adorned with shields surrounded by Renaissance ornament and, on the backplate, a relief of the deceased and family kneeling beside the Resurrection.

The gradual application of Renaissance decoration is also apparent on monuments of the type which consisted of a tomb-chest standing under an enriched four-centred arch between chancel and side-chapel or similar position. This was happening, for example, in Hampshire in the 1520s, notably on a Lisle monument at Thruxton (*c*.1520) and more tentatively on that of Ralph Perall (*c*.1525–30) at Sherborne St John. Chantry chapels, too, until finally made obsolete in England by the ending of Roman Catholicism at the death of Mary I in 1558, compromised between Gothic and Renaissance decoration while retaining their late medieval structure. The best and most lively example is the Delaware chantry of *c*.1532 in Boxgrove priory (Sussex): its lowest stage is still entirely Gothic, but from it rise cylindrical shafts heavily encrusted with Renaissance decoration; which support a roof canopy spectacularly combining rectangular Renaissance panels with Gothic tabernacled niches. Renaissance ornament is also present, though far less obtrusively, on the chantries of Prior John Draper (dated 1529) and Margaret countess of Salisbury (before 1538), both in Christchurch priory (Hants), and of Bishop Nicholas West (d.1533) in Ely cathedral. Even the last to be completed in England, that of Bishop Stephen Gardiner (d.1555) in Winchester cathedral, retains large Perpendicular traceried openings along the sides and a medieval vault under the roof, despite the fact that its enrichment, outside and especially inside, incorporates up-to-date and beautifully executed High Renaissance features.

Renaissance Architectural Forms

After 1550 things began to change more radically. The effect of the Renaissance now began to extend beyond surface decoration to the shape and structure of monuments, as new types of architectural design appeared which were conceived wholly in a Renaissance spirit. This happened first in respect of standing canopied wall monuments and those set in openings between chancel and chapel and exposed on two sides. Here a number of progressive craftsmen, some no doubt working under directions from advanced-minded patrons, broke with tradition by transforming the medieval canopy into a Renaissance superstructure incorporating tall pilasters or columns to support an entablature and in some cases completing the elevation with a straight-sided pediment. The degree of classical correctness, especially as regards proportion, varied in these compositions, but in general they revealed confidence and some maturity in handling classical architectural elements and on occasions achieved remarkably pure results. In most examples a traditionally-shaped tomb-chest or the novel feature of an antique sarcophagus was included, but often there were no effigies. It seems likely, too, that the monuments were not coloured. At first their numbers were small and very localized, comprising for the 1550s mainly a group in Wiltshire and individual monuments in Leicestershire and Buckinghamshire.

The early group in Wiltshire is of particular interest in that they still retain the depressed four-centred arch lingering on from the medieval period, but now set in a Renaissance frame. The group consists of the monument of Sir William Sharington (d.1553) at Lacock (50), the similar but simpler version for Sir William Wroughton (d.1559) at Broad Hinton, and the two related monuments of Sir Robert Brydges (d.1558) at Ludgershall and Sir Francis Choke (d.1562) at Shalbourne. They all incorporate tomb-chests, the first two without effigies, and their decoration is almost entirely Renaissance, including the new device of strapwork. The Lacock and Broad Hinton monuments

have superstructures of enriched or fluted pilasters carrying an entablature upon which stands a framed shield of arms held by cherubs and flanked by large scrolls; the four-centred arch is inserted below the entablature and could (one feels) have been replaced by a Renaissance round arch without serious interference to the overall scheme. At Ludgershall and Shalbourne the design is not dissimilar, but the entablature rests on tall columns, has a rich frieze of foliage scrolls and supports an heraldic shield between mini-pilasters and cherubs, those at Ludgershall riding sea-monsters.

The Leicestershire monument, that of Gregory Cromwell at Launde, dating probably from 1551 but perhaps from 1557, is something quite different. Although a standing wall monument, it projects only a little forward from the wall, there is no tomb-chest or effigy and the design is basically a shallow architectural frame for a large heraldic achievement and inscription panel in the centre. The 'architecture' is made up of enriched pilasters resting on narrow pedestal bases and carrying an entablature and pediment, while the ornamentation is restrained and, if the monument is indeed of 1551, includes probably the earliest occurrence of strapwork on an English funerary memorial, in this case bordering both the inscription panel and a longer plain panel on the base.

Most remarkable of all, however, is the monument of Sir Robert Dormer (d.1552) at Wing (Bucks). This large and impressive piece, regarded by many as the finest monument of its date in England, breaks new ground in the combination of its bold and uncompromising Renaissance design, the noble purity of its classical features and the excellence of its carving. A rectangular sarcophagus without effigy stands against the wall under a high, wide and independent architectural canopy whose front elevation comes well forward of the sarcophagus. The latter is adorned with superbly carved ox skulls linked by looped garlands of leaves and fruit. The canopy is flat, its underside carved with a simple strapwork pattern and its front an entablature resting on two pairs of fluted Corinthian columns with strapwork-panelled bases, the columns being matched at the back by pairs of Corinthian pilasters. A certain amount of mystery surrounds the authorship and derivation of the Dormer monument, for no other in England corresponds at all closely with it, and yet, despite its advanced and possibly French-inspired character, it is constructed almost entirely of local stone and is therefore not an imported work.

A less daring but equally significant departure is evident on the monument of Anthony Lowe (d.1555) at Wirksworth (Derbs). It comprises a Renaissance tomb-chest and effigy set against a wall, but with the addition of a rectangular back-plate of honour rising above and behind the effigy; this, it must be emphasized, is not a canopy, but an 'architectural' frame of shallow projection, made up of two fluted pilasters supporting an entablature and enclosing a richly carved heraldic achievement. This particular combination of the traditional tomb-chest with the new taste for a Renaissance architectural setting was to remain in numerous variations a feature of fairly modest monuments until well into the seventeenth century.

After the 1550s, as more and more regional workshops' adopted similar or related ideas, the number and geographical spread of what might be called these structurally Renaissance monuments increased. The example set by the Launde monument in Leicestershire was followed with variations by those of Richard Neeld (dated 1574) at Tugby (Leics) and members of the Griffin family (*c*.1565–70) at Braybrooke (Northants), the latter distinguished by an exuberant display of tiered balusters. The monuments of the 1st Lord Mordaunt (d.1562) at Turvey (Beds), Alexander Denton (d.1576) at Hillesden and Anthony Cave (dated 1576) at Chicheley (both Bucks) form an interesting trio, in that, although differing markedly as individuals, they are known all to be by the same obscure mason-carver, Thomas Kirby; and indeed a common hand might have been suspected from the similar and very idiosyncratic treatment of the sarcophagus on each and the preference for a plain pediment at the top. Lord Mordaunt's, the most accomplished of the three and the only one to have recumbent effigies proper, has the added distinction of a semi-circular arch over the sarcophagus and effigies in the lowest stage, which may well be the earliest instance of a structural round arch (as distinct from a four-centred one) on an English Renaissance monument. Equally innovatory is the use of small caryatids to support the pediment in the upper parts, a device which also appears in a larger version on the monument of Anthony Cave at Chicheley. Further afield we may note the monument of John Harford (dated 1573) at Bosbury (Herefs), a work by John Guldo of Hereford, with its pediment resting on columns and its deep semi-circular arch sheltering the effigy; the effigy-less

monuments of Sir John Chichester (d.1569) at Pilton (Devon), George Fane (d.1571) at Tudeley (Kent) and members of the D'Arcy family (dated 1578) at Hornby (Yorks); and the extraordinary two-sided composition for Katherine Lady Willoughby (d.1580) and her husband at Spilsby (Lincs), one façade of which includes tiny demi-figures of the deceased and coarsely executed caryatid-like figures. These and several more standing wall monuments in other parts of the country testify to a more general adoption of Renaissance architectural forms as well as Renaissance decoration in the early Elizabethan period.

This final shuffling off of the constraints of late medieval tradition came in the 1560s to affect also the designs of free-standing or virtually free-standing monuments, for, although in these situations simple tomb-chests with recumbent effigies remained popular, a number of such tomb-chests now began to be provided with Renaissance canopies or superstructures. Since these commonly consisted of a flat top resting on four, six or more columns, they have become known popularly as 'four-posters', 'six-posters' and so on. A particularly early instance is the monument of Margaret countess of Bath (d.1561) at Hengrave (Suffolk), in which the tomb-chest stands under a heavy Renaissance superstructure supported on thick Tuscan columns. It is not entirely free-standing and not quite a six-poster, being set into a corner and having only five columns, but, despite this and its somewhat crude and heavy-handed character, it is an important precursor of the elaborate architectural monuments of the later Elizabethan and Jacobean periods.

Other and more original experiments in tomb design in the 1560s can be seen at Bottesford (Leics) in the free-standing monument of the 2nd earl of Rutland (d.1563), and in Canterbury cathedral in the monument of Dean Nicholas Wotton (d.1567), which abuts a pier of the Trinity Chapel arcade. Although each is unique and found no exact followers, they nevertheless stand as striking evidence of a willingness on the part of some designers, who may have been foreigners, to try out completely new compositions related in no way to what had gone before. In the Bottesford monument there is no tomb-chest at all, the effigies lying on a slab slightly above floor-level beneath what looks for all the world like an Elizabethan table in alabaster with four bulbous 'legs' at the corners; however, upon the 'table' stands a large heraldic achievement richly framed and surrounded by small kneeling figures of the earl's three children. Dean Wotton's monument at Canterbury shows him kneeling as in life at a prayer-desk on a sarcophagus-like tomb-chest, facing a high architectural frame resembling a reredos and flanked by excellent Corinthian columns, while behind him stands a single tall obelisk. The scheme was no doubt thought appropriate for a divine, but, though the kneeling attitude, prayer-desk and obelisk were all to have prolific futures, this precise combination was not repeated.

The Later Elizabethan and Jacobean Periods

To summarize the situation in the early years of Elizabeth's reign: monumental craftsmen working in England had by then not only absorbed the decorative schemes and begun to employ the architectural forms of the Renaissance style, but some of them (perhaps aliens) were developing under its influence a pragmatic approach to monumental design which was leading to the evolution of new types, even though a good deal of conservative tradition remained, especially in the northern alabaster workshops. Two factors now began to operate which did much to produce the full flowering of the later Renaissance style on church monuments in the latter part of Elizabeth's reign and in that of James I (1603–25). These were the Elizabethan Church settlement and the influx of a fresh wave of continental Renaissance influence from the Low Countries.

Monument-making had undoubtedly suffered a set-back during the intense, image-smashing Protestantism of Edward VI's reign (1547–53), when monumental effigies were at times as vulnerable to damage or destruction as religious images were, and, although such acts of secular impiety naturally ceased under the Catholic Mary I (1553–58), they threatened to break out again at the accession of Elizabeth I until expressly forbidden by the queen in 1560. Thereafter, the success and comparative moderation of the Elizabethan Church settlement, which aimed to embrace as wide a spectrum of religious opinion as possible, coupled with the firm rule of the queen and her ministers, ensured a long period of domestic and religious peace in which monument-making not only fully recovered but positively seized hold of nearly all who could afford to indulge in commemorative display. The inclusion of effigies became once more as normal as it had

been suspect in some quarters in the middle of the century – and not only effigies of the deceased, but those of their children as well. This period is pre-eminently the age of the great architectural monument in which the deceased and his family are portrayed beneath a proud and exuberantly enriched canopy, brightly painted and gilded and containing much display of heraldry exhibiting the family's pride in its lineage and marriage connections. But these years also saw the production of large numbers of smaller monuments to suit more slender pockets: apart from the survival of simple tomb-chests with effigies, monumental brasses recovered from their decline at mid-century, incised slabs enjoyed possibly their greatest popularity ever and completely new types of hanging wall monument with effigies were devised and rapidly caught on.

In all, the most spectacular and in general the best monuments of the period owed a direct or indirect debt to Netherlandish influence. The major reason for this was the flight to England of Protestant refugees, including monumental craftsmen, from religious persecution and domestic upheaval in the Low Countries, chiefly after the outbreak of the Wars of Religion there and the arrival of the Spanish Duke of Alba in 1567. Of course, Netherlandish and Flemish influence had been an element in English Renaissance development almost from the start, but in the fields of architecture and sculpture it had been generally on a minor scale and subsidiary to the more important French sources. One notable exception to this, however, was William Cure, who came to England from the Netherlands in 1541 at Henry VIII's instigation to work at Nonsuch Palace in Surrey, and settled in Southwark where he founded what became a family business of mason-sculptors. Research has shown that he was working on monuments in the 1560s and may have been responsible for, among others, that of Sir Richard Alington (d.1561) in the Public Record Office, London. Although French influence did not disappear altogether, it was certainly waning in these years, and the Low Countries now became the principal source of later Renaissance ideas in this country, profoundly affecting the character of English funerary monuments down to at least the 1620s. What made this artistic hegemony so much more forceful and direct than earlier foreign influences was the fact that, following the example of William Cure, Netherlanders settled in England, set up their own workshops and, by the quality of their

49 East Tisted (Hants): Richard Norton (*c.*1540). The deceased and his family kneel before the Resurrection

50 Lacock (Wilts): Sir William Sharington (d.1553)

51 North Walsham (Norfolk): Sir William Paston (dated 1608)

52 Titchfield (Hants): Thomas and Henry Wriothesley, 1st and 2nd earls of Southampton, and the 1st countess. By Gerard Johnson (*c.*1594)

53 Bisham (Berks): Elizabeth Lady Hoby (d. 1609)

54 Bottesford (Leics): John Manners, 4th earl of Rutland. By Gerard Johnson (1591)

55 Holcombe Rogus (Devon): Richard Bluett (d. 1614) and wife

56 Great Stanmore (Middx): John Burnell (d. 1605)

designs and excellence of execution, not only succeeded in cornering much of the market for the most lavish and fashionable monuments, but attracted into their workshops English craftsmen-apprentices seeking training in the Netherlandish style. In this way, quite apart from the dissemination of their own products to most parts of England, native workshops came under their influence and, though often with a lower level of sculptural attainment, sought to turn out similar pieces. So it was also that, for instance, two of the greatest English mason-sculptors and tomb-makers of the first half of the seventeenth century, Epiphanius Evesham and Nicholas Stone, spent at least part of their apprenticeship in the Southwark workshops of Netherlandish immigrés, even though each was to stamp his individual genius on the grounding he received there.

Some of the Dutch refugees are not immediately recognizable as such from their names, since these frequently became anglicized after they had settled here. Among the best known of those who came in 1567 were Isaac James and Gerard Johnson (these being their English names), the latter of whom founded a distinguished workshop which descended to his sons, one of whom was also called Gerard. Later in the century the most eminent arrival was Maximilian Colt, who came to England in 1596. These all established themselves in London, mostly in Southwark, but a few settled elsewhere, notably Jasper Hollemans, who set up business in the old alabaster centre of Burton-on-Trent (Staffs). Although the monuments which these, the Cure family and others produced can be separately identified by their own distinguishing features, and much amusement can be had in attempting to assign a particular monument to this or that workshop, nevertheless they all shared certain general characteristics which permeated directly, or at one or more removes, the entire gamut of monumental output in the later sixteenth and early seventeenth centuries.

Alabaster and stone remained the chief materials used in the production of monuments, although black marble (touch) was common for inscription panels and, especially after 1600, both black and white marble increasingly supplemented the traditional materials. The architectural forms continued to be made up of basically classical elements – columns, entablatures, round arches and so on (though pediments were now rare) – but these elements were used freely to create compositions which were on the whole unclassical and further transformed by bright colours and lively Netherlandish ornament into effects distinctly different from earlier Renaissance works. The results have been rightly termed 'Mannerist', on account of their mannered and 'incorrect' use of classical features and their disregard of classical principles. The keynote was confident and self-assertive display, particularly in the great canopied monuments reaching sometimes to the roof of the church, and great play was made with heraldry and certain characteristic decorative motifs to produce results both impressive and appealing. The long-term effect of the Reformation was now most strikingly apparent in the absence of specifically Christian imagery, for instead of saints, religious panels and the like, decorative schemes were composed entirely of secular and antique pagan motifs transmitted through the Renaissance tradition. Toward the turn of the century symbols of death and immortality and personifications of virtues began to come in, but they too were expressed in idioms which were religiously neutral or antique pagan in inspiration. The sole exception was that in the second decade of the seventeenth century angels reappeared, dressed not in religious vestments, as they had mostly been in the Gothic era, but in classical attire.

Decorative Features

Several purely decorative motifs survived from earlier Renaissance styles, including mermaids, sea-monsters, masks, military trophies, acanthus scrolls and so on, but by far the most typical in this period, almost to the point of ubiquity, were strapwork, ribbonwork and obelisks.

Strapwork tended now to be more 'static' than earlier and, though still used on flat surfaces to frame inscriptions and the like, was most characteristically found enlivening the tops of canopies, where it served as a decorative surround for heraldic achievements. It appears in this form on, for example, the monuments of Sir William Dormer (completed in 1590) at Wing (Bucks) and the 4th earl of Rutland (a work by Gerard Johnson finished in 1591) at Bottesford (Leics) (*54*), the latter having the amusing variation, which some others share, of lions' heads terminating the major curls of the strapwork. Ribbonwork, on the other hand, continued to act purely as surface decoration, most commonly on pilasters, as in the case of Thomas

Arnwaye (d. 1603) in St Margaret's, Westminster, or on the backplates of wall monuments, as on that of Robert Kelway (d. 1580) at Exton (Rutland). Obelisks, symbols of eternity deriving ultimately from ancient Egypt and sometimes topped by a ball, heart or other device, appeared most frequently as prominent but comparatively small ornamental motifs on the tops of canopies, often in association with strapwork and heraldry. In this position they occur, for example, on the monument of Sir William Paston (dated 1608) at North Walsham (Norfolk) (*51*). On occasions, however, they assumed larger proportions, either at the sides of canopies, as on the monument of Sir John Spencer (d. 1586) at Great Brington (Northants), or at the corners of free-standing monuments, as on those of Margaret countess of Lennox (d. 1578) in Westminster Abbey and the 1st and 2nd earls of Southampton (*c.*1594) at Titchfield (Hants) (*52*).

From the late sixteenth century these features were increasingly supplemented by a range of equally decorative but in general more symbolic motifs, including cherubs, allegorical female figures, clusters of fruit and funerary urns.

Cherubs had, of course, been familiar in Renaissance work from the time of Torrigiani's monument for Henry VII, but they were not on the whole much used in the sixteenth century and suffered under Elizabeth I something of an eclipse from which they did not fully recover until after 1600. Thereafter cherubs remained a standard ingredient of monumental iconography down to the end of the eighteenth century, being shown either as complete figures or simply as winged cherub-heads, the latter especially on hanging wall monuments. In general cherubs represented the spiritual world of immortality, but in some cases they were depicted in symbolic poses or actions which signified death, such as resting on a spade or extinguishing a torch. Allegorical female figures, borrowed from classical antiquity and appearing now for the first time, personified either the virtues of the deceased, particularly the Four Cardinal and the Three Theological Virtues, or more rarely aspects of his calling or profession. All were shown in classical or pseudo-classical dress, holding their respective emblems or attributes. The Four Cardinal Virtues occur, for example, on the monuments of Sir William Cordell (d. 1580) at Long Melford (Suffolk), Godfrey Foljambe (d. 1598) at Chesterfield (Derbs) and Sir Augustine Nicholls (d. 1616) formerly at Faxton (Northants) and now in the

Victoria and Albert Museum; while allegorical figures representing the calling of the deceased can be seen on the monument of a mathematician, John Blagrave (d. 1611), in St Laurence's, Reading (Berks) (*57*), where they hold geometrical solids, and on that of Sir Thomas Bodley (d. 1613) in Merton College chapel, Oxford, where they display emblems appropriate to his various scholarly achievements. The urn was similarly derived from antique origins and served in general as a symbol of death. In this period, however, and throughout the seventeenth century the urn was most typically shown with flames emerging from it, in which form it represented not death, but immortality. The flaming urn should not be confused with the burning lamp, a symbol of faith, which also began to appear in the early seventeenth century, although it did not become widespread until later.

In addition there appeared a whole range of symbols for death, mortality and the transitory nature of this earthly life, most of which were to enjoy a prolific future. Among them were skulls, bones, hourglasses, spindles and thread (alluding to the Fates of ancient mythology), personifications of Time as an old man with his scythe, and so on. These will be considered more fully in a latter chapter.

It is also toward 1600 that we find the first examples of a significant new feature on monuments that was to become more common later, namely, the depiction of important events in the life of the deceased. It occurs very early at Quorndon (Leics), where the monument of Sir John Farnham (d. 1587) consists of a tomb-chest with effigies and, on the wall, a rectangular relief of Sir John standing in front of a siege scene. Another early and particularly poignant instance is the monument of members of the Hales family (dating after 1596) in Canterbury cathedral, which focusses by contrast on the tragic deaths of two members of the family: it includes not only a painted scene of the elder Sir James's suicide by drowning, but also a relief of the younger Sir James's burial at sea after dying aboard a disease-ridden man-of-war in 1589. Among other examples, the somewhat later monument of Sir Michael Dormer (d. 1616) at Great Milton (Oxon) has on one end of the tomb-chest a finely carved relief of a military engagement in which he had taken part.

Throughout the Elizabethan and Jacobean periods a small and often overlooked decorative feature occurred on the edges of effigy-bearing slabs, whether on free-standing tomb-chests or incorporated into larger designs. The edges were not infrequently bevelled and gadrooned, that is, carved on their upper surface with tiny convex ridges lying parallel with each other and usually at right angles to the edge, forming a continuous embellishment all round. This can be seen, for example, on the monument of Robert Dudley earl of Leicester (d.1588) in St Mary's, Warwick. More often the decoration consisted of a rhythmic alternation of gadroons and pairs of dots (sometimes single dots) along the edges of the slab. This was very much a Netherlandish device and may be regarded virtually as a trade-mark of the Southwark workshops of the period. Large numbers of monuments display it, including those of the 4th earl of Rutland (1591) at Bottesford (Leics) (*54*) and Richard Bluett (d.1614) at Holcombe Rogus (Devon) (*55*).

At the end of the period some canopied monuments began to include a new feature which was strictly speaking neither decorative nor structural, but which had the effect of undermining the purely architectural character of canopies. This was the looped-up curtain or drape, executed in stone or marble, 'hanging' from the top of the canopy and held or tied back to reveal the effigies behind. This beguiling conceit was rare before the 1620s and only came into widespread use later in the century, but it occurs, for example, on the hanging monuments of Anne Herrys (d.1613) at Chevening (Kent) and Sir Thomas Chaloner (d.1615) at Chiswick (Middx), on accessories to the standing wall-monument of Sir Charles Morrison (dated 1619) at Watford (Herts) and, most impressively, on the great free-standing monument of Sir Anthony Mildmay (d.1617) at Apethorpe (Northants).

Monumental Types

The forms of the monuments on which this decoration and imagery were lavished in the later sixteenth and early seventeenth centuries were more varied than ever before.

The free-standing tomb-chest with effigies was now becoming rather old-fashioned and, apart from its use of up-to-date ornament, requires little further comment. Occasionally, however, the formula was varied by placing additional features upon the slab, such as the four symbolic figures which stand on the corners of Sir George Hart's tomb-chest (dating after 1603) at Lullingstone (Kent), or by enlarging the composition to include adjacent kneeling figures, like the monument of Henry Howard earl of Surrey (beheaded 1547, monument 1614) at Framlingham (Suffolk), which has three kneeling children at the head and two at the foot of the tomb-chest.

A quite new development, on the other hand, was the tripartite tomb-chest in which the central section was raised above the outer portions. The opportunity for this variation arose from the desire to include three effigies, although it did not make it essential, since many monuments ranging from the fifteenth to the seventeenth centuries comprised three effigies side by side on broad flat tomb-chests. Perhaps the best known tripartite tomb-chest is that of the 1st and 2nd earls of Southampton (*c.*1594) at Titchfield (Hants) (*52*), a stately work by Gerard Johnson which shows the 1st earl's countess on the high central section, flanked lower down on each side by her husband and son. The raised portion is pierced with three round arches, thus relieving the rather solid mass and enabling the eye to see through from one side of the monument to the other, and an impression of quiet grandeur is achieved by nobility of proportion and, especially, by four tall and elegant obelisks placed one at each corner. Another good example of rather later date can be seen at Blore (Staffs), where the monument of William Bassett (d.1601) has his effigy on the raised centre and, on the outer sections, his wife (d.1640) and son-in-law (d.1616), with two daughters kneeling behind the heads of the effigies. In the case of the 2nd Lord Mordaunt (d.1571) at Turvey (Beds) the tripartite structure is employed beneath a grand eight-poster canopy, he lying in the middle raised above his two wives.

This last belongs to the group of free-standing canopied monuments in which more commonly the principal effigy or effigies rest immediately or ultimately upon a level base. An early example has already been noted in the countess of Bath's monument at Hengrave (Suffolk). Here the columns supporting the superstructure rise directly from the floor, thus enabling canopy and tomb-chest to be structurally independent, but, although this can be paralleled in other cases, usually the design was integrated into a single whole by placing the columns on the corners and sides of the tomb-chest, a resort which inevitably led to the lateral enlargement of the tomb-chest and in time to its gradual transformation into little more than a solid base for the architectural superstructure. The effect of this can clearly be seen in two very different but equally fine monuments of the 1580s, those of Sir

Thomas St Pol (d.1582) at Snarford (Lincs) and John Leweston (d.1584) in Sherborne abbey (Dorset), each of which has recumbent effigies under a six-poster canopy standing directly on a tomb-chest slightly enlarged at the points of contact to provide bases for the upright supporters. Later still, all suggestion of a tomb-chest at the base of such structures utterly disappeared, as in the cases of Sir Francis and Lady Knollys (d.1596) at Rotherfield Greys (Oxon) and Henry Lord Norris (d.1601) in Westminster Abbey. Indeed, in the latter example, which is by Isaac James, the memory of a tomb-chest has been so obliterated that here the effigies lie on a separate sarcophagus raised upon the base and there is room also for six kneeling life-size effigies of Lord Norris's sons.

The Knollys monument at Rotherfield Greys is a particularly impressive member of the group. It is enormous, almost filling the chapel specially built on to the church to house it, and appears splendid in its paint and gilding. Constructed mainly of alabaster, it has a heavy tester-like canopy supported on six columns of black or pink marble and two reinforcing arches set longitudinally in the middle of the composition separating Sir Francis from his wife, both of whom lie on the flat base. On the top of the canopy kneel their son and his wife, somewhat smaller in size and facing each other across a prayer-desk, while smaller still the other children kneel against the two long sides of the base. The rich and varied decoration includes cherubs, flaming urns, ribbonwork and reliefs of musical instruments and military devices.

In addition to these flat tester-like canopies, there were others which incorporated the device of a coffered arch, that is, an arch decorated on its soffit (or underside) with a regular pattern of sunk squares (less commonly hexagons) separated by slightly raised flat strips and frequently occupied by roses or similar motifs. One type of six-poster canopy, for example, comprised two coffered arches rising from entablatures running through the monument, the whole being surmounted by a flat top. It is exemplified at an early date by the monument of Sir William Puckering (d.1574) in St Helen's Bishopsgate, London, (perhaps by William Cure) and, rather later and in more elaborate form, by that of William Cecil Lord Burghley (d.1598) in St Martin's, Stamford (Lincs). Another version, which came into vogue in the early seventeenth century, consisted in the lateral division of the canopy into three sections (most clearly seen when viewed from

the sides), the centre taking the form of a great coffered arch under a flat top rising higher than the flat end sections. This type is seen at its most splendid in two royal monuments in Westminster Abbey, namely, those of Queen Elizabeth I (d.1603), by Maximilian Colt, and Mary Queen of Scots (executed in 1587), a work commissioned from Cornelius Cure by King James I and erected *c.*1612, after the king had had her body transferred to the abbey from Peterborough cathedral. On the whole Elizabeth's monument, though grand, is remarkably restrained in its ornament and, in its reliance for effect on the contrast of white and black marble with a minimum of gilding and paint, looks forward to the predilections of later decades. It is sumptuous without being in the least vulgar, a danger which (it must be admitted) could so easily entrap the over zealous decorator of monuments of this period. Somewhat similar in design is the monument of Chief Justice Sir John Popham (d.1607) at Wellington (Somerset), save that here the upper side of the canopy is uniformly flat. In a few cases the canopy consisted solely of a thin coffered arch supporting nothing but purely decorative features. This rather unstable-looking phenomenon occurs, for example, on the monument of Sampson Lennard (erected before 1611) at Chevening (Kent) and, later, on that of Robert and Marmaduke Jennings (d.1625 and 1630) at Curry Rivel (Somerset).

Fairly frequently what was in conception almost a free-standing canopied monument was prevented from being wholly so by being set against a wall and provided with an ornamental backplate to complete the design. An especially fine example is the monument of Sir William Cordell (d.1580) at Long Melford (Suffolk), whose canopy consists of six columns supporting two coffered arches and a flat top, the enrichment including early figures of the Four Cardinal Virtues. More restrained is that of Frances Lady Tawstock (d.1589) at Tawstock (Devon), a modified five-poster with a flat canopy resting on four round arches. Other examples include the monuments of Sir Thomas Fulford (d.1610) at Dunsford (Devon) and Richard Berney (dated 1623) in St Peter Parmentergate, Norwich. The first of these is of added interest in that here advantage is taken of the backplate to display the kneeling effigies of the deceased's children. A highly unusual form occurs at Hunsdon (Herts), where the monument of Sir Thomas Forster (d.1612) has a canopy which is almost a six-poster, but which has above the entablature a steeply sloping, tent-like roof ornamented with an overlapping scale motif.

From such monuments as these it is but a short step to the far more numerous canopied wall-monuments unequivocally designed as such. Their greater popularity was due chiefly to the fact that in general they took. up less floor space, but the grandest of them compensated by rising high into the roof of the church. Among the most spectacular, for example, are the enormous edifice commemorating Henry Lord Hunsdon (d.1596) in Westminster Abbey, which rises to a height of 36 feet, and the only slightly less lofty monument of Edward Seymour earl of Hertford (d.1621) in Salisbury cathedral. Both are so tall that their upper stages partially obscure windows behind them, while their architecture is so elaborate and their embellishment so richly varied that they stand as supreme expressions of monumental display at this time.

All canopied wall monuments have a solid base to support the effigies, though when two or three recumbent or reclining effigies are included, these are often set on different levels rising into the back of the monument, necessitating a stepped base. Above the base, most have a superstructure of fundamentally rectangular outline defined by free-standing side columns and a flat entablature, but the rectangularity of the design is frequently obscured by complex and sometimes bulky additions on the top. Beyond that, although the variations in architectural and decorative detail are legion, certain basic forms can be discerned with, as might be supposed, many hybrids between them.

Some canopies consist simply of a projecting flat tester supported by free columns at the sides, creating the effect of a rectangular frame, as can be seen, for instance, on the monuments of Sir Roger Manwood (d.1592) in St Stephen's, Canterbury (*45*), and Sir Edmund Uvedale (d.1606) in Wimborne Minster (Dorset). By way of variation some examples of this type have one, or two, shallow arched recesses on the backplate. Elizabeth Lady Hoby (d.1609) at Bisham (Berks) has a single arched panel in this position, (*53*), while Sir William Dormer (dated 1590) at Wing (Bucks) and Sir Henry Poole (d.1616) at Sapperton (Glos) have two. The arched panel behind the effigies of Robert Dudley earl of Leicester (d.1588) and wife in St Mary's, Warwick, is distinguished by a display of heraldic pennons rayed around the inscription plate; and the same idea is exploited even more effectively on the monument of Sir George Fermor (*c*.1612) at

Easton Neston (Northants), where the effect of a peacock's tail is consciously aimed at.

A second major type differs mainly in that the underside of the canopy is not flat, but takes the form of a coffered arch framed by the side columns and entablature. Such, for example, are the very similar monuments of Anne duchess of Somerset (d.1587) in Westminster Abbey and Sir William Paston (dated 1608) at North Walsham (Norfolk) (*51*), the trio of similar monuments of Sir John Puckering (d.1596) in Westminster Abbey, Elizabeth countess of Shrewsbury ('Bess of Hardwick' who died in 1607) in Derby cathedral and Sir William Spencer (d.1609) at Yarnton (Oxon), and that of Robert Kelway (*c*.1600) at Exton (Rutland). The monuments of Giles Reed (d.1611) at Bredon (Worcs) and Humphrey Bridges (*c*.1620) at Cirencester (Glos) also belong to this group, although each is flanked by small rectangular pavilions occupied by kneeling children.

A third category is similar to the preceding, except that the arched central portion, with the entablature above, is recessed between the flanking columns, which stand forward supporting their own entablatures projecting at right angles to the wall. Examples include the monuments of Edmund Walter (d.1592) at Ludlow (Salop), Dean Matthew Hutton (d.1606) in York Minster and Lady Elizabeth Periam (d.1621) at Henley-on-Thames (Oxon). A variant of this type has two arches rather than one, as can be seen in the case of the 4th earl of Rutland (1591) at Bottesford (Leics) (*54*). The canopies of William Cotton (d.1616) at Badingham (Suffolk) and Sir Richard Mompesson (d.1627) in Salisbury cathedral are each exceptional and very attractive in the enrichment of their side columns, those of the former having vertical lines of heraldic shields, the latter climbing vine trails.

In a fourth group the basic rectangular outline is missing, the canopy consisting solely of a thin coffered arch supported at the sides by pilasters or columns. The monument of Edmund Plowden (d.1584) in the Temple Church, London, is of this kind, as are also those of Sir John Glanvill (d.1600) at Tavistock (Devon), Richard Bluett (d.1614) at Holcombe Rogus (Devon) (*55*) and Sarah Vincent (d.1608) and Sir Thomas Vincent (d.1613), both at Stoke D'Abernon (Surrey). In most cases the arch is surmounted by strapwork rising to an heraldic shield at the top.

Many other variations of canopied wall monuments are found, notably where the effigies of the deceased are kneeling rather than recumbent, but the only other form that needs special mention here is the tripartite type in which the principal figures of the deceased and wife kneel in a central section, which is generally wider and more impressive, and the children kneel in the flanking sections. An early version occurs on the monument of Sir Anthony Cooke (d.1576) at Romford (Essex), which shows him and his wife kneeling below a straight-sided pediment, his children at the sides under flat entablatures. Others are to be seen at Cranford (Middx) on the splendid monument of Sir Roger Aston (dated 1612) and at Ingatestone (Essex) on that of John Lord Petre (d.1613). By contrast, that of Sir William Garrard (d.1607) in the charming little church of Dorney (Bucks) has, like others, the deceased and wife kneeling under separate arches, while their children kneel against the base.

Finally in this section we should note those standing wall monuments which do not possess canopies proper, but comprise a tomb-chest with effigies set length-wise in front of a shallow but often elaborate backplate rising behind on the wall. An excellent and quite early example is provided by the monument of Sir Philip and Sir Thomas Hoby (c.1566) at Bisham (Berks), where the two effigies lie on a tomb-chest in front of a thin and shallow arched backplate. Other instances with variously shaped backplates include the monuments of Godfrey Foljambe (d.1598) at Chesterfield (Derbs), Edward Rous (d.1611) at Rous Lench (Worcs), Lady Elizabeth Brocket (d.1612) at Hatfield (Herts) and Henry Grey 5th earl of Kent (d.1614) at Flitton (Beds). The first of these, at Chesterfield, is distinguished by rich decoration, including two standing and two reclining allegorical figures.

In one sense all the forms of monument looked at so far were versions of long-established types originating in the middle ages and now transformed out of all recognition by late Renaissance features, but there were others which were quite new. The later sixteenth century in effect invented the hanging wall monument, that is, a monument not standing upon the floor but wholly suspended on the wall into which it is fixed by mortar and iron ties. The degree of projection from the wall is predictably shallow and such monuments are in general fairly small, sometimes very small. The type had, it is true, been foreshadowed in a few isolated late medieval pieces, but to all intents and purposes there was now a new beginning. Being comparatively cheap, it rapidly caught on, appealing to a

wide circle of clients of middling rank for whom grand monuments were alike too expensive and inappropriate. In the majority of cases the effigies were shown kneeling, but occasionally and particularly after 1600 the novel form of frontal demi-figure occurred; at the same time the long series of wall tablets began, comprising an inscription panel in an ornamental surround and no effigy at all. The 'architectural' designs of these monuments reflected *en miniature* the structural features of contemporary standing monuments, and their decorative schemes were made up from the same range of motifs.

The commonest type incorporates an effigy or effigies kneeling sideways to the viewer, normally at a prayer-desk (or prie-dieu). Examples are so numerous all over the country that no adequate selection is possible, but some idea of the variations upon the basic theme can be suggested. In its simplest form only the single figure of the deceased is shown, as in the case of Henry Tomworthe (d.1608) at Heckfield (Hants). Far more frequently both husband and wife are represented: usually they face each other across the prayer-desk, like James Harrington (d.1613) and wife at Ridlington (Rutland), but on occasions both face the same way, one behind the other and with individual prayer-desks, as on the monument of Thomas Pledger (d.1599) at Bottisham (Cambs). Often the children are included as well, appearing as smaller effigies kneeling either behind their parents, as on the monument of Robert Suckling (d.1589) and family in St Andrew's, Norwich, or in a separate compartment below their parents, as on that of John Burnell (d.1605) at Great Stanmore (Middx) (*56*). Occasionally, the number and disposition of the kneeling effigies led to more ambitious hanging monuments. One dating from 1615 at Helmingham (Suffolk), for instance, has four generations of the Tollemache family represented by male figures kneeling each under its own coffered arch; and another at Woodbridge (Suffolk), commemorating Jeffrey Pitman (d.1627) and his two sons with their wives, is a three-decker affair, Jeffrey appearing in the top storey, then the wives and at the bottom the sons. In this case Jeffrey's effigy kneels frontally to the viewer, a much rarer portrayal which is also found, for instance, on the monument of Lady Elizabeth Fane (d.1618) in Westminster Abbey and on that of Sir William Gee (d.1611) in York Minster, who kneels frontally between his two wives kneeling in the conventional sideways position.

57 St Laurence's, Reading (Berks): John Blagrave (d.1611). Note mathematical instruments and geometrical solids

58 Hatfield (Herts): Robert Cecil, 1st earl of Salisbury (d.1612). By Maximilian Colt

Demi-figures are much less common. They are often referred to as busts, but this can be somewhat misleading, since the entire upper third, half or more of the figure is normally represented. The portrayal was invariably frontal and was particularly favoured for divines and academics or for those with pretensions to learning. Examples include John Blagrave (d. 1611) in St Laurence's, Reading (Berks) (*57*), Dr John Radcliffe (d. 1612) at Orwell (Cambs) and several dons and divines in Oxford college chapels. Merton College chapel, in particular, has two very fine specimens, namely, Sir Thomas Bodley (d. 1613), shown in an oval recess surrounded by allegorical figures in a rectangular frame whose sides resemble piles of books, and Sir Henry Savile (d. 1622), who appears as though in a pulpit, flanked by standing figures of ancient pagan and Christian scholars. The demi-figure was not, however, restricted to the worlds of Church and scholarship. Indeed, one of the earliest examples falls into neither category, namely, the memorial in St Margaret's, Westminster, of Cornelius Vandun (d. 1577), a Yeoman of the Guard portrayed in uniform within a strapwork surround; while another, certainly the most famous of the group, commemorates a playwright (though admittedly one with unimpeachable claims to Renaissance learning), William Shakespeare (d. 1616), in Holy Trinity, Stratford-on-Avon (Warks). Among others of note are the military demi-figure, one hand resting on a helmet, of Edward Fenner (d. 1615) at Hayes (Middx) and the twin demi-figures of William Goddard (d. 1609) and wife at Bray (Berks).

The wall tablet, with inscription panel and no effigy, was destined to become the most popular of all forms of funerary monument, growing increasingly frequent as the decades passed and varying from period to period in accordance with changing tastes in architecture and ornament. However, in this period, when the first examples occurred, the type was not particularly common and did not 'take off', as it were, until a generation or so later. A good early example is that of Sir William Gerrarde (d. 1581) in Chester cathedral; it comprises an arched inscription panel contained within a rectangular frame defined by a ledge on brackets at the bottom, fluted Ionic columns at the sides and an entablature surmounted by strapwork at the top. Slightly later comes the fine piece for Nicholas Hare (d. 1597) at Stow Bardolph (Norfolk), with exquisite carving of foliage trails and arabesque decoration, all beautifully painted and gilded. Of a different kind is that of Anne Lytton (d. 1601) at Knebworth (Herts), whose inscription is set in a rectangular frame decorated with ribbonwork and numerous symbols of mortality and death. In several instances the stone or alabaster frame surrounds a brass or other plate engraved with figures and inscription, a type to which we shall return later.

A number of monuments not easy to classify were also produced at this time and deserve to be noticed, despite their rare and unusual character, since they indicate an increasing scope for individualism in the design of monuments which was to have freer rein in the next period.

The two-tiered form of free-standing monument without canopy, tried out first in the 1560s for the 2nd earl of Rutland at Bottesford, was adopted for two of the most arresting monuments of the early seventeenth century in England, those of Sir Francis Vere (d. 1609) in Westminster Abbey and the 1st earl of Salisbury (d. 1612) at Hatfield (Herts) (*58*). The former is possibly by Maximilian Colt, the latter certainly by him, and their immediate derivation is probably not the Bottesford monument, but Dutch and possibly French exemplars. In any case they both differ from the Bottesford monument in that the upper tier in each case is a slab borne not on columns but on the shoulders of near life-size figures kneeling on one knee. There, however, the resemblance between the two ceases. The Vere monument is of black marble and alabaster, the Salisbury monument of white and black marble, and, while the former shows Sir Francis recumbent on the lower stage beneath a slab supported by warriors and bearing the various parts of his armour separately carved, the latter has the earl's effigy on the upper slab, which is here borne by Virtues, and a skeleton below. The same basic structure was to be employed later in the seventeenth century for, among others, the monument of Sir John Hotham (d. 1689) at South Dalton (Yorks), which has a scheme almost identical to that of the Salisbury monument at Hatfield.

The originality of Maximilian Colt is apparent on another unusual and probably unique monument in Westminster Abbey, that of Princess Sophia, James I's daughter who died as a baby in 1606. Although of alabaster, the form is that of a baby's cradle in which the infant princess is represented as though asleep beneath the coverlet. The latter's realistic carving can be paralleled on the near-contemporary monument of the 3rd Lord Mordaunt (d. 1601) at Turvey (Beds), which has no effigy and consists simply of a tomb-chest covered apparently by a black cloth. This last conceit was later to be used by Colt in the more elaborate monument of Alice countess of Derby (d. 1637) at Harefield (Middx).

The monument of Lady Margaret Hoby (d. 1605) at Bisham (Berks) is also of a highly original type. It consists of a single tall obelisk, topped by a heart and with four swans at its foot, standing upon a high plinth; originally four more obelisks stood on the floor at the corners of the plinth, but these have long since disappeared. The form failed to establish itself, however, although it was employed in a simpler version for the contemporary monument of Anne Harlay (d. 1605) in Westminster Abbey and was chosen for a handful of monuments later in the century.

Then there are the two famous painted wooden triptychs at Burford (Salop), dated 1588, and Lydiard Tregoze (Wilts), dated 1615 (*59*), commemorating respectively Richard Cornwall (d. 1568) with his parents, and Sir John St John (d. 1594) with his wife and children. Each stands against a wall and has folding doors which can be opened, like the wings of a triptych, to reveal the effigies painted on the fixed centre-piece. The Lydiard Tregoze triptych is more complicated, however, for there are other subsidiary panels which can also be moved. At Burford the paintings of the deceased and family are shown standing, at Lydiard Tregoze either standing or kneeling, and both pieces have in addition a wealth of other painting, mainly of a religious or heraldic import, which extends to the outsides of the folding doors. To these very remarkable memorials must be added the smaller and less well preserved monument in similar form of a member of the Harewell family (late sixteenth century) at Besford (Worcs).

Effigies

Hitherto, this chapter has concentrated primarily on the development of monumental forms and ornamentation, and, although effigies have necessarily come into the story, little direct attention has been paid to them. In fact, however, the history of the effigy in this period is hardly less absorbing. Apart from the value of effigies for the study of sculpture and of dress and armour, interest centres mainly on two aspects: the changing postures adopted by effigies, and the development of various family groupings of effigies on individual monuments.

The standard late medieval portrayal of the deceased as a recumbent figure with hands closed in prayer remained almost universal until the mid-sixteenth century, but thereafter, despite its continued use well into the seventeenth century, its ascendancy was gradually destroyed by the introduction of alternative attitudes for the effigy, and in some versions the recumbent effigy itself underwent changes both in presentation and in form.

Although many recumbent effigies produced by provincial workshops remained stiff and rather unlifelike, others (especially those emanating from the Southwark school) displayed greater competence and accuracy in the carving of a human figure, excellent early examples being the effigies of the 1st earl of Bedford (d. 1555) and wife at Chenies (Bucks) and Lord Williams (d. 1559) and wife at Thame (Oxon). A little later male effigies in armour were often shown lying on a straw mattress placed upon the tomb-chest, the mattress being commonly rolled up at one end to provide a rest for the head. Again, some effigies abandoned the attitude of prayer: that of Elizabeth I (d. 1603) at Westminster shows the queen holding the symbols of majesty, while royal ministers are occasionally portrayed holding their wands of office, like William Cecil Lord Burghley (d. 1598) at Stamford and the 1st earl of Salisbury (d. 1612) at Hatfield. Of far greater significance, however, was a development which reflected the deeper penetration of Renaissance humanist ideals into English figure sculpture. The best and most advanced examples began to display a more natural and relaxed treatment of the effigy, with the hands not raised in prayer but allowed to lie in easy positions on or by the body. This culminated in the second decade of the seventeenth century in the realistic portrayal of the deceased as a figure recumbent and asleep in death, quite different from the rather ambiguous state of most sixteenth-century and late medieval effigies, which manage in a curious way to be neither fully alive nor completely dead. Although Dutch influence was very important in these trends, the finest examples of the new interpretation of the recumbent effigy were the work of the celebrated English sculptors, Nicholas Stone and Epiphanius Evesham, the former producing, for instance, the moving effigy of Elizabeth Lady Carey (d. 1617) at Stowe-Nine-Churches (Northants), the latter that of Christopher Lord Teynham (d. 1622) at Lynsted (Kent). But undoubtedly the most remarkable manifestation of this development is Stone's stark high-relief effigy of Sir William Curle (1617) at Hatfield (Herts), a nude figure

59 *Above* Lydiard Tregoze (Wilts): Sir John St John (d.1594) with wife and children. Painted wooden triptych monument, erected 1615

60 *Below* Cranford (Middx): Sir Roger Aston and family. By William Cure II (dated 1612)

partially covered by a shroud and lying dead on a slab at floor level.

A further consequence of the movement toward realism was the growing tendency to portray the deceased as he was, or might have been, in life, a tendency which naturally encouraged the adoption of various non-recumbent postures for the effigy. As a result, this period witnessed the full emergence of the reclining and kneeling attitudes, the introduction of upright demi-figures and the first examples of seated and standing figures.

The reclining attitude differed from the recumbent in that the effigy was represented lying not on its back but on its side 'propped up' on one elbow, turned toward the viewer and never at prayer. It had been used on very rare occasions in the middle ages, but there was no direct link between these and the fashion of the late sixteenth and early seventeenth centuries. The new attitude first appeared with the monument of Sir Philip and Sir Thomas Hoby (c.1566) at Bisham, which may indicate a French source of inspiration, but it was popularised a generation later by the Netherland masters and their English followers. Reclining effigies at this time often appear stiff and uncomfortable. Apart from some armoured male figures which have their legs crossed or bent, such as Sir Thomas Vincent (d.1613) at Stoke D'Abernon (Surrey), the body is normally straight and rigid. The effect can sometimes be faintly comical, especially where more than one effigy is present, as on the well-known monument of members of the Fettiplace family (c.1613) at Swinbrook (Oxon), which has three such figures reclining on separate shelves one above another. In the most awkward examples there is no support for the head, as on the monuments of Sir Arthur Acland (d.1610) at Landkey (Devon) and Lady Elizabeth Brocket (d.1612) at Hatfield, but more frequently the figure supports its head against its hand. In such cases the hand supports either the side and back of the head, like Sir William Paston (dated 1608) at North Walsham (Norfolk) (*51*) and Edward Fagg (d.1618) at Faversham (Kent), or the cheek, like Thomas Owen (d.1598) in Westminster Abbey and Lady Mary Eure (d.1613) at Ludlow (Salop). The latter position inspired the amusing and oft-quoted comment of the dramatist, John Webster, that persons so represented looked 'as if they died of the toothache.' However, while the result was frequently rather clumsy, even quaint, the intention was clearly to depict the deceased in quiet, semi-

recumbent contemplation, and was to give rise in subsequent periods to portrayals of the highest elegance which were eventually to supersede the truly recumbent attitude.

The other favourite at this time was the kneeling posture in which, unlike the preceding, the effigy was almost invariably shown in prayer, normally at a prie-dieu. The kneeling posture had appeared in the middle ages, but almost exclusively on brasses, where it had been used mainly for the portrayal of children, and occasionally for ancillary figures on three-dimensional monuments. In the earlier half of the sixteenth century, too, brasses and relief effigies on the backplates of wall monuments were commonly in this form, but it was only in the later sixteenth century that the bold use of the kneeling posture for the principal effigies began. It was ultimately a French convention, dating back to the late fifteenth century, but once more its popularity in England was chiefly the result of Netherlandish influence. As we have seen, it was pre-eminently suitable for hanging wall monuments, but was also employed on free-standing monuments, the largest of which might include up to ten life-size kneeling effigies. Moreover, the larger monuments gave greater scope for the frontal kneeling figure, of which several examples exist, including the pleasantly provincial monument of Richard Goddard (d.1615) at Aldbourne (Wilts), which has six such figures of varying sizes on a tomb-chest in front of a rich backplate.

The upright frontal demi-figure, which we have already met on hanging wall monuments and in use particularly for divines and scholars, was also sometimes featured on standing monuments as part of larger designs. In St Peter Mancroft, Norwich, for example, the unusual monument of the lawyer, Francis Windham (d.1592), depicts him as a demi-figure beneath a small projecting canopy set upon a tomb-chest, while in St Stephen, Canterbury, Sir Roger Manwood (d.1592) (*145*), a judge, appears likewise in an arched recess at the back of a monument whose tester-like canopy shelters also a tomb-chest bearing a skeleton on a straw mattress. In Eton College chapel (Bucks) the demi-figure of Provost Murray (d.1623) is particularly small in relation to the large and elaborately decorated monument of which it forms a part, and here again a skeleton is incorporated in the design.

Seated and standing effigies did not occur until after 1600 and even then were very rare for some decades, no doubt on account of their revolutionary form and lack of specifically religious feeling. Notable examples of the seated posture include Margaret Legh (d.1605) in All Saints Fulham (London) and John Stow (d.1605) in St Andrew Undershaft, London, the monument in each case being narrow and upright with the effigy seated on a solid base within an architectural frame. The former is the less life-like of the two, for Margaret Legh sits very stiffly, one hand holding a baby, the other placed against her breast, but John Stow, the historian of London, is more realistically portrayed seated at a table and holding a quill pen, as though in the act of writing; moreover, his quill is real and ceremonially renewed each year.

The standing posture was not employed for the sole or principal effigies before the 1620s, but it was used for additional figures on at least two earlier seventeenth-century monuments which also commemorated other persons represented in more conventional attitudes. At Chiddingly (Sussex), for example, a monument of 1612 commemorates not only Sir John Jefferay (d.1578) and his wife, who lie in the centre, but also their daughter and son-in-law, who stand life-size in flanking niches; while at Spilsby (Lincs) the monument of Peregrine Bertie 10th Lord Willoughby (d.1601) and his daughter (d.1610) depicts the lady semi-reclining under a canopy and, in an arched niche on the top, the standing figure of Lord Willoughby, possibly the earliest such figure of any size on an English monument.

The wider range of postures now available for effigies facilitated another significant development of these years, namely the growing practice of including several effigies on a single monument, which enabled the deceased to be represented not only with his wife but also with his children and other members of his family. The development was not entirely new, however, for one can trace a certain trend in this direction from the end of the thirteenth century. It was then, as we have seen, that husbands and wives were first shown together and that other members of the family began to appear as 'weepers' on the tomb-chest, often accompanied by their individual armorial bearings. In the fifteenth century monumental brasses commonly included, in addition to the deceased and wife, small-scale figures of their children, and the inclusion of children became still more marked on early sixteenth-century brasses which depicted kneeling family groups. But these earlier indications of family awareness were distinguished by their reti-

cence, for on the whole their representation of other members of the family was schematic and did not detract from the prominence given to the principal deceased.

To some extent this also applies to a good deal of later sixteenth-century work, especially where the deceased were represented as recumbent effigies and the children confined to the sides of tomb-chests or to the bases (and occasionally the backplates) of canopied wall monuments. In these situations it was common to show the children kneeling in a row, often in descending order of age and size and sometimes including such variations as a young child seated or a baby in a cot or in swaddling clothes. (Very occasionally the figures were not solely those of children, as is clear, for example, from the monument of Sir William Perryam (d.1605) at Crediton (Devon), which has on the base seven kneeling females who represent his three wives and his four daughters by the second wife, but such cases were exceptional.) Frequently little or no attempt was made to differentiate the children other than by sex, all the sons and all the daughters on a single monument being commonly shown alike in dress and features, but, on the other hand, the eldest son might be distinguished by wearing armour and a child's premature death indicated by a skull placed in its hand. Sometimes the concern for identity was taken a step further by carving or painting not only the coats of arms but also the names of the children separately above their figures, as can be seen, for instance, on the monument of Sir William Garrard (d.1607) at Dorney (Bucks), and, as the seventeenth century unfolded, the figures themselves were to be treated in an increasingly individualised manner. Nonetheless, despite this new and widespread practice of depicting the deceased's children, the little figures were relatively unobtrusive and retained something in common with the medieval 'weeper' convention.

By contrast, a number of monuments broke entirely new ground by giving almost equal prominence both to the deceased and wife and to their children or other relatives, and took on somewhat the character of celebrations of the whole family occasioned by the death of its leading member. The frequency of this fashion on hanging wall monuments with kneeling figures has already been discussed, but it is seen at its best on large standing monuments, including particularly those of Sir Anthony Cooke (d.1576) at Romford (Essex), Lady Elizabeth Hoby (d.1609) at Bisham (Berks), Sir

Roger Aston (dated 1612) at Cranford (Middx) – these being all standing wall monuments – and Henry Lord Norris (d. 1601) in Westminster Abbey, which is free-standing. On the first three all the major effigies are in the kneeling attitude. Sir Anthony Cooke and his wife face each other across a prie-dieu, flanked by two sons and four daughters of virtually the same dimensions as their parents; Sir Roger Aston's scheme is similar, save that he faces his two wives and the central figures are flanked by four daughters in pairs (*60*). By contrast, Lady Hoby, who died a widow, is accompanied by neither of her two husbands, thus necessitating a different arrangement of the other figures. Moreover, the effigies vary in size, Lady Hoby's being the largest and those of her children differing according to their order of birth or whether they predeceased her. In the central compartment Lady Hoby appears at a prie-dieu with three daughters behind her, while on the left of the monument and outside the canopy Lady Hoby's eldest surviving daughter faces her across the prie-dieu, balanced on the right by two sons also outside the canopy. (*53*). The whole is a very attractive and unusual ensemble. Different again is Lord Norris's monument, which, being free-standing, has greater freedom in the disposition of its effigies and employs different postures for parents and offspring. It depicts Lord and Lady Norris as recumbent figures upon a raised sarcophagus, and six sons as kneeling figures flanking their parents in two rows of three.

In a number of instances a distinction was made between the eldest son, who was given the sort of prominence just described, and the remaining children, who were relegated to the more common position against the base. Examples include the monuments of Sir Francis Knollys at Rotherfield Greys (Oxon), Sir Alexander Culpeper (dated 1608) at Goudhurst (Kent) and John Lord Petre (d. 1613) at Ingatestone (Essex).

The Culpeper monument has a further point of interest, for it includes a frontal demi-figure of a man who may be Sir Alexander's father, thus increasing the number of generations represented to three. It was not unique in this respect, since a number of monuments extended their family portrayal to the parents or other relatives of the deceased, whether or not his own children were included. The three generations of Fettiplaces (*c*. 1613) at Swinbrook (Oxon) and four generations of Tollemaches (1615) at Helmingham (Suffolk) have been mentioned earlier, but these omit child-

ren. A far more impressive testimony to this wider family sentiment is provided by the monument of Richard Chernocke (d. 1615) at Hulcote (Beds) (*61*), for it incorporates the effigies not only of Richard, his two wives and their children, but also of his father and his two wives with their children. It is a family piece *par excellence*, in the form of a tall standing wall monument of three tiers containing no fewer than 29 kneeling effigies, though none are of any great size and several are in relief only. As a further indication of Richard's filial piety, the effigies of his father and two wives are larger and more prominent than his own.

Family sentiment, aided by the trend toward realism in effigies, also manifested itself at the end of the period in a conscious though restrained portrayal of grief and devotion, particularly between man and wife. Hitherto feelings of tenderness had broken through only rarely in the middle ages with effigies of married couples holding hands, but such depictions had been purely symbolic and the fashion had died out well before 1500. Now the relationship between husband and wife came to be expressed through the rather stylized device of combining different attitudes for their respective effigies, the suggestion being that one partner had died leaving the other in mourning contemplation or prayer. This might be achieved by depicting the one as recumbent, the other reclining alongside and turned toward the dead partner, as is the case on the monument of Richard Bluett (d. 1614) at Holcombe Rogus (Devon) (*55*), the lady having died first. It must be admitted, however, that such combinations will not always bear this interpretation, as is clear, for example, from the similar scheme for Sir Thomas Vincent (d. 1613) at Stoke D'Abernon: here Sir Thomas is reclining and looks across his recumbent wife, yet the inscription records that she did not die until 1619. Alternatively, in the case of a dead husband the widow might be shown kneeling in prayer on a lower level beside his recumbent effigy, as on the monument of Sir Thomas Lucy (d. 1605) at Charlecote (Warks), or beside his reclining effigy, as on that of Sir John Glanvill (d. 1600) at Tavistock (Devon). The latter example is known to have been erected by Sir John's widow in 1615 and, as a further indication that he was indeed already dead, he rests his hand upon a skull. The combination of dead husband and grief-stricken widow was later to be interpreted with deep emotional content by Epiphanius Evesham, as will be seen in the next chapter. Other family relationships were more rarely treated in this way, but a remarkable case occurs on the monument of Richard Lord Rich (d.1568) and his son (d.1581) at Felsted (Essex), which dates probably from *c*.1619 and may well be another work of Epiphanius Evesham. Here, however, the nature of the feelings between the two is ambiguous, for the reclining father turns to look somewhat equivocally upon his son kneeling at a lower level behind his head, but of the intention to express intimate emotion of some kind there can be no doubt.

Inscriptions were another vehicle by which personal details about the deceased – his descent, his wife and her descent, his children, his offices and exploits – were conveyed to the viewer. In the course of the sixteenth century a major change came over the character of monumental inscriptions. Whereas in 1500 they were still in the medieval form of thin lines of carved lettering along the edges of the tomb-chest slab, by 1600 they commonly consisted of square or rectangular framed panels set with far greater prominence into the sides of the tomb-chest or into the canopy, particularly (in the case of canopied wall monuments) into the backplate. Moreover, as we have seen, some hanging monuments now consisted solely of an inscription within an ornamental frame. Inscriptions were thus enabled to increase in length and to contain a great deal of information for which there had not been room in the past. This change was brought about partly by the spread of literacy among the laity, which the Renaissance fostered, and equally by a desire to advertise the 'virtue' of the deceased, not so much in a spirit of boastful pride as in order to set forth a pattern of virtuous achievement which others might emulate. Although Latin remained frequent, many inscriptions were now in English, the use of this language having steadily grown since the mid-fifteenth century, notably on brasses, and reflecting now its increased status and the patriotic pride which Englishmen took in their native tongue after the Reformation. Another change was the result of Renaissance influence. Gothic lettering (or 'black-letter') was gradually replaced after the mid-sixteenth century by Roman lettering of the type first used in England on Torrigiani's monument for Henry VII.

Incised Slabs and Monumental Brasses

The popular medieval forms of two-dimensional memorial, namely, the incised slab and the monumental brass, persisted throughout this period. Little need be said here about the large incised slab, for it continued in all essentials as it had been in the middle ages, except, of course, that figures now appeared in the appropriate armour or dress. Many were in alabaster and the quality of the work was often even lower than in the medieval period, designs being stereotyped and their execution often crude. However, quite good later sixteenth-century examples can be seen at Blithfield (Staffs), Claverley (Salop), Hornsey (Middx), Packington (Leics) and elsewhere. At the same time a new practice emerged, whereby smaller incised panels, commonly of black marble, with kneeling portrayals of the deceased were set into modest hanging wall monuments, as, for instance, in the case of Robert Rychers (d.1588) at Wrotham (Kent).

Developments in the monumental brass were on the whole more interesting and varied. Brasses suffered a severe blow in the iconoclasm unleashed by the Reformation, when large numbers were destroyed and there was for a time a much reduced incentive to produce new ones which might undergo the same fate. One ought not to exaggerate this, however, for manufacture of brasses did not cease, save perhaps in the most destructive years of Edward VI's reign. An instructive case in point is the brass of William Barton (d.1538) in St Laurence's, Reading (Berks). It is a palimpsest brass, that is, a brass re-used by engraving a new memorial on the reverse of an older, in this case part of the brass of Sir John Popham (d.1463), which had been in the London Charterhouse until that was dissolved by Henry VIII. Clearly Sir John's brass had been taken up and acquired by a brass-maker, who had re-used it for William Barton's memorial at Reading (a not uncommon occurrence in this period), but the important fact which emerges is that, despite the destruction of the earlier brass along with countless others, no demur was felt in immediately using its material for another. Nor can the Reformation be blamed for the decline in design and technique evident on brasses of Henry VIII's reign, for this had already become apparent soon after 1500 and was the result of factors other than that of religious change.

In any case, the making of figured brasses recovered under Elizabeth and endured thereafter until the late seventeenth century, when to all intents and purposes it died out until re-introduced during the nineteenth-century Gothic Revival. However, although Elizabethan and Jacobean brasses in general displayed better drawing of the human figure than earlier sixteenth-century work, the metal plates were thinner and the quality of the engraving was often far inferior to that of the best medieval work. It was very shallow and attempted a depiction of minute details of dress, etc., which was difficult to bring off successfully without obscuring the main lines of the figure.

Brasses of this period took a variety of forms, some traditional, some new. The medieval English type, in which the figures and other features were separately cut out and set into a slab (whether in the floor or on a tomb-chest), continued, although the two-dimensional brass canopy disappeared early in Henry VIII's reign. The type is represented in the 1530s by the excellent brass of Thomas Bullen earl of Wiltshire and Ormond (d.1538) at Hever (Kent) and, later in the period, by those of John Ayshecombe (d.1592) at West Hanney (Berks), Dean Humphrey Tyndall (d.1614) in Ely cathedral and Nicholas Wadham (d.1618) at Ilminster (Somerset). Perhaps the best Elizabethan ones, however, are two brasses engraved by Gerard Johnson, dated 1595, commemorating members of the Gage family at West Firle (Sussex). In many cases the figures of the deceased appear with several other items, such as portrayals of children, shields of arms and large rectangular inscription plates, all of which are also set separately into the slab.

Brasses located in the backplates of canopied wall monuments and depicting kneeling figures of the deceased and his family remained popular under Henry VIII. As time passed, however, such brasses ceased to be cut to the outline of the figures and were left as rectangular or arched plates engraved overall with figures and such other features as heraldic shields and inscriptions. Moreover, from soon after 1550 the plates began to be set into ornamental stone or alabaster frames fixed to the wall in the form of comparatively small hanging monuments, an arrangement which became common in the later sixteenth and early seventeenth centuries. Good examples of rectangular plates from this period, showing the whole family kneeling at prayer, include the brasses of Thomas Inwood (d.1586) at Weybridge (Surrey), Thomas Duport (d.1592) at Shepshed (Leics) and Edward Younge (d.1608) at Durnford (Wilts). These and many like them clearly reflect the same concern for the family as appears on contemporary three-dimensional monuments with their groups of effigies in the round, but even the most elaborate of

the latter are surpassed by the remarkable brass plate of Thomas Beale (d.1593) at Maidstone (Kent), which is engraved with a total of six generations, each with children and arrayed on separate 'shelves'.

The engraving on brass plates might represent the deceased in other ways. A type fairly widespread for women who had died in childbirth depicted them lying in a four-poster bed. It is exemplified by the brasses of Alice Harrison (c.1600) at Hurst (Berks) and Anne Savage (d.1605) at Wormington (Glos), the latter showing her baby upon the bed-cover. Again, in York Minster the brass of John Cotrel (d.1595) portrays him as a gesturing demi-figure, while another at Watford (Herts), dating from c.1613, depicts three servants of the Morrison family as standing figures.

Finally, a few words must be devoted to the subject of low-relief effigies, for, although very rare in England as a whole at this time, they enjoyed a particular local popularity in Cornwall. There numerous examples carved on Cornish slate slabs survive from the later sixteenth century onward. The slabs vary in size and location, some being placed upon tomb-chests, some set against a wall or in the floor, and the effigy is usually depicted either full-length or kneeling. Their carving is for the most part naive and primitive and, although not devoid of Renaissance influence, stands rather as a manifestation of independent and localized folk-art. Typical examples, ranging in date from 1567 to 1620, are to be seen at Lansallos, Lelant, St Cleer, St Martin-by-Looe, St Neot and St Tudy, followed by others later in the seventeenth century. Among them, the full-length figure of Margaret Smith (d.1579) at Lansallos, carved in low relief and sunk in the surface of the slab, is strikingly reminiscent of the earliest twelfth-century effigies in England.

A Note on Armour and Costume

Throughout this period monumental effigies remain a major source of evidence for developments in armour and dress, although they can now be supplemented by increasing numbers of paintings and even by the survival of original pieces. Among the more significant aspects are the changes in armour and female costume.

Despite the declining value of the fully armed knight in battle, armour continued to be important in the lists and for display, and numerous male effigies were in consequence depicted in suits of armour until well into the seventeenth century. In its most typical forms the armour displayed was of the 'Greenwich type', deriving from the armoury established by Henry VIII at Greenwich and characterized in particular by the 'peascod' breastplate, which had a more or less pronounced ridge down the centre and came to a bulge at the waist. This was worn with plate armour defences for the arms and legs, but, although the thighs might be similarly protected, in many cases in the latter part of the period long tassets of horizontally laminated plates were simply strapped over stuffed trunk hose. The appearance of this type of armour can be appreciated, for example, on the figure of Sir Roger Aston (dated 1612) at Cranford (Middx) (*60*), who also wears a splendidly full ruff round the neck.

In the sphere of female dress the most significant developments concerned the changing forms of head-dress, the appearance of the ruff and the introduction of the farthingale. The pedimented head-dress, which had come into vogue in the early years of Henry VIII, was succeeded before the mid-sixteenth century by the so-called 'Paris hood', or 'Mary Queen of Scots head-dress', a close-fitting cap, often depressed to a point above the middle of the forehead, with a veil hanging down behind. It is shown, for instance, on the figure of Lady Williams, whose husband died in 1559, at Thame (Oxon) (*62*) and on the brass of Anne Staverton (d.1585) at Sonning (Berks) (*63*). Somewhat later the veil was not infrequently pinned up over the back and top of the cap, but by the early seventeenth century the hair was sometimes more stylishly not covered but gathered high on the head in complex dressings, as can be seen, for example, on the effigy of Anne Herrys (d.1613) at Chevening (Kent) (*64*). At the same time, other female effigies were shown in an extraordinarily capacious hood, frequently pleated and extending down over the back of the figure. Although, as in the magnificent example worn by Lady Elizabeth Hoby (d.1609) at Bisham (Berks) (*65*), the suggestion might be that of widow's weeds, it was emphatically not confined exclusively to widows. Less commonly after 1600, female effigies were depicted in a brimmed high-crowned hat of the type that would be worn out-of-doors. In the case of one of the wives of Richard Humble (d.1616) in Southward cathedral, a hat with a narrow brim is worn, but a little later the brim was to become very broad, as, for example, on the effigy of Edward Skynner's wife (*c.*1631) at Ledbury (Herefs).

An early stage in the evolution of the ruff can be seen on the effigy of Lady Williams at Thame (*62*), already mentioned, the neck of whose dress has a simple and unobtrusively frilly edge. From this were to develop the elaborate ruffs so typical of both female and male attire in the Elizabethan and Jacobean periods, examples of which are worn by the figures on the Aston monument at Cranford (*60*). Alternatively, the ruff might take the form of a starched lace collar rising high behind the head, a form fashionable in the early seventeenth century and worn, for instance, by the figure of Anne Herrys at Chevening. (*64*).

Female dress of the Elizabethan and Jacobean periods was equally characterized by the farthingale, which gave an exaggerated spread to the skirt. Its first form, introduced from Spain in the 1550s and known as the Spanish farthingale, relied upon a petticoat hooped with bands of cane, whalebone or

61 Hulcote (Beds): Richard Chernocke (d.1615) and family

wire, which imparted to the dress worn over it a cone-like shape from waist to foot. The result is apparent, for example, on the brass of Anne Staverton (d. 1585) at Sonning (*63*). Then, in *c.* 1580, a new fashion, the French farthingale, was introduced and remained in vogue for much of James I's reign, in which the skirt was thrust out at the waist over a wheel-like base tilted forward, from which it hung down more or less vertically to the ground. Its characteristic appearance can be seen, for example, on the wives and daughters of Sir Roger Aston (dated 1612) at Cranford (*60*) and on the figure of Anne Herrys (d. 1613) at Chevening (*64*).

The various forms of professional dress in this period remained generally much as they had been in the middle ages. Thus, the official robes of a judge in the mid-sixteenth century, worn, for example, by Chief Justice Bromley (d. 1555) at Wroxeter (Salop) (*66*), were similar to those of medieval judges, save that the cap was now provided with a broad flat top. Later effigies of judges were shown in essentially the same robes and cap with the addition, however, of a

ruff at the neck, as in the case of Sir John Glanvill (d. 1600) at Tavistock (Devon).

However, as a result of the Reformation, major changes came about in the dress of the clergy and were reflected in monumental effigies after the 1530s. Eucharistic vestments were no longer permitted and processional vestments became rare, the clergy being depicted normally in their academic robes. Likewise, bishops abandoned their mitres and other pontificals, and, although episcopal effigies occasionally appear in copes, like, for instance, Bishop Martin Heton (d. 1609) in Ely cathedral, they wear close-fitting caps on their heads. The standard dress of a bishop after the Reformation consisted of a rochet and chimere, the former being a white alb-like vestment whose sleeves grew increasingly in size as the period unfolded, the latter a sleeveless gown, commonly black in colour, worn over the rochet and reaching to the ground. A good example occurs on the monument of Bishop William Cotton (d. 1621) in Exeter cathedral (*67*), where the ensemble is completed by an academic cap.

62 Thame (Oxon): Lord Williams of Thame (d. 1559) and Lady Williams. Detail

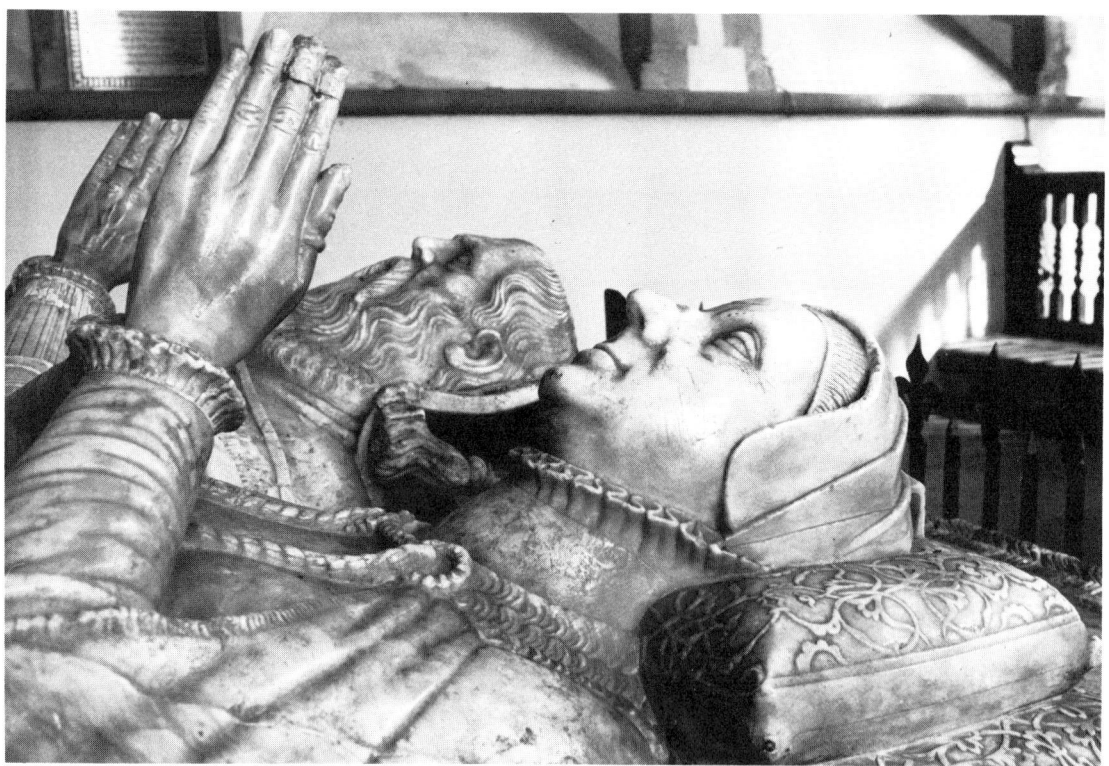

HERE LYETHE BVRYED THE BODY OF ANNE STAVERTON
DAVGHTER AND SOLE HEIRE OF WILLIAM BARKER THE DER
ESQVIER DECEASED LATE THE WIFE OF WILLYAM STAVERTON
OF OCKYNGAM IN THE CONTI OF BARKE GENTELMAN
BY WHOM SHE HAD ISHEW 4 SONES VID FRAVNCES WILL:
YAM GEORGE AND IOHN WHO DEPARTED THIS WORLDE
THE 21 DAY OF SEPTEMB IN TE YEARE OF OVR LORD GOD 158

AFREND VNTO THE WIDDOO FATHERLES SYCKE AND POORE
A COMFORTE AND ASVCKER CONTYNEVED SHE EVER MORE

63 *Above* Sonning (Berks): Anne Staverton (d.1585).
Rubbing of brass

64 *Above right* Chevening (Kent): Anne Herrys (d.1613)

65 Bisham (Berks): Elizabeth Lady Hoby (d.1609). Detail of head-dress

66 Wroxeter (Salop): Chief Justice
Bromley (d.1555) and Lady Bromley

67 Exeter cathedral: Bishop William
Cotton (d.1621)

4 The Seventeenth Century & the Rise of the Baroque Style
c.1620-c.1720

This period marked the next important stages in the development of Renaissance funerary monuments in England. It opened with a phase of increased classical influence, coinciding roughly with the reign of Charles I (1625–49), and came to a climax with the emergence and flowering of the Baroque style, which dominated the character of monuments in the later seventeenth and early eighteenth centuries. These two aspects of the period were closely linked, for, although peaceful evolution of the one into the other was disrupted by the Civil War and Interregnum (lasting in total from 1642 to 1660), the establishment of the Baroque thereafter owed much to advances made before the Civil War.

The increase in classical influence under Charles I was brought about basically by greater knowledge of ancient Roman art and architecture and by closer contact with the mainstreams of classical Renaissance development on the Continent, especially in Italy. These intimately related movements had their origins in the reign of James I (1603–25) and resulted partly from a political and religious toning-down of the rather embattled, fiercely patriotic Protestantism that had prevailed under Elizabeth I and severely blinkered England's later Renaissance experience.

Under James I two developments in particular, resulting from the initiative of Englishmen themselves, were to be of great importance in enhancing the country's classical awareness, though their immediate effect must not be exaggerated. In the field of architecture Inigo Jones introduced England in the second decade of the seventeenth century to principles of classical Roman building purer by far than anything she had yet seen. These principles he had learnt from personal experience of Italy and, in particular, from the writings and works of the sixteenth-century Italian Renaissance architect, Andrea Palladio. Jones's use of Palladian classical features in such buildings as the Queen's House at Greenwich and the Banqueting House in Whitehall

rubbed off in due course on the designers of monuments. In the same decade Thomas Howard earl of Arundel, having acquired what was for the time a remarkable interest in antique Roman sculpture, travelled to the Mediterranean in furtherance of this interest and began his collection of classical pieces and contemporary copies (now in the Ashmolean Museum, Oxford), which was to encourage a similar pre-occupation in the mind of the future Charles I and ultimately to exercise an influence on English mason-sculptors. Moreover, the increasing dissemination of prints and drawings of ancient Roman ruins and sculpture or of Renaissance achievements in Italy and elsewhere was steadily exposing English patrons and craftsmen to exemplars which invited imitation, and the richly decorated title-pages of imported books were another vehicle by which similar influences could be widely circulated. Under Charles I these cultural forces gathered momentum. The classical commitment was intensified by more serious study and deeper appreciation of antique art, especially sculpture, fostered primarily now by the royal court, and was further enhanced by the arrival in England of craftsmen from Flanders, France and Italy.

For some decades, however, the effect on monumental effigies was minimal, except for the introduction of pedestal busts, and the most telling signs of greater classical influence on monuments were to be seen in modifications of 'architectural' design and in a gradual change in decorative motifs. The most important architectural innovation was the incorporation of segmental pediments into the design of canopies, whether free-standing or against a wall. The straight-sided or triangular pediment had been used on occasions in the sixteenth century, as we have seen, but not widely and seldom with much confidence. Now, although straight-sided pediments were sometimes employed, the segmental type became popular. The segmental pediment is so called because its shape is that of a segment of a circle, its base being, as it were, the chord of the circle and its upper line the arc. However, in addition to this difference of shape, both segmental and triangular pediments might also be either 'broken' or 'open', both variations being very common. If they are broken, the centre of the base is missing, if open, the centre of the upper line is missing. Hybrid forms are also found in which, while the complete outline is present, the central portion of base or top, or both, is slightly recessed. In the case of open segmental pediments, the interrupted parts of the arc sometimes terminate in simple scrolls, a type described as a 'scrolly' pediment, and on occasions assume an ogee line as they approach the scrolls, this being known as a 'swan-necked' pediment. In its various forms the segmental pediment was most typical of the seventeenth and early eighteenth centuries.

Changes in the range of decorative motifs were equally significant, though the sequence of developments was more complicated. The three most characteristic motifs of the Elizabethan and Jacobean periods – obelisks (used as decoration), strapwork and the crinkled type of ribbonwork – gradually disappeared, along with several exuberant features of the early Renaissance, such as candelabra, balusters, sea monsters and mermaids. By contrast, other features not only survived but were exploited with vigour and enthusiasm, many of them having a symbolic or personal significance, notably cherubs (either full-body or head only), allegorical figures, urns, burning lamps, scenes from the life of the deceased and the multiform symbolism of death and mortality. Moreover, angels, which had lain under a cloud of 'popery' for much of the sixteenth century and had reappeared on monuments only after 1610, remained in the repertoire. Other features, too, whose use had been but haltingly foreshadowed in the previous period or had appeared very late, now became standard ingredients, namely, garlands of leaves, fruit and flowers, masks, curtains, drapes and objects alluding to the profession of the deceased. Heraldry continued to be a prominent and important element, though now displayed usually not as shields of arms but as ovel cartouches in classical-derived surrounds. Not all these features and motifs can strictly be described as classical, of course, and not all were employed to the same degree throughout the period.

The period also witnessed a general transition to marble (chiefly white, black and grey marble) for the construction of monuments. Marble had been introduced in a limited way in the sixteenth century, mainly at that time black marble, and had steadily become more common under James I, but its adoption was now so accelerated that by 1660 it accounted for most monuments of any consequence. Other materials were progressively abandoned or reduced to minor roles. In particular alabaster, which had predominated for the best English work over nearly three centuries, fell increasingly out of fashion, partly because the purer deposits were being rapidly worked out leaving only heavily veined material of inferior beauty, but chiefly because marble came to be regarded as the most appropriate medium for monuments in a more classical or Baroque idiom. Alabaster continued to be employed on an ever-diminishing scale into the early eighteenth century, but then disappeared until revived for monumental work in the mid-nineteenth century. A variety of local stones of differing quality also remained in use and some bronze work was produced, but pre-eminently the seventeenth century became an age of marble. Hand in hand with this went the gradual disappearance of colour. The painting and gilding of effigies and much of the rest of monuments, which had been so pronounced a feature of the preceding period, gave way gradually to a practice whereby, in imitation of classical Renaissance works, the new marble monuments were left without the adornment of artificial colouring, save for coats of arms and discreet highlighting of certain details in gold paint. The abiding impression of most later seventeenth-century monuments, therefore, is of studies in white, black and grey in various combinations. Shortly after 1700 colour began to creep back, but in the form of marbles of other hues, though the heyday of polychrome monuments of this type was to come later in the eighteenth century.

A further development of some significance was that now for the first time appreciable numbers of monuments were beginning to be 'signed', that is, carved with the name of their maker and possibly the date of completion. The practice had been adumbrated a decade or so earlier, but very rarely, and the growth of the habit from the 1630s onward, despite the fact that the majority of monuments remained unsigned until well after the Restoration, cannot but indicate a certain rise in the status of monument-makers. It has the added advantage, particularly for those interested in individual craftsmen, of placing the authorship of an increasing number of monuments beyond doubt, thus avoiding the many uncertain attributions unsupported by documentary evidence of earlier periods.

These developments were gradual and long-term rather than sudden and immediate. The preceding remarks indicate trends and in the early years of the period apply only to a minority of the monuments produced. In some cases changes were effected by one craftsman or workshop, more progressive than most, adopting or introducing a novel feature which was then taken up gradually by others, but there was inevitably an overlap stage in which the majority of monuments reflected the new influences in hybrid form. On the other hand, forerunners of a more classical approach had already been seen in the reign of James I. In the last chapter note was taken of developments then occurring in monumental forms, in ornamental features and in the use of materials. More striking, however, and belonging properly in this chapter, were certain monuments which, though conventional or basically Mannerist in form, exhibited so pronounced a classical character as to set them in advance of most of their contemporaries.

The splendid monument of Nicholas Bacon and wife (dated 1616) at Redgrave (Suffolk), for instance, consisting of a free-standing tomb-chest with recumbent effigies, is a very traditional type interpreted in a new, forward-looking spirit of classical repose and almost heroic dignity. Constructed of white and black marble, the tomb-chest is severely restrained in its adornment, having merely inscription panels in quasi-classical cartouches with only the faintest echo of strapwork and corner pilasters with bulgy bases and moulded tops, while above lie the effigies of white marble in the easiest of relaxed poses. The same is true, with variations, of the monument of similar type to Lady Elizabeth Carey (c.1617) at Stowe-Nine-Churches (Northants), and indeed both pieces are wholly or principally by the same craftsman, Nicholas Stone. Another equally fine but more elaborate example is the large free-standing canopied monument of Sir Anthony Mildmay (d.1617) at Apethorpe (Northants), again a traditional type (deriving from earlier four-posters) and again transformed by more classical considerations. Of black and white marble, it depicts the deceased and his wife as recumbent upon a severely plain base, from which rises a lantern-like canopy, the centre circular in plan with 'hanging' marble curtains tied back to the corner supports to reveal the effigies. At the four corners stand life-size

figures of the Cardinal Virtues, and three more allegorical figures are seated on the superstructure. Typical Jacobean enrichment and colour are entirely absent. The monument of Lord Knyvett (d.1622) at Stanwell (Middx) shows the same sort of development on another familiar type, the standing wall monument with kneeling effigies, although in this case the materials are black marble and alabaster. The figures appear on a high base carved with garlands and skulls, beneath a flat canopy, from which hang curtains tied back to the supporting side columns. Above the entablature is a rudimentary segmental pediment open in the centre to contain a rich cartouche of arms and, again, there is no trace of Jacobean ornament.

In each of these examples, however, the effigies are unaffected by classical considerations. All are excellently carved, with fine and lovingly observed details of dress and armour, and all share the more naturalistic and sympathetic treatment noted toward the end of the last chapter, especially in relation to face and hands, but the latter characteristic owed its inspiration not to classical influence as such, but to the spirit of Renaissance humanism. These monuments involved, therefore, a combination of increased classical influence in architecture and decoration, on the one hand, and humanistic realism in effigies, on the other. The same combination was to be typical of monuments of Charles I's reign.

Before considering these, however, we must pause to take note of two unique monuments of the 1620s in Westminster Abbey, both by Nicholas Stone, for, though of alabaster and stone, they display not only a conscious attempt at an Italian classical style, but a revolutionary departure in English monumental design. In particular, they are remarkable for their undoubted if indirect inspiration from the Medici tombs by Michelangelo in Florence, which their creator can have known only from drawings or engravings. The monuments in question are those of Francis Holles (d.1622) and his brother, Sir George Holles (d.1626). The former stands free, without canopy or architectural setting, and comprises a drum-shaped pedestal on which the effigy sits dressed in antique Roman armour, feet together, knees apart, its face turned slightly to one side gazing upward. The impression is very much that of an independent statue which one might expect to find in a nobleman's private house or out in the open. The other monument is set against a wall of the north transept: between two mourning

68 Chipping Campden (Glos): Baptist Hicks, Lord Campden (d. 1629)

69 Harefield (Middx): Alice countess of Derby (d. 1637)

women Sir George is depicted in the same Roman armour, but this time standing upon a high plinth above a base carved with a military scene, one knee slightly bent and his head slightly turned. Despite their somewhat clumsy execution, these compositions were strikingly original in England at this time and mark, as it were, the emancipation of English craftsmanship from the heavy hand of Netherlandish influence or, put another way, the coming-of-age of the classical Renaissance in this country.

The Holles monuments reveal an urge to experiment similar to that which we have seen at work earlier in James's reign, and indeed equally striking though different innovations were to occur under Charles I. Nevertheless, at the time of Charles I's accession the number of monuments which were so daringly conceived or broke so sharply with customary practice was not large. Well-established monumental types held on tenaciously for some decades, in many cases exhibiting classical influence only in their decorative enrichment or in subtle modifications of their structural design. This can be seen in each of the main categories: simple tomb-chests, free-standing canopied monuments and standing and hanging wall monuments.

Monumental Types under Charles I

The rectangular tomb-chest with recumbent effigies was by now a conservative type and became markedly less common as the period proceeded. Even so, several examples were produced with classical enrichment (or perhaps one should say classical restraint) on their sides and ends, particularly those constructed of white and black marble. A case in point is the singularly pure tomb-chest of Anne Lady Kinlosse (d.1628) at Exton (Rutland), which is articulated by a series of beautiful Ionic colonnettes interspersed by heraldic cartouches. Others include those of William Standen (d.1639) at Arborfield (Berks), with Doric colonnettes, and Abraham Blackleech (d.1639) in Gloucester cathedral, with plain pilasters, the intervening panels being occupied in each case by inscriptions or heraldic cartouches. In another typical group the sides of the tomb-chest are given over to big rectangular inscription panels which occupy virtually their entire length, the corners of the chest being formed by angle pilasters which are frequently shaped, with bulging bottoms, and sometimes carved with classical decoration. This type is well exemplified by the tomb-chest of Sir George Villiers (dated 1631) in Westminster Abbey, whose shaped corner pilasters are heavily enriched with acanthus leaves, garlands and heraldic cartouches, and by that of Sir Richard Wilbraham (d.1643) at Acton (Cheshire), where they are plain. At Godstone (Surrey), by contrast, the tomb-chest of Sir John Evelyn (d.1641) has straight, unadorned pilasters. Notable in most of these is the depiction of coats of arms no longer as shields enclosed in strapwork, but as oval cartouches of arms in scrolly surrounds, though full heraldic achievements (comprising shield, crest and mantling) are frequently carved on the ends of tomb-chests. The oval heraldic cartouches might alternatively be enclosed in wreathed surrounds, as on the very fine tomb-chest of Sir John Kyrle (d.1650) at Much Marcle (Herefs). Increasingly less common in this period was the inclusion of small figures of children kneeling along the sides of tomb-chests, but where they occur they appear against a plain ground in association with classical details or cartouches of arms. The chest of two members of the Unett family (*c.*1630–40) at Castle Frome (Herefs), for instance, has a row of kneeling children under looped drapes tied at the ends, and that of Sir William Sandys (d.1640) at Miserden (Glos), which is of alabaster, has rows of beautifully carved children each with a scrolly cartouche of arms.

Among the best free-standing canopied monuments exhibiting similar or related developments is that of Sir Baptist Hicks, Lord Campden (d.1629), at Chipping Campden (Glos) (*68*). This comprises a broad base with two recumbent effigies, above which rises a massive twelve-poster canopy resting upon Doric columns. Thus far it departs but little from its precursors in the previous period, but the new influences are spectacularly apparent in the design of the canopy and in the *sotto voce* treatment of the monument as a whole. The elevation of each side consists of four columns supporting an entablature surmounted by the novel feature of a segmental pediment, which in this case is open to accommodate a square heraldic panel topped by a small triangular pediment. Moreover, the monument is constructed of white and black marble and, apart from the painted and gilded shield of arms, entirely lacks colour. Likewise, although all elements are finely moulded, decorative enrichment proper is conspicuously absent. A starker contrast with the obelisks and strapwork of earlier years would be difficult to imagine, and the piece may be regarded in its noble restraint as typical of the most advanced work of its date. Slightly less successful, but equally striking, is the eight-poster canopied monument of William Lord Spencer (d. 1636) at Great Brington (Northants), but, though similarly of black and white marble and devoid of colour, it lacks pediments. The six-poster of Sir Lawrence Tanfield (d. 1625) at Burford (Oxon) is somewhat similar, but differs in being made of black marble and alabaster, in having small figures of Virtues above the columns and in retaining the obsolescent feature of obelisks on top of the canopy.

A few free-standing or nearly free-standing canopied monuments of Charles I's time were provided with domed or dome-like superstructures which, though ultimately of classical origin, were in each case treated in ways which lessened their 'architectural' character. An excellent example is the unusual monument of Lewis Stuart duke of Richmond and Lennox (d. 1624) and his duchess (d. 1639) in Westminster Abbey, which is among the most important funerary works of Hubert le Sueur, a Frenchman who operated in England under royal patronage from 1626 to the outbreak of the Civil War. Carried out in black marble and gilt bronze (a material favoured by le Sueur), it comprises two effigies recumbent upon a large sarcophagus adorned with cherubs, the whole sheltered by a delicate openwork dome supported on the heads of four life-size standing Virtues. The immediate derivation of this piece is undoubtedly north European rather than Mediterranean, and some such origin may also be inferred for another impressive example, that of Alice countess of Derby (d. 1637) at Harefield (Middx) (69). Most probably a late work by Maximilian Colt, this resembles Jacobean monuments in being largely coloured and gilded, but is otherwise quite distinct. The countess lies upon a substantial tomb-chest covered with what appears to be a pall executed in black marble, while above the upper two-thirds of her effigy stands a domed canopy apparently of rich cloth rising from curving entablatures supported on four black marble columns. The *trompe-l'oeil* effect is very convincing, for the 'cloth' of the dome apparently extends below the entablature in the form of curtains which are tied back to the supporting columns. The conceit is clearly intended to represent a baldacchino.

Standing wall monuments with canopies were far more numerous than either of the preceding categories and varied considerably in the degree to which they displayed classical features or took on a classical character. It is impossible here to itemize every variation in form, since, apart from the survival or earlier types for some years, the range was now much extended by experiments in design and particularly by greater freedom in the arrangement of effigies. The more progressive canopies opted for a segmental pediment to crown the design or incorporated curtains either tied back to side columns or held back by angels or other figures. Ornament was usually restrained or quite absent on these, the carving of classical elements such as the capitals and bases of columns was generally of a high order and, in the absence of colour, contrast was achieved by the use of black and white marble or black marble and alabaster.

The elevations of canopies incorporating segmental pediments consist basically of an upright rectangular shape defined by base, side columns and entablature, save that the entablature carries a segmental pediment which imparts a distinctively curved outline to the top of the canopy. Segmental pediments occur in numerous variations of detail and their curves may be interrupted or uneven in the ways described above. A fairly typical example, in which the feature is employed somewhat tentatively, is provided by the monument of Sir William Pitt (d. 1636) at Stratfield Saye (Hants), a work in alabaster and black marble signed by John and Matthias Christmas, with Corinthian side columns and a segmental pediment which is both broken and open for the insertion of an arched heraldic achievement. More noble and showing better understanding of classical forms is Nicholas Stone's black and white marble monument for Sir Edward Coke (d. 1634) at Tittleshall (Norfolk), whose entablature rests on Tuscan Doric columns and carries an open segmental pediment, upon which four Virtues recline. These and other related monuments have effigies of the deceased, but among the most notable instances of the use of segmental pediments are those which dispense with effigies altogether. The monuments of Humphrey Packington (d. 1631) at Chaddesley Corbet (Worcs) and Sir Thomas Puckering (dated 1639) in St Mary's, Warwick, for example, consist of large inscription panels in classical settings surmounted by segmental pediments. The latter is by far the purer piece, on account not only of its extreme reticence but also of its total lack of carved enrichment. It is by Nicholas Stone, whose later years were distinguished by other equally austere classical monuments, includ-

70 Croome D'Abitot (Worcs): Thomas, 1st Lord Coventry
(d.1639)

71 Shinfield (Berks): Henry Beke (dated 1627)

ing that of Sir Edmund Paston (d. 1632) at Paston (Norfolk), which substitutes for the effigy an urn placed upon a plain base beneath a projecting canopy supported on Tuscan columns and topped by an open segmental pediment.

The use of curtains on standing wall monuments was pioneered in the later years of James I by such monuments as that of Lord Knyvett (d. 1622) at Stanwell (Middx), mentioned earlier, where the curtains are tied back to side columns and hang from behind what appears to be a 'cloth' fringe fixed to the entablature. The combination of curtains and fringe was standard under Charles I, occurring, for example, on the fine alabaster and black marble monuments of Sir Edwin Sandys (d. 1629) at Northbourne (Kent) and Sir Edward Lewis (d. 1630) at Edington (Wilts), and somewhat later on that of Sir Henry Griffith (d. 1645) at Burton Agnes (Yorks) (*144*). In these cases the curtains are tied to side columns. Alternatively they are held back by figures, though such compositions are often unclassical in feeling and coarsely executed, as can be seen in the monuments of Sir William Clarke (d. 1625) at Hitcham (Bucks) and Thomas Thornhurst (d. 1627) in Canterbury cathedral, where the curtains are held by military figures in armour. A more accomplished instance occurs at Hurst (Berks), where the monument of Lady Margaret Savile (d. 1631), a tripartite design with the centre bulging forward, has heavy looped curtains held at the sides by angels and lifted at intermediate points upon the necks of projecting cherub busts. On the idiosyncratic canopy of Sir Edward Carr (d. 1637) at Hillingdon (Middx), the curtains are shorter than normal and gathered into knots above their hem.

Space forbids mention of the many canopied wall monuments which compromise in a bewildering variety of ways between Jacobean traditions and the more progressive trends, but room must be found for two extraordinary monuments which individually display curiously disturbing equilibriums between both idioms. They are those of Sir Henry Yelverton (d. 1629) at Easton Maudit (Northants) and Sir Henry Fryer (d. 1631) at Harlton (Cambs). Both must be described as fundamentally Mannerist, since the coffered arch of each rests ultimately upon standing figures (bearded bedesmen in the former case, terminal caryatids in the latter), and both are much coloured and gilded, but their enrichment represents an advance on Jacobean models, for each includes heraldic cartouches and that of Sir Henry Fryer is topped by an open scrolly

pediment.

Toward the end of Charles I's reign a number of advanced monuments began to move beyond the classical as such toward incipiently Baroque designs and ornament. The standard media were by now black and white marble and classical influence was still very marked, but the compositions were less classical in tone, and the ornament, though for the most part classically inspired, became more elaborate and intrusive. The effects are neither unpleasing nor inelegant, but they undoubtedly represent a departure from the cool poise of classical monuments in the direction of the grand, opulent monuments of the High Baroque period. This is admirably illustrated by the monument of the 1st Lord Coventry (d. 1639) at Croome d'Abitot (Worcs) (*70*). It depicts the deceased semi-reclining beneath a richly panelled segmental arch, which rests upon pairs of side columns and is crowned by what appears to be the upper part of an open segmental pediment whose base-line is missing. Outside the columns on each side sit small allegorical figures holding objects appropriate to the deceased's office as Keeper of the Great Seal of England, and on top of the canopy recline two angels flanking an heraldic achievement. The capitals of the supporting columns are wilfully unclassical, for, though apparently Ionic in origin, they have tiny festoons hanging from them, while garlands of foliage hang from tied ribbons at the sides of the monument and winged cherub-heads appear upon the backplate and above the arch. Finally, on a ledge in front of the effigy are placed the mace and bag for the Great Seal excellently carved in white marble.

All that has been said in reference to standing wall monuments applies *mutatis mutandis* to hanging monuments. Standard Jacobean types continue for a time, though with the application of more or less classical enrichment, alongside others which, in varying degrees of classical correctness, have segmental or triangular pediments or tied-back curtains. Special mention should be made of one distinctive and attractive form which is first found under James I and remains popular for part of Charles I's reign. This type depicts the effigy (or effigies) beneath a fringed, forward-bulging canopy, from which hang curtains held back by angels who stand against side pilasters. In most examples the effigies are kneeling, commonly singly, as in the cases of Margaret Pope (d. 1621) at North Barningham (Norfolk) and Sir Eubule Thelwall (d. 1630) in Jesus College, Oxford, but sometimes in groups of two or more, as on the monument of Henry Beke (dated 1627) at Shinfield (Berks) (*71*), which has three. Occasionally, as with William Langton (d. 1626) in Magdalen College, Oxford, the effigy is by contrast a frontal demi-figure.

Despite the many points of similarity with standing wall monuments, hanging monuments displayed a far wider variety of compositions and decorative schemes, partly no doubt simply because of their greater numbers, but mainly because their hanging nature allowed many to be designed with scant regard for 'architectural' considerations. On occasions quite fantastical combinations of 'structural' and ornamental elements were achieved, a case in point being the monument of Sir Hugh Hammersley (d. 1636) in St Andrew Undershaft, London, which shows kneeling figures beneath a canopy that would be almost inconceivable in a standing monument of this time. By contrast, other hanging monuments abandoned entirely the notion of an 'architectural' canopy, or even of a rectangular or arched frame. Particularly where the deceased was represented by a demi-figure or bust, they might consist simply of circular or oval recesses in scrolly surrounds with separate inscription panels. Examples include the monuments of John Eldred (d. 1632) at Great Saxham (Suffolk) and Robert Burton (d. 1639) in Oxford cathedral, each of which is surmounted by an heraldic cartouche. The trend away from architecture was most marked, however, in wall tablets comprising inscriptions without effigies, for, although these may be found with 'architectural' frames throughout the period, many take the different form of a more or less elaborately enriched cartouche. Their development was prodigious and extremely varied, especially in the Baroque period, and consequently their consideration is better left until later in the chapter.

Effigies in Charles I's Reign

Despite the growing number of inscription tablets, the majority of monuments continued to include representations of the deceased, either as complete effigies or as demi-figures or busts. The most striking aspect of effigies in this period, compared with those earlier, is their great variety. This can be seen not only in the postures and hand positions adopted by individual effigies, but also in the range of particular groupings of figures on individual monuments and the increasing skill of craftsmen in expressing emotions between them. The recumbent, reclining and kneeling postures remained common, but in addition the early experiments with seated and standing effigies noted in the previous chapter were now exploited freely. Similarly, whatever the basic posture assumed by the effigy, a realistic, relaxed treatment of the human figure, with carefully modelled features and fastidiously carved details of dress and armour, became normal. The traditional depiction of the hands closed in prayer, which had tended to produce formal and often stiff effigies, grew less common, especially after 1630, and virtually died out altogether by 1650. Instead, hands were frequently placed in less formal, though sometimes highly eloquent, positions on the breast or at the side of the body, or the effigy was shown holding a devotional or symbolic object (e.g., a book or a skull), female effigies occasionally holding babies and married couples sometimes joining hands in affection.

A few examples of the various postures will illustrate what all this meant in practice. Firstly, the recumbent effigy managed to hold its own and in some cases retained the old-fashioned attitude of prayer until the mid-seventeenth century. More progressive, however, were those which went for a less rigid treatment of the recumbent figure. At South Acre (Norfolk), for example, Sir Edward and Lady Barkham (*c.*1623) allow their hands to rest easily on their bodies, he asymmetrically and holding a book in one hand, she folding her hands at her waist, while at Exton (Rutland) the shrouded figure of Lady Kinlosse (d. 1628) has one hand upon her body, the other by her side and still hidden under the shroud. The celebrated Savage monument (*c.*1631) at Elmley Castle (Worcs) has three recumbent figures, each differently depicted: William Savage is at prayer, but Giles (d. 1631) rests one hand on his breast, the other on the hilt of his sword, while his wife holds a baby in her arms. Three effigies are also present on the monument of Sir John St John and his two wives (dated 1634) at Lydiard Tregoze (Wilts): Sir John himself is similar to Giles Savage and one wife has a babe in her arms, but the second wife has one hand on her breast and with the other holds a book into which a finger is inserted, presumably at the page she has reached in her reading. At Acton (Cheshire) Sir Richard Wilbraham (d. 1643) seems rather less relaxed, with one knee slightly raised and loosely clutching with one hand at the military cape on which he lies.

The reclining figure was, of course, incapable of having its hands closed in prayer, but not of expressing devotional feeling. In this period it lost the intensely uncomfortable stiffness so characteristic of Elizabeth I's and James I's reigns and, more especially, the head was less commonly propped up awkwardly on an elbow. Reclining effigies now appeared in a variety of slightly different positions between the full-length reclining posture and the sitting-up posture, and, depending on the degree to which they approach the latter, some are described as semi-reclining. In this form they were to enjoy considerable popularity in the Baroque period. An early herald of things to come is provided by the splendid effigy of Sir Adrian Scrope (d. 1623) at South Cockerington (Lincs), which has been plausibly attributed to Epiphanius Evesham. Here the deceased is semi-reclining, there is no trace of stiffness in the figure and one hand is placed eloquently on his breast, all of which, coupled with the intensity of religious expression in his face, makes for a satisfyingly natural portrayal. Equally fine, though less charged with emotion, is the slightly later semi-reclining effigy of Lady Katherine Paston at Paston (Norfolk), a work of Nicholas Stone completed in 1629; in this case the deceased appears almost to lounge, so comfortably is she supported by her right elbow on a cushion, while her left hand lies across her body and nonchalantly draws up her mantle. The effigies of Sir Charles Morrison (d. 1628) at Watford (Herts), Thomas 1st Lord Coventry (d. 1639) at Croome D'Abitot (Worcs) (*70*) and Sir Thomas Lucy (d. 1640) at Charlecote (Warks) all lean comfortably on one elbow (the last figure holding the hilt of his sword in that hand), while the other hand lies easily upon the thigh. Some figures continue to prop up their head on an arm, but generally in a more relaxed fashion than earlier, as can be seen in the cases of Sir William Pitt (d. 1636) at Stratfield Saye (Hants), Sir William Dyer (dated 1641) at Colmworth (Beds) and the two wives of Sir Roger Smith (d. 1655) at Edmondthorpe (Leics). A rather curious variation occurs on the monument of Henry Danvers (d. 1654) at West Lavington (Wilts), for here the deceased, though semi-reclining with head propped up on left elbow and legs crossed at the ankles, appears to have fallen asleep while reading, since his right hand has allowed the book to fall from its grasp on to the slab.

The most characteristic use of the kneeling posture continued to be in the depiction of children on monuments, irrespective of the attitudes adopted by the principal figures, but it also remained common for the deceased or the deceased and wife, especially on hanging wall monuments. In some ways it was the most conservative posture. The traditional form in which the figure kneels sideways to the viewer remained standard, as did the closing of the hands in prayer, craftsmen and patrons being apparently reluctant to abandon the obvious close connection between kneeling and prayer. Good examples of this period include the monuments of Edward Skynner (d. 1631) at Ledbury (Herefs), Thomas Lord Fauconberg (dated 1632) at Coxwold (Yorks) and Sir Edward Carr (d. 1637) at Hillingdon (Middx). Variations occurred, however, both in the direction faced by the effigy and in the position of the hands. Occasionally the frontal kneeling attitude was chosen, as in the case of Sir Francis Egioke (d. 1622) in St Margaret's, Westminster, although it was often not feasible owing to the shallow depth of many monuments and commonly resulted in ugly shortening of the legs. Even rarer was the semi-frontal attitude, kneeling on one knee, which is adopted by an eleven-year old boy, Henry Cookin (d. 1627) in St Mark's, Bristol. Neither Sir Francis nor Henry Cookin is at prayer; the former gazes out of the monument, one hand on his breast and the other on the hilt of his sword, while the latter reads from a book held in his left hand and resting on his raised thigh. The placing of one hand on the breast was the commonest variation in effigies kneeling sideways. Examples include the figures of Sir Henry Fryer (d. 1631) at Harlton (Cambs), his other hand being on the hilt of his sword, and Anne Combe (d. 1640) at Abbots Langley (Herts), the other hand in this case holding a book. An interesting and revealing case is presented by the small monument of Giles Humberston (d. 1627) at Walkern (Herts), which was erected by his widow, for, while she in widow's garb is conventionally at prayer, he with a distant expression on his face has one hand on his breast and the other catching loosely at his cloak. Different again is the much larger monument of George Monox (d. 1638) and wife at Cirencester (Glos), which shows the couple kneeling at a prayer-desk but not specifically in prayer, since his left hand reaches across to hold her right hand and each figure places its free hand on its breast.

Seated and standing effigies of the deceased, though much less numerous, exhibited more variation and individuality. Both postures no doubt benefited from having been used by Nicholas Stone for the Holles monuments at Westminster discussed above, but, although their numbers increased in this period, they remained exceptional and unconventional. Human figures so displayed were uninhibited by traditional forms of presentation and could therefore take full advantage of the trend toward realism. In particular, they were never shown at prayer and seldom with any directly religious feeling, tending rather to emphasize ease, pensiveness and in some cases melancholy reflection.

One of the most remarkable instances of seated effigies in Charles I's reign occurs on the large hanging monument of Lady Katherine Mompesson (d. 1633) at Lydiard Tregoze (Wilts), which was erected by her husband, Sir Giles, after her death. Of white, black and grey marble, it depicts both Lady Katherine and her husband seated facing one another under separate arches. Not only are the figures realistically carved, but an overall atmosphere of melancholy contemplation is achieved. Sir Giles, in armour, looks up from reading a book across to his wife, who leans her head languidly against her right hand and rests her left hand on a skull on her lap, this last being a newly poignant treatment of the old device for death. The deep emotions portrayed or inspired by this monument, enhanced by its subdued black-and-white tones, set it apart among contemporary funerary works, but there are others which attempt less intense feelings in similar mode. In particular is this true of a group in Devon. At Crediton, for example, the monument of Elizabeth Tuckfield (dated 1631), which also includes busts of her husband and his father, shows her seated frontally, her right hand holding a skull on her lap and her head leaning against her left arm propped on the back of a prayer-desk. The same pose is adopted by Dulcibella Hodges (d. 1629) at Kenton, while at Newton St Cyres the small monument of Sherland Shore, a scholar who died in 1632 at the age of seventeen, employs a similar attitude, save that he sits beside a table with books and a skull, propping his right elbow on the skull and leaning his head against his hand. Notable seated figures in other areas include Maria Wentworth (d. 1632) at Toddington (Beds), who appears beneath a curtained baldacchino, and, rather later, Lady Jane Bacon at Culford (Suffolk). The latter is part of a large monument commissioned from Thomas Stanton in 1654, depicting a family group at the centre of which Lady Jane sits frontally and seriously with a child on her ample lap.

With the exception of the two semi-nude figures of John and Thomas Lyttelton (dated 1635) in Magdalen College, Oxford, standing effigies in this period are nearly all frontal or virtually so. They include two very similar life-size figures in Devon, namely, John Northcote (d. 1632) at Newton St Cyres and John Coke (d. 1632) at Ottery St Mary, both in armour and each holding a baton in his right hand. The monument of Robert Graye (d. 1635) in St Mary Magdalene, Taunton (Somerset) (72), has the deceased standing in civilian dress, one hand on breast, the other holding gloves. In St Peter's, Wolverhampton (Staffs), the standing bronze figure of Admiral Sir Richard Leveson (d. 1605) survives from the monument made for him in *c.* 1634 by le Sueur, depicting him in armour, left arm akimbo, the other holding his baton out at right-angles to his body. This effigy may have inspired that at Lydiard Tregoze of Edward St John, who died in 1645 of wounds sustained in the 2nd Battle of Newbury, a figure of gilt bronze set beneath a curtained baldacchino, his left arm similarly akimbo, his right hand resting upon an heraldic cartouche. At Broad Hinton (Wilts) is the unusual memorial of another casualty of the Civil War, Colonel Glanville, killed at Bridgewater in 1645. It is a hanging wall monument consisting of an oval-oblong recess in which the deceased stands somewhat stiffly in armour, holding in his right hand the staff of a banner which breaks through the frame of the recess, the banner itself being exceptionally of real (not pretended) cloth. Most of the standing figures mentioned so far are in contemporary armour, but a fine mid-seventeenth-century example at Ross-on-Wye (Herefs) follows the precedent of Sir George Holles's monument at Westminster in choosing antique Roman armour (or what passed for it at the time). The effigy is that of Colonel William Rudhall (d. 1651) (73), who stands upon a free pedestal, one knee slightly bent, his right hand clutching the hilt of his sword and his left holding a shield by his side.

Three effigies (one standing, two seated) display in exceptional measure the qualities of realism and repose gently charged with melancholy which were inherent in the best funerary sculpture of this period. They are those of Sir William Slingsby (d. 1634) at Knaresborough (Yorks), Sir Francis Bacon (d. 1626) in St Michael's church, St Albans (Herts), and Dean John Boys (d. 1625) in Canterbury cathedral. The first, dressed in everyday clothes and wearing a hat, stands in calm repose in an arched recess. His weight is taken mainly on his

72 St Mary Magdalene, Taunton (Somerset): Robert Graye (d.1635)

73 Ross-on-Wye (Herefs): Colonel William Rudhall (d.1651)

74 St Michael's church, St Albans (Herts): Sir Francis Bacon (d.1626)

75 Canterbury cathedral: Dean John Boys (d.1625)

right leg, the other crossing over it at the ankles, and the upper half of the body turns slightly to his left, as the head leans against the left hand, the elbow in turn being supported on the hilt of his sword, while his right hand holds an heraldic cartouche. The sculptor, who may have been Epiphanius Evesham, has here brilliantly portrayed the relaxed and natural pose of a man standing at rest. Sir Francis Bacon's effigy, set in a recess to the north of the high altar, represents the same idea translated into the sitting posture (*74*). Similarly wearing everyday clothes and an almost identical hat, he lounges back comfortably in his chair, one hand supporting his head which leans to one side, the other dangling over the arm of the chair. The figure of Dean Boys at Canterbury (*75*) is somewhat different, for its large canopied recess is transformed into the interior of his study, where he is revealed seated in academic robes by a table bearing the open book which he has been reading. In his contemplations he turns away from the table to gaze upward in the direction of the altar and, like the other figures, leans his head against his arm supported by its elbow on the table. The realism of all three of these effigies is utterly convincing and could scarcely be improved upon.

The frontal demi-figure also remained in vogue, losing now any special association with scholars and divines. It was featured largely, but not exclusively, on hanging wall monuments, of which many for a decade or so were similar in form to those of the previous period. However, by being displayed in an oval or circular surround the demi-figure was often reduced in effect to a head-and-shoulders bust. Such can be seen, for instance, on the monuments of John Eldred (d. 1632) at Great Saxham (Suffolk), Richard Hooker (1633) at Bishopsbourne (Kent) and the two wives of Haynes Barley, Margaret (d. 1653) and Mary (d. 1658), who have separate monuments at Clavering (Essex). The portrayals of Nicholas Slake (d. 1634) at Barnstaple (Devon) and Lady Dorothy Selby (d. 1641) at Ightham (Kent), though similarly in oval surrounds, show rather more of the figure with the hands disposed in ways already observed in complete effigies. Very occasionally a semi-frontal position was adopted, as in two early examples almost certainly by Epiphanius Evesham, namely, John Troughton (d. 1621) at Ingatestone (Essex) and Robert Rich earl of Warwick (*c.*1619) at Snarford (Lincs). The latter is of peculiar interest in that it also depicts the earl's wife behind him and slightly to the right, not frontal but in relief facing

to the right. Though not in this exceptional form, the inclusion of two figures for husband and wife was a feature of an increasing number of such monuments. In some the demi-figures or busts are in separate ovals, as in the cases of Sir Thomas Merry (dated 1633) at Walthamstow (Essex) and Ralph Hawtrey (d. 1638) at Ruislip (Middx), but they may appear as demi-figures together in the same basically rectangular frame, as though on a balcony or looking out from a curtained window. An early instance is the monument of John Clenche (d. 1628) at Great Bealings (Suffolk), which depicts the couple as strictly frontal and stiffly at prayer, while that of Sir Robert and Lady Barkham (d. 1644) at Tottenham (Middx), a work of Edward Marshall, uses the same idea in a more relaxed and accomplished form, the figures slightly turned toward each other and not at prayer. In these cases there is no physical contact between the couple, but in others the figures, turning toward each other, join hands in affection, a touching device which enjoyed a certain popularity. It occurs quite early at Ampton (Suffolk) on the monument of Sir Henry Calthorpe, made in 1638 by John and Matthias Christmas, and, later, on those of Richard Combe and wife (d. 1649) at Stratford-on-Avon (Warks), Walter Roberts (d. 1652) at Brenchley (Kent), where the depiction of conjugal affection is particularly apparent, Jonathas Sacheverell (d. 1662) at Morley (Derbs) and John Oneby (d. 1662) at Hinckley (Leics) (*76*). The last three each have curtains tied back or held open by angels.

These various forms of the demi-figure or head-and-shoulders bust were all in some sense derived from Jacobean prototypes, but the pedestal bust depicting head and shoulders on a small low pedestal was quite new. It first appeared on funerary works in the 1620s, possibly the earliest instance being the monument of the celebrated composer, Orlando Gibbons (d. 1625), in Canterbury cathedral, produced by Nicholas Stone in 1626. It undoubtedly owed its introduction to the greater interest in classical sculpture and its acceptance in part to the influence of foreign artists working in England at this time. For example, both le Sueur and the Italian, Francesco Fanelli, produced bronze pedestal busts for monuments in Westminster Abbey, the former those of Sir Thomas Richardson (d. 1635) and the wife of Lord Cottingham (*c.*1634), the latter that of Sir Robert Aiton (d. 1638). Pedestal busts became more widespread in the 1630s and were well established by the mid-seventeenth century. They were normally made in marble or less frequently in alabaster and, like demi-figures, were most typically used on hanging monuments, where they were commonly set in oval niches. The earliest tended to occur in courtly or scholarly circles, but a fairly early case to which this does not apply is the monument of Richard Atkins (d. 1635) at Sherborne St John (Hants) (*77*), in which the deceased is represented by a pedestal bust set in a richly decorated oval niche. Its comparatively early date is perhaps betrayed by the fact that the bust includes rather more than head and shoulders, and one of the deceased's hands is shown pulling his cloak round him. Others with head and shoulders only include Sir Austin Palgrave (d. 1639) and wife at North Barningham (Norfolk), Lady Anne Clarke (d. 1653) at Sonning (Berks), Charles Cocks (d. 1654) at Dumbleton (Glos) and Judith Strode (d. 1660) at Knebworth (Herts). The last of these is a superbly classical bust, displayed in a noble black marble setting of bold and simple classical design totally lacking in enrichment of any kind. The oval niche was not, however, universal. The bust of Sir William Paddy (d. 1634) in St John's College, Oxford, appears in an arched niche enclosed in a rich segmentally-pedimented frame, while that of William Harvey (d. 1657), who discovered the circulation of the blood, at Hempstead (Essex) (*78*), a fine portrait by Edward Marshall, is set in front of a shallow arch in a rectangular frame. Pedestal busts were less commonly employed on standing monuments, a particularly impressive example being the great wall monument to members of the Verney family at Middle Claydon (Bucks) made by Edward Marshall in 1653. It incorporates the white marble busts of Sir Edward Verney (killed at Edgehill in 1642), his wife Lady Margaret, their son Sir Ralph Verney (who commissioned the monument and lived until 1696) and his wife Lady Mary, each being housed in its own arched niche. By contrast, the standing monument of Edward Perry (d. 1646) at Marholm (Northants) looks forward to the late seventeenth and eighteenth centuries in displaying the bust not in a niche or recess, but quite free; the single bust is set in front of a tall obelisk above an heraldic cartouche supported by two small doleful cherubs, the entire scheme being carried on a rectangular plinth which bears the inscription.

Family Groups in Charles I's Reign

The combination of effigies in family groups was in many cases no less important than the forms of individual portrayals. The depiction of married couples with all their children, living and dead, remained a feature of numerous monuments, although it declined in the later years of Charles I and became rather rare thereafter. Until then children continued most frequently to be displayed as small kneeling figures, except that now they were generally less stiff and more carefully individualised. Those who had been stillborn or died soon after birth were shown in swaddling clothes and those who had died as very young children appeared in cradles or cots. Older children who predeceased their parents were depicted holding skulls. Such little figures remained common on hanging monuments, where they were usually displayed in compartments below their parents, and along the sides of tomb-chests or the bases of standing wall monuments, but many other variations in the location of children were tried out.

So numerous are the hanging monuments with kneeling effigies of parents and children, the majority being closely similar to earlier types, that no reasonable selection can be made, but a few of the more unusual may usefully be cited. The monument of Thomas Wood (d. 1649) in St John's, Hackney (London), for instance, is fundamentally traditional in form, save that the deceased and wife are exceptionally in a standing posture, facing each other across a prayer-desk, with the children kneeling behind them in varied naturalistic poses. Another odd but rather affecting variation occurs on the monuments of Thomas Parke (d. 1628) at Wisbech (Cambs) and John Hugessen (d. 1634) at Lynsted (Kent). Each has husband and wife kneeling and conventionally facing one another across a prayer-desk, but the latter is adapted to form a housing for the small figure of a child, in the former case a girl kneeling at her own prayer-desk, in the latter a boy seated under a tiny curtained canopy and leaning his head disconsolately against one hand propped on the arm of his chair. A related idea is employed on the standing wall monument of Sir Edward Carr (d. 1637) at Hillingdon (Middx), which depicts the parents kneeling at prayer and, in front of their prayer-desk, two girls standing frontally and holding hands. Again, at Ibsley (Hants) Sir John Constable (d. 1627) and his wife kneel toward each other, but neither in prayer nor at a prayer-desk, for between them there grows a vine, whose stem they grasp and which bears not only grapes but their five children appearing as busts

76 *Above* Hinckley (Leics): John Oneby (d.1662)

77 *Above right* Sherborne St John (Hants): Richard Atkins (d.1635)

78 Hempstead (Essex): William Harvey (d.1657). By Edward Marshall. Detail

79 Noseley (Leics): Sir Arthur Heselrige, 2nd Baronet Heselrige (d. 1661). Detail

80 Hambleden (Bucks): Sir Cope D'Oyley (d. 1633) and family

among the leaves and fruit, a conceit characteristic of the seventeenth-century love of symbolism and allegory. Rows of kneeling children are sometimes found on hanging monuments in which the deceased and wife are depicted not as kneeling effigies but as frontal demi-figures or busts. This can be seen, for instance, on two Suffolk monuments, those of John Clenche at Great Bealings, already mentioned, and Sir Martin Stuteville (d. 1631) at Dalham, the children in each case kneeling below their parents. Later examples of this type may depict the children themselves as frontal busts in a row below their parents, as in the case of John Oneby (d. 1662) at Hinckley (Leics) (76).

Among many instances of children kneeling against the bases of standing wall monuments, good examples are provided by those of Sir Peter Vanlore (d. 1627) at Tilehurst (Berks) and Sir Arthur Heselrige (d. 1661) at Noseley (Leics). The former has a total of eight daughters charmingly split into three groups, the figures differing in size and all holding skulls, with a ninth child lying as a baby in swaddling clothes in front of one of them. The Heselrige monument (79), though a rather late example, has an exquisite line of boys and girls markedly varied in size, some half-turned to the viewer, some holding skulls or roses and all with their hands arranged other than in prayer. By way of variation, that of Sir William Dyer (1641) at Colmworth (Beds) shows the children standing frontally, the boys under one arch, the girls under another, the hand positions being slightly different for each figure. However, children were not restricted to the base in such monuments, for, while remaining smaller in size than their parents, they might be located in closer association with them, continuing and expanding Jacobean moves in this direction. Sir Peter Vanlore's monument, for example, has, in addition to the daughters below, two frontally kneeling children placed on the same level as their parents, one on each side. A further development, in which the children appear on three sides of the parents, can be seen in the case of Sir Henry Lee (d. 1631) and wife at Spelsbury (Oxon). At the heads of the principal effigies two daughters kneel facing them at prayer; at their feet is a third daughter in the same attitude and a son who kneels semi-frontally on one knee, while in front of Sir Henry and lying alongside him are three recumbent children, of whom one clearly died as a baby, for he appears tucked up in a tiny bed, and the others must have died very young. The scheme expresses, in a

way that the more conventional arrangement could not, the mutual affection between parents and their children, as the latter (even the dead ones) gather round their recumbent figures. But perhaps the most moving example is the monument of Sir Cope D'Oyley (d. 1633) at Hambleden (Bucks) (*80*), for here the family is completely integrated into a single sculptural group, all kneeling together in pairs on the same level, father and sons to the left, mother and daughters to the right, the children already dead holding skulls. Moreover, although the effigies vary in size and the parents' are the largest, the difference in scale between them and the eldest children is no greater than that between the eldest and youngest children. The ideal of a loving, united family was never more cogently expressed on an English funerary monument.

This monument clearly makes its point by an apt and felicitous grouping of the effigies, but no particular emotions are expressed in their faces or attitudes. Other monuments, however, developing early seventeenth-century trends, emphasized more intimately the sense of grief and loss occasioned by the death of a member of the family, especially the distress felt by the surviving spouse. This is nowhere more movingly displayed than on two monuments in Kent, one signed by Epiphanius Evesham, the other probably also by him. That of Christopher Lord Teynham (d. 1622) at Lynsted (*81*) depicts him lying peacefully at the point of death; alongside him his grief-stricken wife kneels at prayer, hardly daring to look upon her husband, while on the front of his tomb-chest the children are depicted in two exquisite relief panels, at prayer or in agonized mourning, the sons having set aside the pleasures of the field to attend their father's demise. At Otterden Sir Justinian Lewin (d. 1620) lies in the stiffness of death upon a tomb-chest, in front of which at a lower level kneels his distracted widow, leaning in grief against the top of the chest and endeavouring to comfort her small daughter who clutches appealingly at her knees. By contrast, on the monument of Elizabeth and Arthur Coke (d. 1629) at Bramfield (Suffolk) it is the earlier death of the wife which is the focus of attention. Here Nicholas Stone has created a strikingly beautiful and pathetic image of a woman who died in childbirth. Her mattress, pillows and covers have, as it were, been transported to the top of the tomb-chest where she lies at rest holding a swaddled baby in her arms, her body concealed beneath the bedclothes, while in the wall above her husband kneels concernedly at prayer in an arched recess. The monument of Thomas Lord Scroope (d.1609) at Langar (Notts), which was made *c*.1630, is notable for its depiction of filial devotion: Lord and Lady Scroope appear as recumbent figures, at the feet of whom kneels their son facing them, not in prayer but reading mournfully from a book held in his right hand. Finally, we may recall the melancholy of the seated figures on the Mompesson monument at Lydiard Tregoze, mentioned earlier, in which the surviving husband contemplates, and seems almost to commune across the grave with, his deceased wife.

In their various ways all these monuments stressed the importance of the deceased's immediate family relationships, but others, as earlier, laid emphasis less directly on the domestic than on the dynastic aspect of the family. A case in point is that of Meriall Coke (d.1636) at Holkham (Norfolk), which includes the kneeling effigies not only of herself and her husband, but also of her parents and grandparents, while her 15 children kneel lower down and, at the top, appears a bust, possibly of her husband's father, Sir Edward Coke. The portrayal of the lady's immediate family, though certainly there, is thus subsumed in a more extended family memorial.

Common, however, to both types of family monument (domestic and dynastic) was a desire to stress the individuality of the deceased in the context of his own particular family. At the same time personal identity was established in other ways, by a wider resort to portraiture in figures and, of course, by the details set forth in inscriptions, each enhanced in many cases by appropriate allusions in the embellishment of the monument. For example, scenes from the life or of the death of the deceased became more widespread, as did the inclusion of objects associated with his calling or profession, such as books for a scholar, military trophies for a soldier, and so on.

Another feature very characteristic of seventeenth-century monuments, especially those before the Restoration, was a pre-occupation with symbolism and allegory. It is apparent not only in the frequent use of cherubs, angels, urns and various symbols of death as part of the carved enrichment, but more strikingly in the treatment of certain monuments entirely as allegorical vehicles. The latter fall mainly into the category of so-called 'resurrection monuments', most of which show the deceased as a shrouded figure rising or having risen

from the dead. In other cases the deceased is portrayed as a recumbent shrouded figure without suggestion of a resurrection. These and other related aspects are reserved for fuller discussion in a later chapter.

The Development of Baroque

During the Interregnum which followed Charles I's execution in 1649 funerary monuments, though continuing to be produced in some numbers, were cast mainly in conservative moulds and showed little or no fresh development. With the Restoration of the monarchy in 1660, however, a new phase began and lasted unchallenged until about 1720, in which monuments were predominantly Baroque in character. In part the ascendancy of Baroque was built upon the foundations laid earlier, but it rested equally on the results of increased contacts with the Continent which were more intimate and regular and extended to a wider range of potential patrons and craftsmen than at any time since the Reformation. With the return of Charles II and his fellow exiles in 1660 and with the consolidation of the Grand Tour of Europe as part of the education of young noblemen, the English establishment became (or had the opportunity to become) more fully aware of artistic movements on the Continent. Equally, visits of English craftsmen abroad, notably to Italy, and the settlement of foreigners, especially from the Low Countries, in England served further to encourage the development of Baroque in this country. The Baroque style in architecture and sculpture was, in truth, a European-wide phenomenon, manifesting itself to a greater or lesser extent in all regions, but receiving its supreme and most dramatic expression in Italy, dominated by the massive genius of Gian Lorenzo Bernini (d.1680). English monumental designs and effigies seldom approached Bernini's dynamic and emotional style, however, assuming instead a rather subdued and insular form which corresponded more closely with the less extreme version predominating in the Netherlands and elsewhere in northern Europe.

The term 'Baroque' is notoriously difficult to define, but in the context of English funerary monuments it denotes a style which is firmly classical in origin and employs for the most part classical forms and motifs, but which departs from classical nobility by exaggerating the elements of display and movement, and retains something of the Mannerist propensity for using classical features in

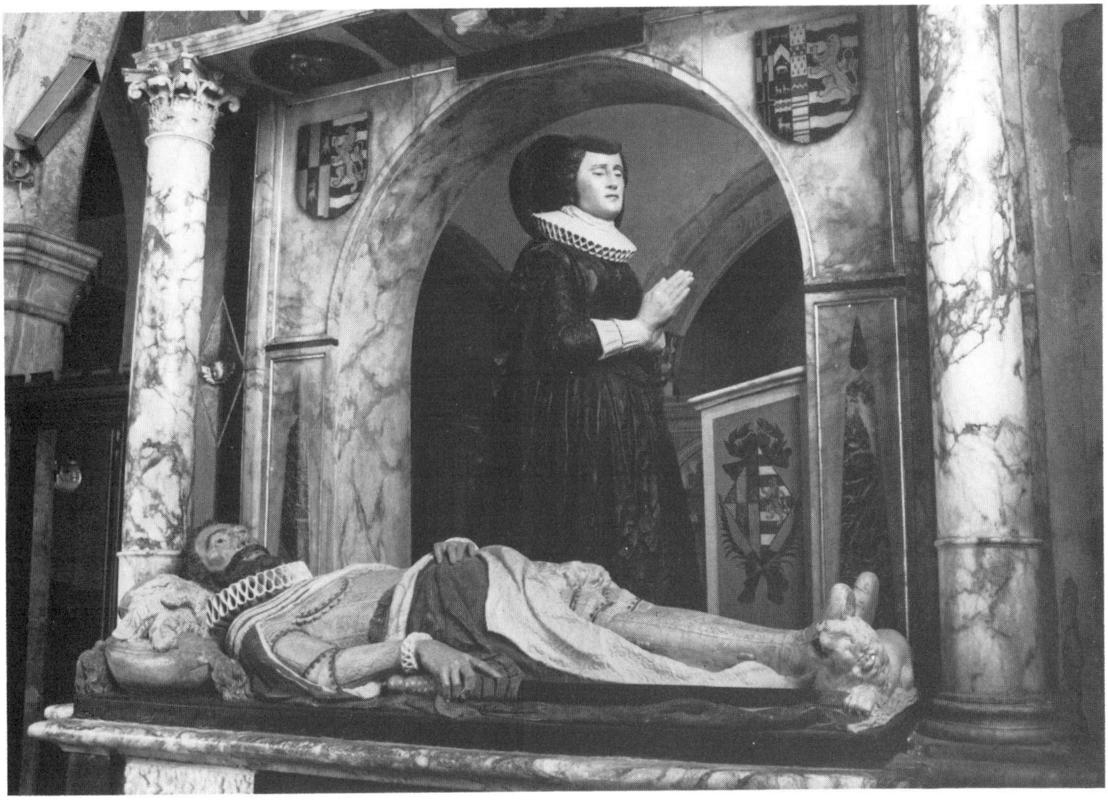

81 Lynsted (Kent): Christopher, 2nd Lord Teynham (d. 1622). By Epiphanius Evesham

82 Kingsclere (Hants): Sir Henry and Lady Kingsmill (dated 1670)

THE LADY BRIDGET KINGSMIL WHOE ERECTED THIS
MONVMENT, HAVEING LIVED A WIDOW FORTY EIGHT
YEARS IN GREAT REPVTATION AND HONOVR, IS AT
LENGTH IOYNED TO HER DEARE HVSBAND ON
THIS FOVRTH DAY OF SEPTEMB IN THE YEARE OF OVR LORD
1672, WHERE THEY BOTH REST IN PEACE, TO Y COMFORT
AND SATISFACTION OF THEIRE NVMEROVS & HONOVR-
ABLE OFSPRING, WHO HAVE NO SEEN HER DECEN-
LY DEPOSITED IN THIS PLACE, CAVSED THIS INSCRIP-
TION TO BE INGRAVED HERE.

individual and often 'unacademic' ways. Baroque monuments are rich and ostentatious, whatever their size, the larger ones being made almost exclusively of costly imported marbles. They are characterized by unashamed opulence and grandeur, lively and richly carved ornament, an almost theatrical presentation of effigies often with grandiloquent gestures caught in arrested animation and, in some cases, a degree of uninhibited emotionalism. At their best such monuments are grand and impressive, at their worst pompous and vainglorious.

Carved enrichment was on the whole more urbane and secular than in the first half of the seventeenth century, less emphasis in particular being laid on the macabre, though this aspect was far from absent and various symbols of death, mortality and eternity remained in use. In addition to these and, of course, the ever-present displays of heraldry, the most typical motifs were festoons of leaves, flowers and fruit (with or without ribbons), ears of wheat, palm-branches, cherub-heads, masks and curtains and draperies employed now in a new variety and freedom of treatment. All were carved in a lively, realistic and deeply undercut manner, especially leaves, flowers and other natural subjects, the depiction of which frequently achieved a level of excellence comparable with that of contemporary wood-carvings. A number of the best examples were indeed carved by Grinling Gibbons or in his workshop, for, apart from his more famous masterpieces in wood, he also worked in marble and produced funerary monuments, where, however, he revealed himself as sadly less skilled as a sculptor of effigies. The edges of effigy-bearing slabs and the like were not infrequently gadrooned in a distinctive and sumptuous fashion, larger and more rounded then in the Elizabethan and Jacobean periods and without intervening dots.

The carving of such architectural elements as columns, entablatures and pediments was of a generally high standard, and here again it was typically the richer and more showy forms that were favoured. Columns were commonly of a Corinthian or Composite order with shafts which were often fluted or, as on the monument of the 1st duke of Beaufort (d. 1699) at Great Badminton (Glos), covered in arabesque decoration. Spirally twisted columns, revealing the playful side of Baroque, enjoyed a certain popularity. They can be found on standing monuments, like those of Mary Wolryche (d. 1678) at Quatt (Salop) and Sir Henry Bendyshe

(d. 1717) at Steeple Bumpstead (Essex), and on hanging monuments, including those of Charles Rich (d. 1657) at Sonning (Berks) and Sir Richard Newdigate (d. 1678) at Harefield (Middx) (*95*). The segmental pediment retained its ascendancy over the triangular type, occurring in a variety of broken, open or partially recessed versions, none more original than that on the enormous monument of Sir Robert Clayton (d. 1707) at Bletchingley (Surrey) (*92*).

Monumental Forms in the Baroque Period

The simple tomb-chest with effigies now became rare, especially the form with recumbent effigies, which disappeared altogether by 1700 and was not revived until the nineteenth century. Its latest manifestations include the rather fine monument of Sir Henry and Lady Kingsmill (erected 1670) at Kingsclere (Hants) (*82*), which is unusually still free-standing and looks back in its details to thirty or forty years earlier, and, exceptionally late (and in all probability the last), the three monuments to members of the Sherburne family at Mitton (Yorks), which were completed by 1699. In every instance the recumbent effigies are, of course, not at prayer but in relaxed repose. More normally effigies on tomb-chests were shown reclining or semi-reclining with arms and legs variously disposed, as in the cases of Sir Thomas Master (d. 1680) at Cirencester (Glos), Lady Dyonis Williamson (d. 1684) at Loddon (Norfolk) and Mary duchess of Norfolk (d. 1708) at Lowick (Northants). At Quainton (Bucks) the tomb-chest monument of Richard Winwood (erected 1691) combines the two postures, for, while he is comfortably recumbent with crossed legs, his wife reclining alongside raises herself on one arm to look upon him.

The great free-standing canopied monument of earlier days passed similarly out of fashion, partly because it took up a disproportionate amount of space and partly, one suspects, because it could not display effigies in other than the outmoded recumbent attitude to equal advantage on all sides. This is apparent on the otherwise excellent black and white marble monument of the 1st earl of Nottingham (d. 1682) at Ravenstone (Bucks), with its grand four-poster canopy, from which hang white marble curtains tied back to the corner columns and beneath which the earl appears semi-reclining in dignified and splendid self-importance.

Viewed from one side, however, the effigy presents only its back, which cannot but detract from the dignity of the portrayal.

On the other hand, certain kinds of free-standing monument, without either canopy or effigies, were a particular feature of the age, though not produced in any great numbers. At Wingham (Kent), for example, the Oxinden family are commemorated by a magnificently Baroque piece of 1682, which harks back to Margaret Hoby's obelisk monument of 1605 at Bisham. It comprises a high square base, enriched with ox-heads and looped drapes, upon which stands a tall three-sided obelisk covered in garlands of fruit and flowers and surrounded by four putti, two standing, two kneeling. An almost exact replica was later provided for the monument of John Whitfield (d. 1691), placed under the tower which alone remains from the church of St Mary Magdalene at Canterbury. Two-tiered monuments without effigies, consisting of an upper slab supported by figures or objects on a lower slab, occur in a variety of configurations. The type derives ultimately from such effigied monuments as that of the 1st earl of Salisbury (d. 1612) at Hatfield and can be traced through a series of examples in succeeding decades, all of black and white marble, in which the plain upper slab is carried by angels, as at Framlingham (Suffolk) for Sir Robert Hitcham (dated 1638), or by urns, as at Roxby (Yorks) for Lady Boynton (erected 1634), or by bulbous balusters, as at Maidstone (Kent) for Jacob Lord Astley (1653). In this period come two fine instances of standing putti taking on the supporting role, they and other features being in white marble, the slabs in black. On the monument of Sandford Neville (d. 1673) at Royston (Yorks) they carry a slab which bears only the inscription and an heraldic cartouche, but on that of Sir Thomas Rich (d. 1667) and his son at Sonning (Berks) *(83)* they have to support not only the slab but two large urns standing upon it, the combined weight of which is convincingly portrayed by their bowed necks.

When it came to large-scale memorials, however, the Baroque age undoubtedly preferred a characteristic type of standing wall monument with a grand, classical-derived canopy or superstructure which no longer served so much to shelter the effigy as to provide an imposing 'architectural' frame or setting in which it might be displayed. The 'architecture' was commonly made up of side columns or pilasters, typically of a Corinthian or Composite order, supporting a more or less elaborately detailed segmental pediment or panelled arch, though all sorts of variations and idiosyncracies (such as twisted columns or flat-topped designs without pediments) were possible. Such monuments were in most cases tall in relation to width, often not projecting far from the wall, and, in their fully-developed form, are known as 'reredos-type' monuments, on account of their many resemblances in design and enrichment to contemporary wooden reredoses. The first instance of the reredos-type in fact occurred as early as 1640 in Nicholas Stone's monument of Dudley Carleton, Viscount Dorchester, in Westminster Abbey. Here, by placing a semi-reclining effigy beneath one of his late classical canopies, consisting of fluted side columns and an open segmental pediment, Stone produced the prototype for dozens of others, very diverse and usually richer in detail, of the later seventeenth and early eighteenth centuries. Another source of this type of monument was, however, the tomb-chest set in front of a shallow back-plate, a form which had first appeared in the mid-sixteenth century, had persisted through the intervening years reflecting successive fashions in design and was now treated in the current Baroque manner.

There was much scope for variety at this time, not only in design, enrichment and the degree to which the superstructure protruded from the wall, but also in the depiction of the deceased, for the reredos-type could be adapted to accommodate effigies in any attitude. Even so, the semi-reclining and standing postures were the most popular. Of the former, good examples are provided by the monuments of Archbishop John Dolben (d. 1686) in York Minster, the 1st earl of Coventry (d. 1699) at Elmley Castle (Worcs), John Viscount Lonsdale (d. 1700) at Lowther (Westmorland) *(84)* and Sir Henry Bendyshe (d. 1717) at Steeple Bumpstead (Essex); while standing effigies, sometimes in an arched niche encompassed by the 'reredos' design, are found, for example, on the monuments of Sir Hugh Wyndham (d. 1684) at Silton (Dorset), Col. John Birch (d. 1691) at Weobley (Herefs), Sir Robert Clayton (d. 1707) at Bletchingley (Surrey) and Lytton Lytton (d. 1710) at Knebworth (Herts). Recumbent effigies were predictably rare by this time, though an instance is provided by the monument of the 1st duke of Newcastle (d. 1676) and his duchess in Westminster Abbey; and the kneeling and seated postures were distinctly uncommon, the first because it simply fell out of fashion, the latter because it had not yet become widely acceptable.

Pairs of frontally kneeling effigies in curiously unsatisfactory poses occur on the monuments of Richard Crich (d.1709) at Northfleet (Kent) and Luke Lillingstone (d.1713) at North Ferriby (Yorks), while among examples of seated effigies are the huge and splendid monuments of Chief Justice Sir John Holt (d.1710) at Redgrave (Suffolk) and the 1st duke of Bedford (d.1700) at Chenies (Bucks), the duke and duchess sitting below a medallion of their son, executed in the aftermath of the Rye House Plot in 1683, and flanked by medallions of their other children. Busts and demi-figures might also be depicted on reredos monuments, the former, for example, on that of Thomas Catesby (dated 1700) at Whiston (Northants), the latter on that of Sir John and Lady Brownlow (c.1679) at Belton (Lincs), in which the couple appear holding hands.

On occasions (though much less frequently than earlier), the representation of figures on such monuments extended to other members of the deceased's family. Various family combinations were depicted, for example, on three monuments which have been plausibly attributed to the Flemish sculptor, John Nost (or Jan van Ost), namely, those of Sir Thomas Spencer (d.1684) at Yarnton (Oxon), Sir Josiah Child (d.1699) at Wanstead (Essex) and Sir John Banks (d.1699) at Aylesford (Kent). The first of these, in particular, stands out as a Baroque version of the earlier family monument. It includes three life-size standing effigies of the deceased, his wife and son, flanked lower down by two smaller seated daughters, all supported on a base whose front is carved with two more daughters in relief.

In many cases, however, although additional figures appear prominently in the design, they represent not members of the family, but angels or personifications of Virtues. The semi-reclining effigy of the 1st earl of Coventry at Elmley Castle, for instance, is flanked by standing angels, tall and elegantly posed, and similar figures accompany that of Sir William Lytton (d.1705) at Knebworth. The seated effigy of Sir John Holt at Redgrave, on the other hand, is flanked by the large standing figures of Truth and Justice appropriate to his office as a chief justice. In these and other cases the symbolic figures are similar in scale to the main effigy, that is, they are nearly life-size, but often smaller Virtues, angels or putti are found standing, sitting or reclining at various points on monuments, and attractive groups of cherub-heads in clouds or 'glories' adorn the tops or backplates of canopies, like that of Archbishop Dolben at York.

The inclusion of marble drapes and hangings played an important part in enhancing the impression of sumptuous grandeur. Simple curtains on the earlier model became less common, though more richly carved, as can be seen on the monuments of Sir Thomas Tyrril (d.1671) at Castlethorpe (Bucks) and the 1st duke of Beaufort at Great Badminton, but more interesting was a development whereby the centre, or even the whole, of the 'architectural' canopy was replaced by a baldacchino with pendant curtains. On Grinling Gibbons's monument for Admiral Sir Cloudesley Shovell (d.1707) in Westminster Abbey, for example, the deceased appears semi-reclining on a sarcophagus between pairs of Corinthian columns supporting short entablatures, but, instead of having a pediment, the monument is crowned by a baldacchino whose curtains are looped up to the flanking entablatures. A similar case is found at Rockingham (Northants), where Margaret Watson (d.1713) stands beneath a curtained baldacchino between fluted Corinthian pilasters surmounted by urns. The culmination comes in such monuments as that of Sir William and Lady Ashburnham (made in 1675 by John Bushnell) at Ashburnham (Sussex) (*85*), which has no 'architecture' properly speaking at all, but merely a plain back-plate surmounted by a baldacchino whose curtains are held open by small putti. In a similar vein the effigies of Leonard Bartholomew (d.1721) and his wife at West Peckham (Kent) appear in front of a large inscription plate crowned and bordered by a baldacchino and its looped-up curtains. On occasions the Baroque love of gorgeous silks extravagantly employed to no 'functional' purpose resulted in the depiction of great lengths of material simply draped over the 'architecture', a very fine example of which is provided by the monument of Sir Thomas Powys (d.1719) at Thorpe Achurch (Northants). Here the composition is side columns carrying a broken and open segmental pediment, but on the latter recline two putti who between them endeavour to hold up a heavy 'silk' band draped over the pediment and looped in rich cascading folds, its ends hanging down outside the columns. Very characteristic, too, in this period was the carving of the inscription on a marble 'sheet' richly bordered and fixed to the backplate, as, for example, in the case of Sir Robert Clayton at Bletchingley (*92*).

There was also at this time a growing fashion, which was to become more widespread in the eighteenth century, of erecting standing wall monuments without effigies or busts. Such monuments focussed attention either on a prominently displayed inscription or on some symbolic object. The former is illustrated as early as 1655 by two fine monuments by John Stone for Sir Peter and Sir John Osborn at Campton (Beds), each comprising a plain tomb-chest set in front of a shallow backplate consisting of an enriched inscription panel topped by a small segmental arch. Later versions of this type, lacking the projecting tomb-chest, tended to be flatter and more uniform in depth. For instance, that of Henry Jermyn earl of St Albans (d.1684) at Rushbrooke (Suffolk) (*86*) has a simple base, above which rises the inscription surmounted by a scrolly pediment and flanked by leafy volutes and cherub-heads, the entire scheme being of the same shallow projection throughout. That of the 1st earl of Lichfield (d.1716) at Spelsbury (Oxon) is somewhat similar, while four early eighteenth-century bishops of Ely, beginning with Bishop Patrick (d.1707), are commemorated by variations of the same type in Ely cathedral. Of the symbolic objects which alternatively formed the focus of the design, the flaming urn was the commonest, occurring on monuments widely diverse in detail. It appears in an especially charming setting on the monuments of Sir John Nicholas (d.1704) at West Horsley (Surrey), Francis Newport earl of Bradford (d.1708) at Wroxeter (Salop) and Admiral George Churchill (d.1710) in Westminster Abbey. The last is known to be the work of Grinling Gibbons and the others, so nearly identical, must also be by him. In each case the design comprises, between pilasters and beneath an entablature, an arched recess containing a flaming urn conspicuously displayed upon a flared pedestal, against whose sides nestle small cherub-heads with their wings closed. A much larger treatment of the same basic idea is found on the monument of Sir Thomas Winford (d.1702) at Astley (Worcs). Among numerous other variations of the use of urns in place of effigies, we may cite the very stylish monument of Sir Thomas and Lady Ursula Putt (d.1674) at Gittisham (Devon), in which, within a deep black-marble recess, two exquisitely garlanded flaming urns stand upon a tomb-chest in front of a pedimented backplate, a remarkably metropolitan piece to come across in a remote country church. Less frequent than the urn alone was the depiction of a sarcophagus or a column surmounted by an urn. A good example of the former is to be seen on the monument of German Pole (erected 1684) at Radburne (Derbs),

and of the latter on the monument of Sir William Harvey (d.1719) at Hempstead (Essex).

Effigies in the Baroque Period

The Baroque period witnessed a continued decline of the more conservative postures for effigies, coupled with further development of the more progressive forms observed earlier in the seventeenth century. Thus, while recumbent and kneeling effigies fell out of fashion, the semi-reclining attitude reached a height of popularity and the standing posture was widely employed for the first time. As yet, however, seated effigies remained for some reason uncommon. The major new element, irrespective of the posture, was the Baroque sense of movement and display, which generally, though not in every case, superseded the calm, pensive atmosphere of earlier years. It is apparent especially in the turn of figures (sometimes as if posing in grand and elegant manner), the frequent depiction of hands not in repose but caught in a rhetorical or symbolic gesture, and occasionally in the suggestion that the figure's attention has been arrested by some unseen external force, such as a divine vision or revelation. Often, it must be said, the feelings portrayed are those of earthly pride and self-satisfaction, but they may equally be of a religious nature, expressed in idioms unfamiliar to modern eyes, or, exceptionally, of a deeply emotional character.

Where the effigy is charged neither with religious nor with emotional overtones, the impression of self-display is irresistible, for, whereas earlier effigies seem, as it were, unaware of the viewer, many Baroque effigies with their demonstrative gestures appear very conscious of his presence. The effigy of Sir William Jones (d.1682) at Ramsbury (Wilts), for example, comfortably semi-reclining on a mattress and cushion, looks out at the viewer, drawing attention to the open scroll which he holds in one hand and raising the other in an elegant upward-pointing gesture. Sir William Gore (d.1707) at Tring (Herts), also semi-reclining, fingers his chain of office as Lord Mayor of London with one hand and extends the other with the thumb pointing oddly upward, while Sir George Strode (d.1707) at Knebworth raises a hand to direct the eye toward his inscription panel. The effect of Baroque animation and stylish posing is most marked in standing effigies, the figure being commonly slightly turned at waist and neck, with one leg a little in front of the

83 *Above left* Sonning (Berks): Sir Thomas Rich (d. 1667) and son

84 *Above* Lowther (Westmorland): John Viscount Lonsdale (d. 1700). By William Stanton

85 *Far left* Ashburnham (Sussex): Sir William and Lady Ashburnham. By John Bushnell (1675)

86 *Left* Rushbrooke (Suffolk): Henry Jermyn, earl of St Albans (d. 1684)

87 *Above* Knebworth (Herts): Lytton·Lytton (d.1710)

88 *Above right* Redgrave (Suffolk): Chief Justice Sir John Holt (d.1710). By Thomas Green

89 Withyham (Sussex): Thomas Sackville (d.1677). By Caius Gabriel Cibber

other and the hands in animated display. It can be seen clearly at Tawstock (Devon) in the figure of Rachel countess of Bath (d. 1680), whose turning motion is emphasized by the folds of her heavy robes, at Little Easton (Essex) in the figures of Sir William and Lady Maynard (late seventeenth century), who are gesticulating toward an urn set between them, and at Knebworth in that of Lytton Lytton (d. 1710) (*87*), who poses with head turned slightly to the left, his left arm elegantly akimbo and the right gesturing outward to balance the turn of the head. Many other standing effigies display the same characteristics in varying degrees, but undeniably the supreme and most Berninesque example is John Bushnell's figure of John Lord Mordaunt (d. 1675) in All Saints, Fulham (London), with its commandingly theatrical pose and its satisfying rhythm of contrasted but balanced motions. For animated display in a seated figure, there is the effigy of Sir John Holt (d. 1710) at Redgrave (Suffolk) (*88*), who sits robed as a chief justice in wonderful complacency, the sense of balance being achieved by turning the head to the left and placing the left leg slightly forward to the right, as the right hand points elegantly outward.

Other effigies appear less concerned with display than with conveying a symbolic, religious or emotional message. A number, including, for example, that of the 4th Lord Coventry (d. 1687) at Croome D'Abitot (Worcs), take part in scenes suggesting their impending immortality and will be discussed in a later chapter. In a different idiom, Margaret Watson (d. 1713) at Rockingham (Northants) stands in a markedly animated state, robed in garments disturbed by her anxiety as she points to a skull at her feet and turns her head away in dismay. Archbishop Dolben (d. 1686) in York Minster, on the other hand, is clearly reassured by an unseen vision of salvation, as he reclines below a glory of cherubs, who bring down a wreath of victory.

The portrayal of personal emotions, representing a culmination of developments dating back to the early seventeenth century, resulted in the most quintessentially Baroque effigies of all. In this context John Bushnell and Caius Gabriel Cibber approached nearer than any other craftsmen working in England to the style of Bernini, the master of Baroque emotionalism, the former producing the remarkable monument of Sir William Ashburnham (d. 1675) and his wife at Ashburnham (Sussex), Cibber the equally stunning monument of Thomas Sackville (d. 1677) at Withyham in the same county.

The first (*85*) depicts a dramatically emotional scene in which Lady Ashburnham semi-reclines at the point of death, as a putto flies down to place a wreath upon her head, while her husband kneels facing her, his face anguished by grief and his hands outstretched in desperate entreaty. The second monument is more subdued (*89*), but, if anything, more moving. Thomas Sackville, dying in his thirteenth year, is shown semi-reclining on a free-standing tomb-chest holding a skull in his left hand, but what lifts the monument to the level of pathos is the fact that life-size effigies of his mourning parents kneel beside the tomb-chest and lean an arm against it, the father gazing upon his son in quiet grief, the mother with head bowed in prayerful contemplation. The piece is full of life and, as one approaches it, the sensation is almost that of trespassing upon the private grief and devotions of parents who are in the very act of mourning their departed son, this effect being clearly deliberate, since the sides of the tomb-chest are carved with conventionally kneeling children in relief, partly obscured by the parental figures, as though the latter have knelt down beside an existing monument. A related but less spectacular case is William Stanton's hanging monument for Sir Richard Harrison (d. 1683) at Hurst (Berks), which treats in Baroque fashion the outmoded type with two figures kneeling at a prayer-desk. Here Lady Harrison is doubly afflicted, for she kneels in mourning not only for her husband, kneeling opposite and looking out at the viewer, but also for their youngest son, who followed his father to the grave four months later and stands at the back of the monument gazing out from behind the prayer-desk.

Apart from the variety of postures and poses of effigies in this period, another notable feature was the growing tendency to portray them in Roman or quasi-Roman dress or armour, a practice which was to become very widespread in the first half of the eighteenth century. However, those not shown in this way were depicted in fashionable clothes, the carving of which was frequently executed in great detail, faithfully reproducing the smallest items of dress. The standing figure of Sir Thomas Wendy (d. 1673) at Haslingfield (Cambs) (*90*), for example, gives an excellent impression of male attire in Charles II's reign, while that of Lytton Lytton (d. 1710) at Knebworth (Herts) (*87*) makes clear the changes that had occurred by the time of Queen Anne. In a number of instances, the lace cravats fashionable for men in the late seventeenth and early eighteenth centuries were carved with amazing fineness of detail, an exquisite example of which can be seen on William Stanton's effigy of the 1st earl of Coventry at Elmley Castle (*91*). Equally fine specimens of female dress were produced, including an example of Charles II's time worn by Thomas Sackville's mother at Withyham (Sussex) and another of Queen Anne's reign worn by Lady Clayton at Bletchingley (Surrey) (*92*).

For partial depictions of the deceased in this period there was the choice of demi-figures, pedestal busts or a new form of relief portrait. The first declined markedly in appeal, however, despite a certain revival at the turn of the century, among the best products of which was Francis Bird's hanging monument for Sir Orlando Gee (d. 1705) at Isleworth (Middx). The head-and-shoulders bust in an oval or circular frame, though enduring for a time, also petered out. The pedestal bust, in contrast, became very popular and remained so throughout the eighteenth century. At this time it was especially favoured on hanging monuments and was often carved in a lively Baroque manner with a characteristic turn of the head. A very fine example is provided by the large and impressive monument of Robert Shiers (d. 1668), his wife and son at Great Bookham (Surrey), which has three excellent pedestal busts within a rich Baroque frame. Other good framed instances include the monuments of Catherine Shuckburgh (d. 1683) at Upper Shuckburgh (Warks), where the bust, with one breast coquettishly bare, is set beneath a garlanded cartouche of arms against a plain arched background, and Sir Edward Wigley (d. 1710) and wife at Scraptoft (Leics), where the busts are in front of arched panels under a baldacchino. Alternatively, the bust was placed entirely free on top of the monument, as in the case of John Hales (d. 1670) at Great Gaddesden (Herts), whose strikingly Baroque bust stands with two urns on a gadrooned ledge above the inscription panel. Among others, with varying designs below the bust, are those of Lady Anne Dormer (d. 1695) at Wing (Bucks) and Martha Fitzherbert (d. 1699) at Tissington (Derbs), the latter being by Francis Bird and having the inscription carved on a hanging marble 'sheet'.

Relief portraits enclosed in oval frames made their first appearance in the Baroque period. Though not yet in the form of antique cameos, which were to be imitated on a large scale in the eighteenth century, they undoubtedly represented a move in that direction. The deceased was normally shown as a head-and-shoulders portrait in a half or three-quarter frontal pose. One of the earliest examples is the beautiful standing monument of Sir Thomas Baines and Sir Thomas Finch in the chapel of Christ's College, Cambridge, the only known work of Joseph Catterns and erected in 1684 (*93*). It has separately framed portraits of the two young men, each festooned and surmounted by an heraldic cartouche, and each resting on a pedestal supported on a tall plinth on which the respective inscription is carved. Normally, however, the relief portrait was to be employed on smaller hanging monuments, often above a framed cartouche or panel bearing the inscription, as can be seen in the cases of Toby Rustat (made before his death in 1695) in Jesus College chapel, Cambridge, Lady Abigail Stawell (d. 1692) at Hartley Wespall (Hants) and others. The monument of Richard Acton (d. 1703) and wife at Acton Round (Salop) (*94*) is of additional interest, since, by depicting the couple as relief portraits holding hands in a horizontally oval frame, it represents an application of the new technique to the older convention for portraying conjugal affection.

Apart from busts and relief portraits, hanging monuments continued in some cases to include full effigies of the deceased, mainly in a standing or kneeling attitude, the former being illustrated by the monument of Sir Thomas Wendy (d. 1673) at Haslingfield (Cambs), the latter by that of Grace Gethin (d. 1697) at Hollingbourne (Kent). At Abbots Langley (Herts) the monument of Lady Anne Raymond (d. 1714) shows her exceptionally in the seated posture with three grandchildren in cradles below.

Wall Tablets in the Seventeenth and Early Eighteenth Centuries

By far the commonest type of hanging monument in the Baroque period was that which dispensed with a portrayal of the deceased in any form, consisting instead solely of an inscription set in an honorific or ornamental surround, usually with a small coat of arms at top or bottom. Such monuments, as we have seen, had originated in the later sixteenth century and, largely because of their relative cheapness, had grown steadily in popularity throughout the seventeenth century. Although often overlooked, they amply reward study, revealing surprising ingenuity on the part of craftsmen in varying the basic format and containing in many instances carving of high quality and delightful detail.

90 *Left* Haslingfield (Cambs): Sir Thomas Wendy (d. 1673)

91 *Above* Elmley Castle (Worcs): Thomas, 1st earl of Coventry (d. 1699). By William Stanton

92 *Above* Bletchingley (Surrey): Sir Robert Clayton (d.1707) and Lady Clayton. By Richard Crutcher

93 *Above right* Christ's College chapel, Cambridge: Sir Thomas Baines and Sir Thomas Finch. By Joseph Catterns (1684)

94 Acton Round (Salop): Richard Acton (d.1703) and wife. By Edward Stanton

The class was capable of much variety, not only in size and shape, but also in the form and degree of embellishment of the surround. In the first half of the century the inscription was usually set in an 'architectural' frame whose design reflected the style of contemporary large-scale monuments, but, while this type persisted in numerous variations throughout the period, it soon had to compete with a new and equally variable fashion which appeared toward the middle of the century. This abandoned any notion of an 'architectural' frame and consisted instead of a roughly oval cartouche bearing the inscription and set in a more or less ornate border carved with a variety of motifs, including garlands, palm-branches, laurels, drapes, ribbons, cherubs, masks, skulls, and so on.

The 'architectural' form consisted of a rectangular inscription panel flanked by columns or pilasters and surmounted by an entablature and pediment of one sort or another, the style becoming increasingly classical under Charles I and predominantly Baroque later on. Thus, at West Horsley (Surrey) the monument of Susan Brisco (d. 1636) has fluted columns at the sides carrying a scrolly pediment with an heraldic cartouche in the middle, and that of Thomas Foley (d. 1677) at Great Witley (Worcs) plain columns and a double open pediment with heraldic cartouche. By contrast, those of George Beverley (dated 1678) at Sherborne St John (Hants) and Sir James Rushout (d. 1711) at Blockley (Glos) have pilasters supporting their pediments, the pilasters of the first being severely plain, of the latter richly carved with cherub-heads, leaves and flowers. On occasions the inscription was enclosed in an oval wreath within the rectangular frame, as can be seen on the monuments of Sir Laurence Washington (d. 1643) at Garsdon (Wilts) and Sir Richard Newdigate (d. 1678) at Harefield (Middx) (*95*), both having twisted columns at the sides and open segmental pediments. Again the frame might lack a pediment, as in the case of Thomas Childe (d. 1708) at Kinlet (Salop), where twisted side columns rise to an irregular flat entablature supporting flaming urns and a shield of arms. In the later seventeenth century other related forms appeared in which the 'architectural' character was much reduced or lost, either by bringing the inscription panel forward of unobtrusive side columns or by doing away with the latter entirely and replacing them with ornate volutes. Memorials of this sort were sometimes very richly decorated, as in the elaborate example for Gen. Charles Churchill

(d. 1714) at Minterne Magna (Dorset), with its dense arrays of military trophies at top and bottom, the drapes and volutes at the sides and the group of cherub-heads above the inscription.

The 'cartouche' type varied enormously in detail, not only from generation to generation, but also, when made by local craftsmen, from region to region, though cherubs and cherub-heads were almost invariably included in the designs. At first the outline of the inscription area was a strict oval, but in the later seventeenth century this was frequently modified to make it more truly egg-shaped (i.e., with its greatest width nearer to one end) and on occasions further altered by turning the direction of each lateral curve inwards in the middle to produce a wavy outline.

In the early examples the borders, on which the decorative features were carved, tended to be fleshy or gristly in appearance. The memorial of Sir Peter Wyche (d. 1643) in Oxford cathedral, for instance, has an oval inscription surrounded by gristly decoration which embraces a total of three coats of arms, with two seated putti at the top and two more turning away from an urn at the bottom. A later example, that of Thomas Isham (d. 1676) at Hillesden (Bucks) (*96*), has a surround of fleshy, even sea-weedy, character surmounted by an heraldic cartouche and seated putti, with a skull and two winged cherub-heads below. Later cartouches were in general either softer or more brittle in appearance and commonly incorporated drapes and/or garlands in their decorative schemes. That of John Oldham (d. 1683) at Holme Pierrepoint (Notts) has beautifully curling lobes from which garlands of fruit and flowers fall to a mask at the bottom , while that of Bishop John Pritchett of Gloucester (d. 1681) at Harefield (Middx) has a richer version with three cherub-heads at the top and two masks halfway down the sides, from whose mouths issue garlands looped to a third mask below. Drapes and putti appear together on the fine Baroque cartouches of Sir George Curteis (d. 1702) at Otterden (Kent) and Thomas Strangways's children (*c.* 1706) at Melbury Sampford (Dorset), the latter with sprays of laurel and both with skulls at the bottom. Perhaps the most exquisite Baroque cartouches, however, are those which have had the carver's skill in depicting flowers, fruit and foliage lavished upon them. It can be seen in countless examples of the later seventeenth and early eighteenth centuries, including that of Lady Mary Howard (d. 1718) at Lingfield (Surrey) (*97*), where flowers combine with drapes

95 *Above* Harefield (Middx): Sir Richard Newdigate (d.1678).
By William Stanton

96 *Above right* Hillesden (Bucks): Thomas Isham (d.1676)

97 Lingfield (Surrey): Lady Mary Howard (d.1718)

and cherub-heads to form a particularly pleasing composition. Finally, there was a new kind of mural tablet which appeared at about the same time and took the form of a richly bordered 'cloth' bearing the inscription. It can be seen, for instance, on the monuments of Sir John Bramston (d. 1699) at Roxwell (Essex) and Robert Wormley (d. 1712) at Riccall (Yorks).

Low-relief and Two-dimensional Memorials

There remain to be considered low-relief effigies, monumental brasses and monumental slabs of various kinds. The low-relief effigies of Cornwall continued to flourish in the first half of the seventeenth century and then largely disappeared, but their odd occurrence later in Cornwall and elsewhere reveals that this primitive folk-art form possessed a vitality immune from more sophisticated developments. It crops up, for instance, at St Devereux (Herefs) on the monument of Ann Goode (d. 1668), who is depicted at prayer in the crudest simplicity, blissfully unaware of dawning Baroque.

This period saw also the rapid disappearance of the incised slab, although one of the latest full-length depictions, that of Elizabeth Havers (d. 1634) at Stockerston (Leics), has claims to be considered the finest ever made in this country. Likewise, the making of monumental brasses with figures virtually came to an end. The types of monumental brass current in the Elizabethan and Jacobean periods remained in use until the mid-seventeenth century, but thereafter the separately cut-out figure became exceptional and the normal form of brasses was that of a smallish square or rectangular plate engraved with the figure or figures and other details. By 1700 even these brasses with representations of the deceased were very rare, and this ancient form of memorial may be regarded as having to all intents and purposes died out, to await revival in the nineteenth century.

The reason lay partly in the introduction of a new class of monument, the memorial slab carved with an inscription for the deceased and, where appropriate, a deeply-cut relief of his heraldic achievement. Such slabs were commonly of black marble, but they might be of white marble, alabaster, slate or, in iron-rich areas like the Weald and Shropshire, of iron. Normally laid in the floor of the church, but occasionally placed upon a tomb-chest, this form was to serve in the later seventeenth, eighteenth and early nineteenth centuries a function similar to that of earlier incised slabs and monumental brasses, except that it lacked a depiction of the deceased. Often walked over and grievously worn, such memorials were as typical of their age as the grander and more obvious monuments around them.

5 The Eighteenth Century

The history of English church monuments in the eighteenth century is one of increasing diversification and change. In the first place, the period was a 'Roman' age, in which the influence of ancient Rome on the arts in England reached its zenith. More especially in architecture, an area closely involved in the making of monuments, it brought to a climax the long and vicissitudinous process of classical Roman revival which had begun in Italy more than three centuries earlier. In seventeenth-century England, as we have seen, the Palladian classical style introduced by Inigo Jones had made but limited progress before being transformed in its later development into the Baroque style. Now a reaction to the Baroque set in, pioneered largely by the 3rd earl of Burlington and his circle, committed to the re-introduction of Palladian ideals, as a result of which the Baroque, while far from disappearing, was modified to a purer classical style. Hence, where architectural elements were employed on monuments, the more correctly classical forms were preferred, so that, for instance, curtained baldacchinos and twisted columns disappeared, triangular pediments were adopted far more frequently than segmental pediments and, though the latter remained in use, the wilder versions of the High Baroque fell out of fashion. No such clear transition was evident in the field of human figure sculpture, whether for effigies or for other figures on monuments, but here, too, despite the continuing vigour of the Baroque tradition, in general a calmer, less dramatic or emotional manner predominated. These developments were aided by an ever-growing and increasingly better-informed interest in the antique, and by the continuing attraction of Rome, where English patrons and artists came into contact with the latest works, which abandoned the dramatic style of Bernini, and brought the new ideas back with them to England. Notable among these were the sculptor, Francis Bird, and the architect, James Gibbs, the latter of whom returned from Rome in 1709, began designing monuments soon afterwards and, in 1728, published an influential set of architectural designs, including many for monuments, which displayed the more classical and much modified Baroque style then in vogue.

At first the reaction to High Baroque in England was partly political in motivation, the revived Palladianism (and through it conscious pursuit of the antique) being associated with the Hanoverian Whig ascendancy after the death of Queen Anne (1714) but it gradually established itself as a dominant style for all. One of the most telling indications of its supremacy on monuments, at least up to about 1750, was the frequent depiction of leading Englishmen as Roman citizens, Roman generals and the like, clothed in ancient dress or armour. The affectation was deliberate, for among other things it reflected a feeling in eighteenth-century England that here, in contrast to most of Europe ruled by absolute and (as they were regarded) tyrannical monarchies, the values and liberties of ancient Rome were kept alive. Living under a king whose powers were limited by Parliament, and protected in the enjoyment of their property and liberties by statute and the Common Law, the English ruling classes could see themselves as true heirs of the senators and citizens of pre-imperial Rome. That they should be portrayed as latter-day Romans in classical settings was therefore wholly appropriate.

Despite this veneration of classical Rome, many aspects of the Baroque style remained. Indeed, apart from its survival in more classical guise for some decades, its continued vitality was separately attested by the rise of the Rococo style, a late and extravagant development of Baroque which was at its height in the period roughly 1730–1770. Though stemming in the Baroque tradition from ultimately classical origins, rococo was far from classical in spirit and in some respects represented the histrionic and picturesque qualities latent in High

Baroque taken to their limits. One of its characteristics was a deliberate disregard of symmetry in monumental designs, coupled with a lively exploitation of contrasting rhythms of movement. This can be seen particularly on some large-scale monuments in which effigies and other figures upset the symmetry of the composition, break out of its basic frame or diversify the direction of movement. It is also apparent, in more modest form, on a number of wall tablets which, unlike their earlier Baroque precursors and more classical contemporaries, have asymmetrical designs with flowing curves and complicated scroll-work reminiscent of elaborate rococo mirror-frames. Moreover, for much of the eighteenth century decorative enrichment on monuments (employed especially where there were no effigies) consisted essentially of Baroque motifs, which, as time went on, tended to acquire a degree of elaborate detail, delicate refinement and elegant charm which may properly be called rococo.

In the later decades of the century both the classical Baroque and rococo styles gave way to the so-called Neo-classical movement, at first affecting monumental forms and decoration, and by the end of the century human figure sculpture as well. By 1770 architecture had been abandoned as an element of monumental design, and the decorative delights of Baroque and rococo ornament, such as cherub-heads and garlands, were being supplanted by a new range of cool, chaste and largely abstract motifs. The most important aspect of the neo-classical movement was the Greek revival, which, in the search for the purest antique authority in art, went back to the primary, pre-Roman civilization of classical Greece. The Greek revival was well under way by the 1780s and was soon to overwhelm the typical eighteenth-century fashions entirely. At the same time, however, another influence had begun to make itself felt on monuments, namely, the Gothic Revival. Although as yet its signs were faint and hesitant, Gothic quietly gained confidence in the background and was destined in the latter half of the nineteenth century to predominate over all other influences, including that of neo-classicism, in determining the form and nature of monuments.

Needless to say, the paramount material from which eighteenth-century monuments were made was marble, but not merely black, grey or white marble, for, despite the total disappearance of paint (save for heraldry), colour was provided by the use of variously coloured marbles on the one monument. Red, pink, green, yellow and purple marbles,

veined and unveined, were imported on a large scale and were employed, in combination with marbles of traditional hues, to produce a wealth of multi-coloured effects. Moreover, monuments were now commonly signed, reflecting the much increased status of their creators, whom in consequence we may generally describe henceforth as sculptors rather than mason-sculptors or craftsmen. Some monuments resulted from the co-operation of two men, a designer (usually an architect) and a sculptor, in which cases the names of both men will be found in the 'signature'. Our knowledge of the designers and makers of monuments in this period, aided by more abundant documentary evidence, becomes so extensive that it is rare for a monument of any size to be totally anonymous. English craftsmanship reached a new level of excellence in the eighteenth century, partly as a result of skills accumulated in the preceding century and partly by way of continuing inspiration from abroad. Apart from the pull of Rome, the other predominant influences were once more Flemish and Dutch, as a fresh group of immigrés settled in England after 1720, including the important figure of Michael Rysbrack from Antwerp, but of all foreign sculptors working in England in the eighteenth century among the most accomplished was a Frenchman, Louis François Roubiliac.

Typical Features

Although the forms of monuments were very diverse and included certain types surviving with suitable modifications from earlier periods, a number of features were particularly characteristic of the eighteenth century. Most typical was the large, two-dimensional pyramid which formed the backplate of numerous standing monuments and, on a smaller scale, determined the shape of countless hanging monuments. Ultimately of ancient Egyptian origin, the pyramid had been introduced into the Renaissance repertoire by Raphael, whence it had been imitated by later tomb-makers in Rome and so was brought to England in the early eighteenth century by such men as Bird and Gibbs returning from that city. However, its first appearance here was as early as 1704 on a monument made in Rome and imported for erection in St Martin's, Stamford (Lincs), namely, that of the 5th earl of Exeter, which shows him with his wife semi-reclining on a sarcophagus in front of a tall pyramid. It did not come into general use until after about

98 High Wycombe (Bucks): Henry Petty, 1st earl of Shelburne. By Peter Scheemakers (1754)

1720, and in its early stages was sometimes incorporated into monuments with 'architectural' frames, in which it was merely set behind the effigies against the backplate. It is employed in this way, for instance, on the monuments of John Holles duke of Newcastle (dated 1723) in Westminster Abbey, Viscount Newhaven (d.1728) at Drayton Beauchamp (Bucks), Richard Ladbroke (d.1730) at Reigate (Surrey), Sir Francis Page (c.1730) at Steeple Aston (Oxon) and, rather late, the 1st earl of Shelburne (dated 1754) at High Wycombe (Bucks) (*98*), the last two of which are surmounted by broken straight-sided pediments. More commonly, however, the architecture was discarded, leaving the pyramid to stand alone and impart its distinctive, controlling shape to the design of monuments, a shape which was to remain a standard into the early nineteenth century. In its grandest versions the pyramid rises behind an effigy of the deceased semi-reclining on a sarcophagus, often accompanied by his wife and attended by other members of his family or by allegorical figures, all in antique dress or armour. Such schemes were used by many of the leading monumental sculptors working after 1720, but were particularly favoured by Rysbrack, who on occasions piled up enormous masses of sculpture in front of the pyramid, as, for example, on the huge monuments of the 1st duke of Marlborough (dated 1733) in the chapel of Blenheim Palace (Oxon) and the 1st Lord Foley (before 1743) at Great Witley (Worcs) (*99*). Notable among his less-crowded compositions in this vein are the monuments of Sir Isaac Newton (dated 1731) in Westminster Abbey, the 1st earl of Harborough (d.1732) at Stapleford (Leics), and the 2nd and 3rd dukes of Beaufort (dated 1754) and the 4th duke (d.1756) at Great Badminton (Glos), the last depicting the deceased as a solitary standing figure. Of similar works by other sculptors, we may note the monuments of Lord Justice Raymond (d.1732) by Henry Cheere at Abbots Langley (Herts), where the judge appears in official robes semi-reclining with his seated wife; Col. Thomas Moore (d.1735) by Thomas Carter senior at Great Bookham (Surrey), a semi-reclining 'Roman' officer in front of a pyramid carved with military trophies; and the 2nd duke of Ancaster (d.1742), probably by Roubiliac, at Edenham (Lincs) (*112*), the duke standing and leaning on an urn above a medallion of his wife. Also by Roubiliac is the remarkably rococo version seen on his monument of John duke of Argyll (completed 1749) in Westminster Abbey (*100*), in which the

deceased leans, in a semi-reclining attitude of dying, against the figure of Fame, who is in the act of writing his inscription on the pyramid behind, while below on either side of the sarcophagus are the standing and seated personifications of Eloquence and Valour, the former gesticulating forward to capture the viewer's attention.

In many other cases the pyramid was used as a background for busts, medallion portraits and a great variety of symbolic groups, including allegorical figures, putti, urns, and so on. The same was true also of hanging wall monuments, hundreds of which were made consisting of a roughly rectangular inscription plate surmounted by a bust or other feature in front of a pyramid.

Other typical features included the urn and the antique sarcophagus. The former, a standard motif of ancillary decoration on monuments since the late sixteenth century, had been increasingly used after 1630 as a major feature at the centre of designs. While it continued in both rôles in the eighteenth century, a prominent position became far more common, especially on hanging monuments but also on a number of standing wall monuments, often in association with a two-dimensional pyramid. The large standing monument of the 9th earl of Huntingdon (d.1746) at Ashby-de-la-Zouch (Leics), for example, consists simply of a big urn, carved with a relief of his widow, in front of a pyramid. Again, at Avington (Hants) that of Margaret marchioness of Carnarvon (d.1768) has, above a high base bearing the inscription, two flaming urns flanking a tall pyramid. Alternatively, the urn might be placed prominently above an inscription plate, as on three hanging Newdigate monuments (dates of death, 1765, 1774 and 1800) at Harefield (Middx) and on two standing monuments at Shepshed (Leics) for Jane Phillipps (d.1761) and Samuel Phillipps (d.1774), the last with the urn placed upon an enormously high plinth and surmounted by an allegory of Religion. Moreover, the symbolic significance of the urn changed in the eighteenth century, for, although the earlier flaming type, standing for immortality, remained frequent for some time, it was increasingly supplanted by a form without flames and commonly draped, serving unequivocally as a symbol of death. Good examples of the draped version occur on the hanging monuments of James Kendal (d.1750) at West Horsley (Surrey) (*101*), where the sumptuously and asymmetrically draped urn has the inscription carved upon it and stands in front of a pyramid, and Robert

Palmer (d. 1787) at Hurst (Berks) (*118*), on which the chastely draped urn surmounts an early neo-classical inscription plate. Increasingly common toward the end of the eighteenth century and into the nineteenth century was the depiction of a classically-attired female (sometimes the widow) leaning in mourning over or against the urn. This can be seen, for instance, in the cases of John Dalton (by John Bacon, 1791) at Great Stanmore (Middx), where the figure places a garland over an urn carved with a relief medallion of the deceased, and John Lord Northwick (d. 1800) at Blockley (Glos) (*102*), where the deceased is lamented both by his widow leaning over the urn and by a cherub extinguishing the torch of life alongside. Variations upon these themes are legion.

The sarcophagus had been employed intermittently from the mid-sixteenth century, rarely alone and normally carrying recumbent or reclining effigies, but only now did it become widespread, being used either to support effigies, allegorical figures and the like, or, in the absence of figures, to form a principal object of attention in its own right. Its design varied from a rounded type, with gadrooned top and embellished edges, to that of a severely plain casket with flat tapering sides and lid, all types being typically supported on monstrous clawed feet. On several standing monuments without effigies the urn and sarcophagus appear together, the former placed upon the latter, as, for instance, on the monument of George Bridges (d. 1751) at Avington (Hants) (*103*), composed of grey, pink and yellow marbles, where the combination is set between columns and beneath a broken triangular pediment. Occasionally, as on the monument of the 1st earl of Hardwicke (d. 1764) and his countess at Wimpole (Cambs), the sarcophagus is carved with relief medallions of the deceased.

Allegorical female figures, attired in loose classical dress, were also a standard feature of the period and grew steadily in popularity as the century unfolded. Coming now to full maturity after a lengthy process of development dating back to the late sixteenth century, they could be used to portray not only the principal Virtues, but almost any conceivable attribute, calling or profession merely by placing appropriate symbolic objects in their hands. They commonly occur either in close association with other figures and features or standing and sitting at cardinal points on a monument, whether or not a representation of the deceased is included. Thus, to take a few examples from hundreds, a splendid seated figure of Hope (with an anchor) appears with a medallion portrait on the monument of Viscount Tyrconnel (d. 1754) at Belton (Lincs), and Medicine (with a caduceus) stands and mourns beside an urn on that of John Dealtry, M.D. (d. 1773), in York Minster. At Flamstead (Herts) Hope and Faith (with a cross) sit flanking an urn on the monument of Sir Edward Sedbright (d. 1782). A supreme exponent of the standing allegorical figure was John Bacon, senior, who flourished in the later eighteenth century and died in 1799, an excellent example of whose work in this idiom is provided by the monument of James Marwood (made in 1781) at Widworthy (Devon) (*104*), on which personifications of Justice (with scales) and Benevolence (with a pelican and her nest of young) stand on either side of a garlanded urn on a column. A similar piece for Sarah Winford (d. 1793) at Astley (Worcs) has Benevolence and Sensibility (with a bowl of foliage). Occasionally, the provision of carved names for the allegories makes their identification doubly clear, as, for example, on the monument of Ann Whytell (d. 1788) in Westminster Abbey, where we are told that they represent Innocence and Peace. Less commonly there occur personifications of countries (normally, of course, Britannia with her familiar helmet, trident and shield), the arts and sciences, economic enterprises like trade and agriculture, and the elements. For instance, John Bacon's massive pile commemorating William Pitt 1st earl of Chatham (completed 1783) in Westminster Abbey has five allegorical figures depicting Britannia with Prudence and Fortitude (two of the traditional Cardinal Virtues), and Earth and Ocean.

Related to allegorical figures are the similarly attired female figures without symbolic attributes which one frequently meets either seated with a medallion portrait (especially before 1750) or, increasingly after 1750, standing or kneeling with a medallion, urn or sarcophagus, and at all times commonly accompanied by one or more cherubs. Such figures are not always easy to interpret in individual cases and there may have been a partial change in their significance in the course of the century. It seems likely, however, that in most cases they represented grieving widows, but that on occasions (especially in the later eighteenth century) they served as anonymous personifications of mourning or stood for the imaginary figure of Sorrow.

Cherubs likewise took on a more central rôle, quite apart from their continued importance in

99 Great Witley (Worcs): 1st Lord Foley. By Michael Rysbrack (before 1743)

100 Westminster Abbey: John duke of Argyll. By Louis François Roubiliac (completed 1749)

101 West Horsley (Surrey): James Kendal (d. 1750)

102 Blockley (Glos): John Lord Northwick (d. 1800)

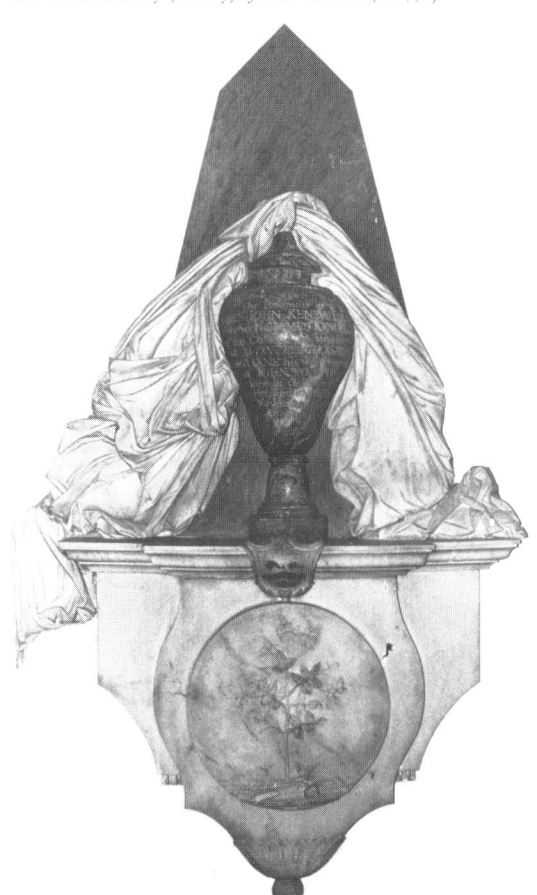

103 Avington (Hants): George Bridges (d.1751)

104 Widworthy (Devon): James Marwood. By John Bacon (1781)

105 Spelsbury (Oxon): Robert Lee, 4th earl of Lichfield (d.1776)

106 Scraptoft (Leics): James Wigley (d.1765). Note the relief of a tree-planting scene

minor decorative enrichment. They were often employed as essential figures in allegorical or mildly sentimental compositions, much favoured in the later eighteenth century, especially where no effigy of the deceased was included. Allegory and tenderness, for example, are displayed on two good standing monuments at Spelsbury (Oxon), each made of several different coloured marbles with a black pyramid background and commemorating, respectively, the 3rd and 4th earls of Lichfield (d.1772 and 1776). The first, designed and executed with considerable refinement, consists of two urns set in an oval recess framed by a serpent biting its tail (a fashionable device for eternity) and, above, growing up in front of the pyramid a young oak tree in whose branches stands a cherub tying a scroll to its trunk. The other monument (*105*), less inventive but equally attractive, shows a large sarcophagus surmounted by two cherubs, one seated, one standing, in the act of placing a garland round a red marble urn. Cherubs garlanding an urn figure also on the more elaborate allegorical monument of the 2nd duchess of Montagu (by Roubiliac, 1753) at Warkton (Northants), where the theme is combined with asymmetrically disposed representations of the three Fates of ancient mythology. The allegorical use of cherubs occurs in different form on the extravagantly rococo monument of Nicholas Magens (d.1764) at Brightlingsea (Essex), a successful businessman with world-wide interests, whose earthly riches are depicted by, *inter alia*, a cherub seated on a huge cornucopia, pointing with one hand to a globe and with the other up to the top of the monument where, amid a 'glory' of billowing clouds and cherub-heads, a second cherub flies down blowing a trumpet and indicating a wreath of victory symbolic of the deceased's heavenly reward. In these examples the deceased is not portrayed, but on many occasions cherubs appear in association with effigies or with busts or medallion portraits, which they sometimes drape or garland, and not uncommonly they accompany mourning or allegorical female figures. Perhaps the most typical depiction of the cherub was in the doleful act of extinguishing a torch, symbolising the end of earthly life.

Angels, too, now acquiring a distinctly female appearance, figured increasingly in the repertoire, especially in the second half of the century, and were employed in the same sort of rôles otherwise filled by cherubs or female figures. Thus, on the monuments of Charlotte St Quintin (d.1762) at Harpham

(Yorks) and Leak Okeover (d.1765) and wife at Okeover (Staffs), both by Joseph Wilton, an angel stands leaning over an urn on a pedestal carved with a medallion of the deceased, the angel in each case holding a wreath in one hand and extinguishing a torch with the other. At Kinnersley (Herefs) the monument of Lady Anne Morgan (d.1764) has a standing angel who looks heavenward and drapes a medallion on which appears a profile of the deceased with unusually bare breasts. One of the most beautiful eighteenth-century angels, however, occurs on Richard Westmacott the Elder's monument for James Dutton (dated 1791) at Sherborne (Glos), where a conventional idea is successfully combined with the theme of triumph over death – the angel stands beside a relief medallion of the deceased and his wife, which she drapes, but in doing so she tramples on a skeleton symbolising Death lying at her feet. In the following century angels were commonly to appear in schemes portraying the related theme of the salvation of the soul, often by taking souls of the deceased with them to Heaven, but the first essays in this genre occurred in the later eighteenth century. A notable case is the exquisite relief by Flaxman for Sarah Morley (d.1784) in Gloucester cathedral. Here Mrs Morley, who died in childbirth while en route by sea from India, is depicted rising from the waves into the arms of hovering angels, the point of the iconography being underlined by the biblical quotation on the containing arch, which reads, 'The sea shall give up the dead.'

One other characteristic feature needs to be mentioned, namely, the incorporation into monumental designs of panels of relief carving depicting scenes of one sort or another. Though stemming from origins as distant as the late sixteenth century and growing increasingly frequent in the later seventeenth, such panels proliferated in the eighteenth century to an extent hitherto unknown and in many cases displayed a new minuteness of detail. They might be placed in any of a variety of positions, sometimes on the frontal base of standing monuments, sometimes forming the central element on hanging monuments, sometimes carved on the fronts of sarcophagi. The subject matter was equally varied and frequently carried inspiring or morally didactic overtones, the latter especially after 1750. It might commemorate a notable incident in the life of the deceased or his death, or it might celebrate his favourite occupations or charitable good works, or, again, it might allude by allegory to his virtues and

achievements. A few examples will suffice to indicate the scope of possibilities. Scenes of naval
encounters commonly occur on monuments of
admirals and the like. A fine instance can be seen on
that of Vice-Admiral Henry Medley (d. 1747) in
York Minster, with its several men-of-war carved in
delicate detail on the front of a sarcophagus, and a
number of similar pieces for other naval celebrities
of the period survive in Westminster Abbey,
principal shrine of the nation's heroes until the end
of the eighteenth century. Scenes of the deaths of
military commanders in action were equally popular. Among several in the Abbey we may cite the
monuments of Col. Roger Townshend, killed at
Ticonderoga in 1759, and Gen. James Wolfe, with
its fine relief of the scaling of the Heights of
Abraham in 1759; and, elsewhere, that of Cornet
Geary at Great Bookham (Surrey), which shows his
death in ambush at Flemington (New Jersey) in
1776 in the American War of Independence. By
contrast, the monument of Bishop John Hough
(dated 1746) in Worcester cathedral depicts an
incident from his life, namely, his temporary ejec-
tion from the presidency of Magdalen College,
Oxford, by James II in 1687–8. On a fairly modest
hanging monument at Scraptoft (Leics) James
Wigley (d. 1765) (*106*) is depicted in relief super-
intending the planting of trees, part of his efforts to
provide work for the poor, while on another at
Powick (Worcs) Mrs Mary Russell (d. 1786) appears
teaching music to her daughter surrounded by
instruments of many kinds. Allegorical scenes of
varying import occur on the monuments of William
Lytton Strode (d. 1732) at Knebworth (Herts),
William Lord Maynard (dated 1746) at Little Easton
(Essex) and John duke of Argyll (completed 1749)
at Westminster, the last of these incorporating a
figure of Britannia and a depiction of Magna Carta
in allusion to the duke's defence of Liberty. On the
ends of the tomb-chest of Bernard Brocas (d. 1777)
at Bramley (Hants) are richly carved high-relief
panels showing, on the one, Charity giving food to
the needy attended by Justice and Fortitude, and, on
the other, War overcoming her enemies with Fame
writing a record of her exploits. Specifically Christian allegory, in the form of representations of
Christ's parable of the Good Samaritan, began to
appear on such panels soon after 1750. It became
increasingly popular in the later eighteenth century,
and, among several examples, can be seen on the
hanging monument of William Pyke (d. 1794) at
Great Somerford (Wilts) (*107*).

Effigies and other Representations of the Deceased

In connection with a number of the pieces mentioned above reference has been made to a medallion portrait. This was of great importance as the
major new contribution made by the eighteenth
century to the range of possible depictions of the
deceased. It consisted of a relief portrait in profile or
semi-profile, sometimes showing head and shoulders but typically head and neck only, set on a plain
and usually unframed oval medallion. Inspired by
study of antique coins and cameos, it was significantly first employed on an English monument by
Francis Bird, who incorporated a medallion of this
kind into his monument for Henry Priestman
(d. 1712) in Westminster Abbey. Once introduced, it
quickly secured a popularity over the more frontal
head-and-shoulders portraits of the earlier Baroque
period and was used in a great variety of compositions. In many cases it occurs against a pyramid
background, as for William Harvey and wife
(erected 1758) at Hempstead (Essex), where the
medallions are draped, and the 4th earl of Gainsborough (dated 1790) at Exton (Rutland) (*108*),
where a total of three medallions are being tied on to
the pyramid by a flying cherub. Alternatively, it is
held by a female figure or by putti, or by both, and
not infrequently draped. A very characteristic
monument of the first half of the eighteenth century
is that of Charles Sergison (d. 1732) at Cuckfield
(Sussex) (*109*), which combines in an instructive
manner many of the standard features of the age: in
front of a two-dimensional pyramid without architecture, a classical female sits upon a sarcophagus
and, with the assistance of a putto, holds an oval
relief medallion of the deceased. It is by Thomas
Adye, whose other major monument, that of
William Mitchell (d. 1745) at Fowlmere (Cambs),
displays a similar though not identical scheme.
Again, relief medallions, commemorating wives or
other relatives, may be held or contemplated by
effigies of the principal deceased, as in the cases of
Lord Justice Raymond at Abbots Langley (Herts)
and the 2nd and 3rd dukes of Beaufort at Great
Badminton (Glos), or medallions of the deceased
may be carved on urns, as at Great Stanmore
(Middx) for John Dalton and at Withyham (Sussex)
for the 3rd duke of Dorset (dated 1802). In yet other
cases medallions were employed in combination
with busts, especially when several members of the
family were depicted, as on the large and splendid

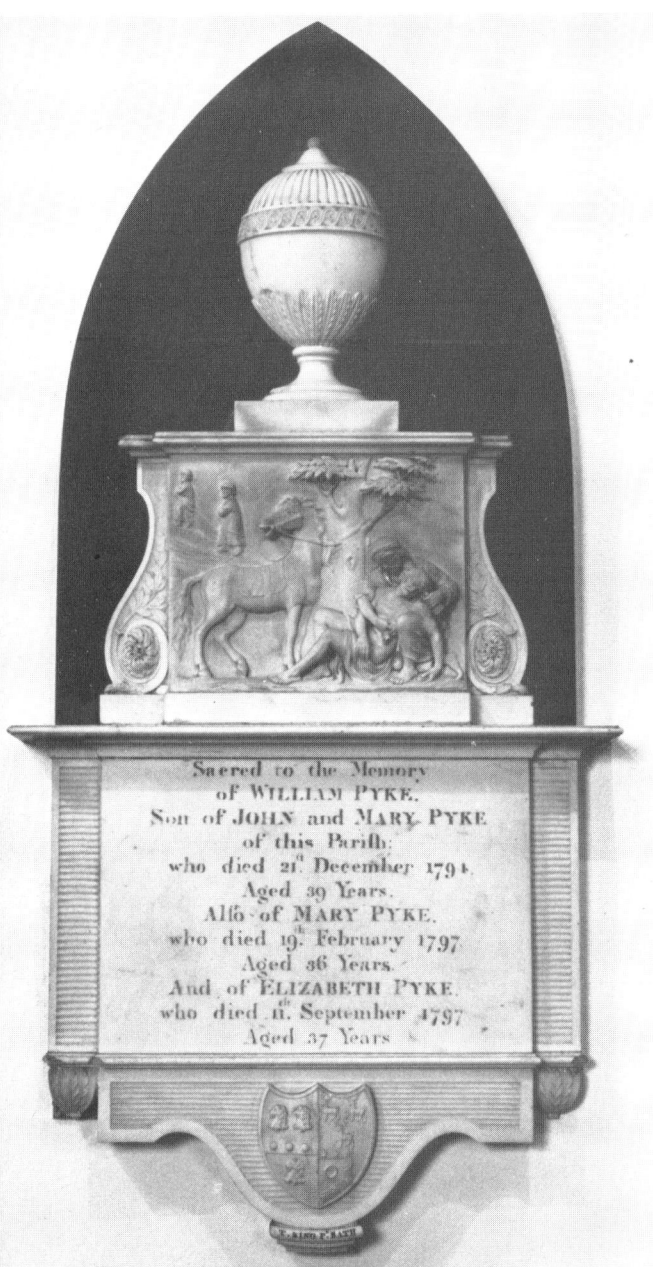

107 Great Somerford (Wilts): William Pyke (d. 1794). By
Thomas King of Bath. Relief of the Good Samaritan

108 Exton (Rutland): Baptist Noel, 4th earl of
Gainsborough. By Joseph Nollekens (1790)

109 Cuckfield (Sussex): Charles Sergison (d.1732). By
Thomas Adye

110 Fifehead Magdalen (Dorset): Sir Richard Newman
(d.1721) and family

hanging monument of Sir Richard Newman
(d.1721) at Fifehead Magdalen (Dorset) (*110*),
which has busts of Sir Richard and his two wives set
against a pyramid, and relief medallions of three
daughters below.

The pedestal bust itself enjoyed a popularity
equal to that of the relief medallion. Either singly or
in family groups, and either on standing monuments
or hanging monuments, busts are found in a
correspondingly varied range of schemes and locations. Not surprisingly, however, its most
frequent occurrence is in association with a pyramid. For example, a single bust will commonly be
set in front of a pyramid, as on the hanging
monuments of William Wither (d.1733) at Wootton
St Lawrence (Hants) and David Polhill (d.1754) at
Otford (Kent), or a pair of busts may be placed on
either side of a central pyramid, as on the standing
monument of Sir Alexander and Lady Denton
(d.1733) at Hillesden (Bucks). But busts may be met
in such other settings as a pedimented rectangular
frame, good examples being provided by an impressive series of hanging monuments to members
of the Halsey family at Great Gaddesden (Herts),
beginning with Thomas Halsey (d.1715); or a
circular recess, as in the cases of Matthew Prior
(dated 1723) in Westminster Abbey and Henry
Medley (d.1747) in York Minster; or displayed in a
variety of combinations with urns, putti and the
like. On occasions, too, busts appear with full
effigies: at Pusey (Berks), for instance, the monument of Jane Pusey (d.1742) depicts her seated
beneath a bust of her husband in an oval recess,
while in St Helen's, Abingdon, in the same county,
that of Mrs Hawkins (dated 1782) shows the
deceased as a seated figure leaning on a relief
medallion of her fiancé and surrounded by four
busts representing members of her family.
Moreover, in the eighteenth century busts were
treated in a more classical manner. The influence of
the antique led not only to the loss of Baroque
animation (though the turn of the head survived),
but especially to the portrayal of persons not as
contemporaries in wigs and fashionable clothes, but
as Roman men and women in loose-fitting classical
dress and Roman hair-styles – short, curly hair for
men, neat tresses and veils for women. Among
many examples, this can be seen to good effect at
Blockley (Glos), where, from the hanging monument to members of the Rushout family (*c.*1775), a
total of five dignified Roman busts, two men and
three women, gaze calmly and timelessly into a

far distance.

For full effigies of the deceased all postures were
employed, but without doubt the semi-reclining
attitude was the most widespread and characteristic.
Although semi-reclining figures had grown steadily
in appeal since the early seventeenth century, there
is little doubt that the particular use of the posture in
the Augustan Age, namely, for effigies in antique
dress on a sarcophagus, resulted from a renewed
and conscious desire to be classical. In its numerous
variations the type derived ultimately from the form
of ancient Etruscan sarcophagi, which survived
(and survive) in some numbers and, being discovered not far from Rome, were believed to be a
classical form worthy of imitation. These showed a
man or married couple semi-reclining on the lid of a
sarcophagus, usually with head and shoulders raised
and without hand gestures. In England the posture
was treated in resourcefully different ways. It might
be employed for single figures, as in the cases of the
1st earl of Uxbridge (d.1743) at Hillingdon (Middx)
and Col. Thomas Moore (d.1735) at Great Bookham (Surrey); or for the deceased alongside a seated
wife, as for John Sheffield duke of Buckingham
(*c.*1721) in Westminster Abbey; or for the deceased
in a family group (the other members being seated
or standing), as in the case of the 1st Lord Foley
(before 1743) at Great Witley (Worcs) (*99*). In some
instances the attitude was adopted for husband and
wife together, one behind the other in the manner of
some Etruscan models, this being so, for example,
on the monuments of Sir Francis Page (*c.*1730) at
Steeple Aston (Oxon) and the 1st earl of Shelburne
(dated 1754) at High Wycombe (Bucks) (*98*). At
Kelham (Notts) the monument of the 2nd Lord
Lexington (d.1723) and his wife consists of a free-
standing tomb-chest (remarkable in itself at this
date) with the two semi-reclining effigies exceptionally back-to-back. Furthermore, the posture itself
was capable of much variety – in addition to the
commoner poses, the effigy might be made to look
back over its shoulder to a wife or allegorical figure,
as in the case of Lord Justice Raymond at Abbots
Langley (Herts), or to look upward to some celestial
vision, as in the cases of John Holles duke of
Newcastle (erected 1723) in Westminster Abbey
and Bishop Richard Willis (d.1734) in Winchester
cathedral. Around the middle of the eighteenth
century the posture was adapted to the theme of a
dying hero, an early instance being the monument
of John duke of Argyll (completed 1749) in Westminster Abbey, where the duke appears to collapse

against a figure of Fame (*100*). The pictorial and allegorical content of this piece is, of course, far removed from Etruscan sources and much overlaid by other influences, yet the position of the duke's body is fundamentally semi-reclining. A little later came the depiction of the deceased in the last moments before death, not as a hero but as an ordinary person dying in the arms of a ministering woman, sometimes his wife. A fine instance at Bramley (Hants) shows Bernard Brocas (d.1777) (*111*) as a nearly recumbent figure lying on a mattress, his body becoming limp as life ebbs away, his head and shoulders held up by a female figure who kneels behind his head and looks tenderly into his face, meeting the already glazed look in his eyes. Finally, at the end of the century the attitude began to be used, by extension of this idea, for effigies lying on their death-beds, either awaiting the final call or roused to heavenly bliss by an attendant woman, a good example of which is to be seen on John Bacon's monument of Samuel Whitbread (d.1796) at Cardington (Beds). In many variations this last idiom was to be deployed widely on monuments of the first half of the nineteenth century.

Standing effigies of the deceased remained frequent in this period, but the posture was less common than the semi-reclining and more often employed for additional members of the family or for attendant allegorical figures. Like other forms, the standing posture was featured normally on large wall monuments, with or without an 'architectural' frame, and typically placed in front of a pyramid backplate. Equally, except for lawyers and high ecclesiastics, who were shown in appropriate robes or vestments, such figures were commonly clothed in antique or quasi-antique dress or armour, the latter being resorted to especially for members of the aristocracy who had held senior military or naval rank. Standing effigies were on the whole less ostentatious and, with notable exceptions, to a degree less animated than in the Baroque era, one pose in particular emphasizing restful contemplation rather than stylish display. This was introduced by Giovanni Guelfi (an Italian brought to England by Lord Burlington) and first used by him in 1727 for the monument of James Craggs in Westminster Abbey. Though now mutilated by the loss of its pyramid background, this piece constitutes an important landmark in eighteenth-century monumental sculpture, for the pose of the effigy established a fashion which persisted in

various interpretations throughout the century. The deceased, in loose pseudo-classical garb, stands with legs crossed, his left arm leaning against an urn and supporting his head, his right arm placed akimbo. In some respects the pose resembles a fashion of the first half of the seventeenth century, notably in the way the head is supported, but the treatment is now in a classical rather than naturalistic idiom. The same attitude is adopted by the effigy of the 2nd duke of Ancaster (d.1742) at Edenham (Lincs) (*112*), who leans in antique armour against an urn above a medallion of his wife; and by that of Charles Polhill (d.1755) at Otford (Kent), who, wearing a toga, stands upon a sarcophagus and leans on an urn. Other such effigies, while assuming the same pose in essentials, do not copy it exactly. That of Sir John Dutton (dated 1749) at Sherborne (Glos), for instance, is very similar, save that his head is not supported by his arm, and slightly further removed is that of William Lord Maynard (dated 1746) at Little Easton (Essex), who neither supports his head nor crosses his legs. Again, Vernon Bowater (d.1735) at Hanbury (Worcs) reads from a book held in one hand, as he leans upon the urn. Apart from several other examples in classical attire, the pose was occasionally used for effigies in contemporary dress, particularly in the late eighteenth century. Two fine instances occur at Ossington (Notts), both by Joseph Nollekens, namely, the monuments of William Denison (d.1782) and Robert Denison (d.1783), the latter in particular being, despite the up-to-date clothes and lack of support for the head, clearly derived from the Craggs effigy at Westminster.

Otherwise, effigies stand on both feet without extra support – but almost never squarely or rigidly. A slight turn of the head and a gentle 'sway' of the body are typical, while the hands may be disposed in a variety of different ways, and one leg may be placed forward or may be slightly bent, as the body weight is taken mainly on the other. These characteristics are present, for example, on the monuments of Sir Samuel Ongley (d.1726) at Old Warden (Beds); Frances Dirdoe (d.1733) at Gillingham (Dorset), where the deceased is portrayed with two sisters who stand on either side and link arms with her; and the 4th duke of Beaufort (d.1756) at Great Badminton (Glos), who appears as a Roman senator in full oratorical flow. These effigies wear classical dress, but, especially in the earlier and later decades of the period, contemporary clothes are worn, as, for instance, on the monuments of Edmund

111 Bramley (Hants): Bernard Brocas (d. 1777)

113 *Below* Shute (Devon): Sir William Pole (d. 1741)

112 Edenham (Lincs): Peregrine Bertie, 2nd duke of
Ancaster (d. 1742)

Humphrey (d. 1727) at Rettendon (Essex), with four standing figures, Sir Nathan Wright and his son (c. 1728) at Gayhurst (Bucks), a splendid late version of the 'reredos-type' with two effigies, and Mrs Mary Ramsden (d. 1745) at Adlingfleet (Yorks), where she appears as a widow alone. The effigies of Robert Earl Ferrers, on a monument of 1775 at Ettington (Warks), and William Pitt 1st earl of Chatham (completed 1783) in Westminster Abbey are similarly in contemporary dress, but with a peer's robes over all, and, as an instance of official dress, there is the standing figure of John Turner, sergeant-at-law (d. 1688, monument c. 1740), at Kirkleatham (Yorks), who wears his proper legal gown and cap.

Very occasionally one encounters standing effigies, not on wall monuments, but on free-standing pedestals. This type of monument, though it had first appeared in England as far back as the 1620s, remained rare before the nineteenth century, when it was to enjoy considerable vogue both for standing and for seated figures. Among eighteenth-century examples, however, we have the impressive monument of Sir William Pole (d. 1741) which dominates the north chapel of the little church of Shute (Devon) (*113*). Upon a high rectangular pedestal with bulging volutes at its corners, he stands splendidly in clothes of the day, bewigged and holding a wand of office in allusion to his having served as Master of the Household to Queen Anne.

The sitting posture now became fairly widespread for the first time, though, as with the standing posture, more common for ancillary figures than for effigies of the deceased as such. It was employed very effectively by Francis Bird for the monument in Westminster Abbey of Dr John Grabe (d. 1711), who sits frontally on a sarcophagus, clothed in skilfully carved robes and holding a book in one hand, a quill in the other, with a lamp and more books beside him on the sarcophagus. Rather later, the monument of Bishop John Hough (by Roubiliac, 1746) in Worcester cathedral has the sitting posture in a dramatically asymmetrical composition characteristic of the sculptor's rococo style: the bishop, seated on a sarcophagus, looks up suddenly to the right, as though startled by a vision, while lower down on the left a standing figure of Religion lifts his robes to reveal a scene carved in relief on the front of the sarcophagus and, on the right, sits a small weeping putto holding a medallion portrait of the bishop's wife. A number of

monuments depict both husband and wife seated, often on either side of an urn in front of an architectural or pyramid background, including, for example, those of the 1st Lord Barnard (d. 1723) at Shipbourne (Kent), John Knight (d. 1733) at Gosfield (Essex) and the 1st Lord King (d. 1734) at Ockham (Surrey). A grand 'reredos-type' monument of c. 1740 at Hope-under-Dinmore (Herefs) has the effigies of the Earl and Countess Conyngsby seated, without urn, in front of fluted pilasters carrying an open segmental pediment, the countess holding on her lap her infant son, who died by choking on a cherry in 1708, a tragedy remembered by the cherry which the baby holds. In some cases, where two generations of deceased are commemorated, one effigy may stand while the other sits, as, for instance, on the monuments of the 2nd and 3rd dukes of Beaufort (dated 1754) at Great Badminton (Glos) and the 3rd and 4th dukes of Ancaster (c. 1779) at Edenham (Lincs). More frequently a seated effigy of the deceased's wife appears beside his semi-reclining effigy. Such a figure for Lady Newhaven (d. 1732) was added to the earlier monument of her husband (d. 1728) at Drayton Beauchamp (Bucks) (*114*), for instance, and several examples exist in which the combination was present from the start. Occasionally, too, the sitting posture was chosen to portray the dying moments of the person commemorated, a notable case being Joseph Wilton's daring monument of Gen. Wolfe (dated 1772) in Westminster Abbey where it is employed in a version of the dying-hero theme. Seated on a couch inside his tent, the victor of Quebec is depicted as an almost totally nude figure expiring in the arms of a soldier in uniform, who stands behind him supporting his sinking body and directing his eyes to a winged Victory flying down with a palm and laurel-wreath, as a second soldier looks on in grief. A further example is provided by Roubiliac's famous monument for Lady Elizabeth Nightingale (dated 1761), also at Westminster, to which, in view of its dramatic portrayal of Death, we shall return in a later chapter.

Compared with these standard postures, others were extremely infrequent. Despite much evidence of devotional and generalized religious feeling, eighteenth-century effigies were very seldom shown in a Christian attitude of prayer or in a specifically religious pose. This no doubt partially accounts for the extreme rarity of kneeling effigies of the deceased, for, apart from their unclassical form, they inevitably suggested prayer. Nevertheless, the kneeling posture did not disappear entirely and, though highly unfashionable, was even on occasions shown with the hands closed in prayer. A case in point is the monument of Anne Haydon (d. 1747) in St Laurence's, Reading (Berks), which, with its effigy kneeling at a prayer-desk under a triangular-pedimented canopy, is an exact eighteenth-century version of the standard Elizabethan and Jacobean type. Equally derivative in scheme, but wholly eighteenth-century and markedly rococo in treatment, is the beautiful high-relief group of Mrs Elizabeth Drake (d. 1757) and her children at Amersham (Bucks); the figures kneel in a line before a prayer-desk, but all are in classical dress and the children appear in delightfully observed variations of attitude reflecting the natural lack of concentration and innocence of childhood.

Recumbent effigies were even rarer, their eclipse being explained by the fact that, while having little antique authority, they were also incapable of the variety of treatment demanded in this period. An exceptional instance occurs on the family monument of Mr Justice Dormer (*c*.1730) at Quainton (Bucks), which incorporates *inter alia* the recumbent life-size effigy of his dead son, but otherwise the posture is virtually unknown until the late eighteenth century. Then it begins to re-emerge, as, for example, at Milton Abbas (Dorset), where the effigy of Lady Milton (d. 1775) appears recumbent beside her semi-reclining husband, who turns to gaze upon her. In the nineteenth century both kneeling and recumbent effigies were to come once more into their own.

Effigies in Family and other Groups

As will have become clear, a common feature of eighteenth-century monuments was the inclusion of two or more effigies in different postures. Especially typical was the depiction in this way of, say, a husband with his wife and perhaps other members of his family, all in classical attire. A favourite type of composition comprised a semi-reclining husband beside a seated wife, such as occurs, for instance, at Stapleford (Leics) on the monument of the 1st earl of Harborough (d. 1732), where the scheme is further elaborated by placing the couple's nude child on Lady Harborough's lap. The 1st Lord Foley's huge monument (before 1743) at Great Witley (Worcs) (*99*) has at its heart a basically similar group, although the child is clothed and the central figures are surrounded on either side and higher up

the monument by the standing effigies of four other members of the family, one leaning on an urn in the pose of the Craggs effigy at Westminster. But the most striking example of a classical family monument is Peter Scheemaker's great piece for the 1st earl of Shelburne (dated 1754) at High Wycombe (Bucks) (*98*), where the earl and his family, all in antique dress, present themselves in the full dignity of an ancient Roman family. In the centre are the deceased and wife semi-reclining on a sarcophagus in front of a draped pyramid, while on either side are placed groups of their children – a standing son and seated daughter-in-law with a child on her lap to the left, two daughters and a boy standing to the right. These flanking groups appear in front of paired columns which support the pedimented architectural frame over all. Its impressive, well-carved architecture and the noble grouping of its effigies combine to make this one of the grandest, consciously classical monuments of the century. The effigies here, as on the Foley monument at Great Witley, range between the semi-reclining, seated and standing postures, the three most frequently encountered in the eighteenth century, but less common postures in more unusual combinations were sometimes employed. For example, the already mentioned monument of Mr Justice Dormer at Quainton (Bucks), very difficult to appreciate now in its cramped position under the tower, to which it was moved in the nineteenth century, comprises three effigies in the standing, kneeling and recumbent attitudes – a dead son is depicted recumbent in the centre, flanked on the left by the standing figure of his father and on the right by the kneeling figure of his mother in tearful grief.

Sometimes, on the other hand, effigies were displayed not in family groups, but in boldly allegorical compositions. Allegory was seldom far removed from eighteenth-century monuments, but in some cases it was made strikingly central and explicit, particularly in the latter half of the century. In one form it can be seen on Roubiliac's celebrated monument for Gen. William Hargrave (dated 1757) in Westminster Abbey, showing the deceased dramatically rising from the dead amid a welter of allegorical carving. This example belongs in the tradition of resurrection monuments and will be discussed more fully in a later chapter. Allegory in a different, less dramatic, form occurs on the same sculptor's monument to the 2nd duke of Montagu (completed 1752) at Warkton (Northants). Here the deceased is represented by a medallion portrait

114 Drayton Beauchamp (Bucks): Lady
Newhaven (d.1732), part of the
monument to her husband, William
Viscount Newhaven (d.1728). By
William Woodman

115 Warkton (Northants): Mary, 3rd
duchess of Montagu (d.1775). By
Robert Adam and Peter Matthias
Vangelder

which is being hung up by a cherubic boy and a standing figure of Charity, the latter with a child in her arms and a third child beside her extinguishing a torch, while on a lower level the widowed duchess stands and leans forward in mourning. More spectacular, but curiously less touching, is the very theatrical monument of Mary 3rd duchess of Montagu (d.1775), also at Warkton (*115*), designed by Robert Adam and sculpted by Peter Matthias Vangelder. It resembles a stage-set on which an allegorical scene is enacted. On a platform in an arched and semi-domed recess, the seated duchess expires against an urn on a pedestal; on the right the standing figure of an elderly veiled woman reaches out to take from her lap a young child (perhaps in allusion to the fact that her only son predeceased her), while in front of her another child points in grief to her earthly coronet on the floor and to the left a large standing angel leans forward, endeavouring by flamboyant gestures to re-assure the dying duchess of a heavenly crown. This is clearly not a portrayal of the lady's actual death, but a symbolic representation of her passage from earthly life to celestial bliss. Again, on the unique monument of Sir Thomas and Lady Salusbury (made by Nollekens in 1777) at Offley (Herts) their two standing effigies in stylized grave-clothes are shown meeting in front of a draped oak-tree and, as it were, renewing after death the troth they had pledged in life. In all these monuments we see, not a family or allegorical group posed or at rest, but an allegorical action frozen at its most poignant moment. Such monuments were not common, but were clearly related to those which depicted scenes of death or the salvation of the souls of the deceased, types which, as we have seen, were becoming increasingly fashionable in the later eighteenth century.

Equally uncommon, and not appearing before the late eighteenth century, were monuments with effigies of the deceased portrayed in the rôles for which they had been chiefly famous in life. Among the best known is that of Thomas Guy (d.1724) in the chapel of Guy's Hospital, Southwark (London), which he founded. The governors of the hospital decided on the erection of a monument in the chapel in the 1770s and awarded the commission to John Bacon, who completed the work in 1779. It is a fine piece, conveying its message in direct and unmannered simplicity. Standing against an arched relief of his hospital, the philanthropist is shown lending a hand to help up a sick man whom he invites to enter the hospital, the sick man representing the many whose fate his benevolence had alleviated. Another example is the dramatic monument of David Garrick (dated 1797) in Westminster Abbey, where the celebrated actor throws back curtains to reveal himself between the seated muses of Tragedy and Comedy. The idea behind such portrayals as these had clear affinities with the older and more widespread practice of incorporating into monuments relief panels of important events or aspects of a person's life.

Wall Tablets in the Eighteenth Century

Despite the undoubted importance of grand monuments with effigies and figured compositions of various kinds, they were by no means the most numerous of eighteenth-century memorials. Far more common were hanging wall monuments, especially wall tablets without portrayal of the deceased in any form. Granted that many hanging monuments displayed busts or medallions of the deceased (and on occasions effigies), and that many others included prominent allegorical figures, cherubs, sarcophagi or urns, nevertheless a greater number consisted merely of an inscription in an ornamental setting or frame. Their only other standard and almost invariable feature was a painted and gilded heraldic cartouche or shield, set usually either at the top or bottom of the memorial. Few parish churches lack specimens of this type and many have quite a number, but most people pay no attention to them or even notice their existence; more is the pity, since, although some are admittedly the work of inexpert local craftsmen, many contain work of a high order. Furthermore, an analysis of the output of almost any major monumental sculptor of the period reveals that, while he might reserve his creative genius for the elaborate monuments of the great, he was not averse to producing less imposing, even minor, memorials for those of lower status or less pretentious aspirations. For the student of decorative enrichment the wall tablet is also on the whole more rewarding than the grand standing monument, for decoration was often richer and was allowed a freer rein less hampered by the need to conform to stylistic or allegorical criteria. It commonly included not only purely ornamental motifs like swags, ribbons and garlands of flowers, fruit and leaves, but other motifs which had originally a symbolic or allegorical significance, such as urns, burning lamps, cherubs and winged skulls, although repeated use was threatening to turn these into mere decorative clichés. Much play was made with marbles of different colours, very charming effects being achieved by placing features in white marble, such as groups of cherub-heads or garlands of flowers, against a coloured ground.

Several different types of basic design were in use, some being contemporary versions of those favoured in the previous century, others new. Firstly, there was the traditional form in which a rectangular inscription panel was enclosed in an 'architectural' frame resting on brackets (commonly of the curved type known as 'consoles') and surmounted by a pediment. The main distinguishing features of this type in the eighteenth century were a more 'accurate' rendering of classical elements in general and, in particular, a preference for the more purely classical straight-sided pediment over the segmental pediment. Memorials of this kind are common, especially in the first half of the period. A fine representative example can be seen at Wheatfield (Oxon) in Peter Scheemaker's monument of John Rudge (d.1739) (*116*), which has the inscription between unfluted Corinthian columns carrying a broken, straight-sided pediment, on which rest two cherubs and an urn, the carved enrichment being otherwise restrained and refined.

Secondly, there was the cartouche, consisting of an inscription of varying (but often basically oval) shape set in an ornamental surround carved with much the same range of motifs as characterized the earlier Baroque period. A significant new element in designs of this type was the introduction of rococo asymmetry, though it was far from being shared by all in the group. It shows itself most clearly in those cartouches whose left side does not exactly mirror the right and whose vertical axis is not straight but zigzags from right to left through the memorial. A splendid example is provided by the monument of Joseph Wade (d.1743) in St Mary Rotherhithe, Bermondsey (London), which is illustrated in Sir Nikolaus Pevsner's *London except the Cities of London and Westminster*. Its vertical axis makes no fewer than four changes of direction, and its decorative border, carved in rich rococo detail, includes a cherub's head prominent on the left, matched by a skull on the right but set lower down to enhance the sense of movement. This rhythm is accentuated by flourishes of rococo foliage and plume-like decoration which break out in alternate directions at certain points, and is further emphasized by the asymmetrical outlines of the inscription itself and of

the heraldic cartouche below.

A third group comprised memorials that were basically little more than plain inscription tablets. Invariably symmetrical in design, they lacked a frame or border in the full sense, though they might have rudimentary arched or pedimented tops and volutes, or 'wings', at the sides. Most were essentially rectangular in outline, but oval, circular, lozenge-shaped and other forms were also produced. Apart from the usual heraldic shield or cartouche, carved enrichment was generally kept to a minimum, often consisting simply of a cherub's head, winged skull, lamp, urn, swag or garland.

Related to these was a fourth type, more elaborate in design and very largely new in the eighteenth century. It comprised memorials which were essentially symmetrical in form, but widely diverse in shape and often enriched with rococo ornament. The inscription, though the most conspicuous feature, was frequently placed between a decorative panel (or 'apron') below and a plate of varying outline above, but in simpler versions the apron was omitted. The monument of Edward Cressett, bishop of Llandaff (d.1755), at Cound (Salop) (*117*) may serve to illustrate the kind of composition that resulted, although it cannot be taken as typical in its precise shape and detail. Shunning any attempt at classical correctness in form, it exploits the picturesque possibilities of contrasting differently coloured marbles and embellishes the result with tastefully executed rococo decoration. It is a piece of delicacy and elegant refinement. At its lower end is the apron of veined red marble edged in white, curved and partially angular in outline and bearing an exquisite group of three winged cherub-heads in white marble; next comes the inscription on an horizontally rectangular tablet of white marble edged in veined yellow, its sides curving outward as they descend; this in turn is surmounted by a red-marble plate, also edged in white, whose shape is that of a concave-sided and truncated pyramid, bearing on its face an heraldic cartouche and flanked by rococo foliage-sprays and objects alluding to the deceased's episcopal office (mitre, crozier, sacred books), all these details being in white marble; finally, on the top stands a small white-marble urn. In numerous other instances the design culminated in a simple two-dimensional pyramid of the standard eighteenth-century type. This might be quite plain or have simply an heraldic cartouche set upon it, but, as we have seen, it commonly served as a background for

In the Family - Vault, near this Place,
lie interred the Remains of

JOHN RUDGE *Esq.*

He went through several important Trusts,
with Prudence, Integrity, & Honor,
particularly that great Trust of Parliament,
having represented the Borough of EVESHAM,
in the County of Worcester,
for 36 Years.

He Married Susanna Daughter of John Letten
of London *Esq.* by whom he had five Children;
two of which survived him; 1763.
Edward who married Elizabeth, Eldest
Daughter of Mathew Howard of Hackney *Esq.*
And Susanna, married to the Honorable
S.r William Stanhope, Knight of the Bath,
second Son of Philip, Earl of Chesterfield.

He departed this Life March, 12. 1749
in the 72.d Year of his Age

Here also lies his abovementioned Son

EDWARD RUDGE *Esq.*

Who succeeded him in the Borough of Evesham,
And serv'd in several Parliaments
with equal Integrity and Worth;
Born Oct.r 22.d 1703. Died June. 6. 1763.

To the Memory of D.r EDWARD CRESSETT
Bishop of *LANDAFF*,
second Son of EDWARD CRESSETT *Esq.r*
who died Feb.ry 13. 1755. in the 58th Year of his Age.
He married first ALBINA the Youngest
Daughter of GRIFFITH RICE of *NEWTON*
in *CARMARTHENSHIRE Esq.r* by whom he
had no Issue.
He afterwards married FRANCES the
Eldest Daughter of THOMAS PELHAM *Esq.r*
of *LEWES* in *SUSSEX*,
by whom he had one Daughter
ELIZABETH who survives him,
to whom he bequeathed his whole Estate

116 *Left* Wheatfield (Oxon): John Rudge (d.1739). By Pet
Scheemakers

117 *Above* Cound (Salop): Edward Cressett, bishop of Lla▪
(d.1755). By Thomas F. Pritchard

a figured group or a large urn placed on a ledge above the inscription, in which cases the monuments concerned were clearly more than mere inscription tablets.

In the last quarter of the century one finds an attractive kind of wall tablet, often oval in shape and without a border, carved in neo-classical detail after the manner of Robert Adam (d.1792). Such Adamesque memorials are for the most part modest in size and reticent in ornament. Individuals vary considerably in detail, but a fairly characteristic example is the memorial of Robert Palmer (d.1787) at Hurst (Berks) (*118*). This consists of a severely plain oval in green marble (somewhat like a large smooth medallion), on which is set, in white and yellow marbles, a square inscription plate within a chaste border of refined Adamesque character surmounted by a draped Grecian urn.

Conclusion

In the previous pages an attempt has been made to indicate with examples the most important and most typical aspects of English funerary monuments in the eighteenth century. The numbers of monuments, however, are so huge and the variations in form and iconography so legion that the merest suggestion of the wealth of interest and aesthetic enjoyment that they afford has been possible. Not only have the origins of the Greek and Gothic revivals been reserved for the next chapter, but all manner of fascinating by-ways and individual peculiarities have perforce been omitted. One such, for example, is the endearing monument of Thomas Pindar (d.1722) in the church of St George-in-Colgate, Norwich, which has, where one would expect an effigy of the deceased, a semi-reclining cherub propping his elbow on a skull and holding an hourglass in his other hand! Inventiveness of this sort is almost boundless in this period, and it is to be hoped that readers will derive pleasure from discovering other examples of its richness for themselves.

118 Hurst (Berks): Robert Palmer (d.1787)

6 The Nineteenth Century

Church monuments of the nineteenth century displayed in the main the influence of two major stylistic movements in the arts, namely, the Greek and Gothic revivals. Both movements, the one drawing inspiration from classical Greece, the other from the Gothic middle ages, had their roots in the eighteenth century and both were in different ways reactions against the classical Baroque style associated especially with Rome. Though not entirely mutually exclusive, they inevitably pulled designers and craftsmen in different directions, so much so that commentators have spoken of a 'Battle between the Styles' in the nineteenth century, as each jostled the other for predominance. As far as funerary monuments were concerned, the Greek movement on the whole prevailed in the first half of the nineteenth century, and certainly in its first three decades, while the Gothic Revival predominated in the Victorian period. The division was far from clearcut, however, for much Gothic evidence is apparent in the early nineteenth century and certain aspects of the Greek revival persisted in the latter half of the century. Moreover, monuments produced in either idiom were throughout the period shot through with the spirit of nineteenth-century Romanticism, descending on occasions to sentimentalism, which was neither Greek nor Gothic.

The Greek Revival

The Greek revival was the most important and crucial aspect of the neo-classical movement which developed in the latter half of the eighteenth century. Stimulated by a belief in the primary authority of classical Greek art, and sustained by an increasing flow of descriptions and engravings of ancient Greek architecture and sculpture, neo-classicism rejected Rome and its Baroque and rococo derivatives in favour of Greece. Although neo-classicism was a European-wide movement, its particular growth in England was aided by the publication of such important works as Robert Wood's *Ruins of Palmyra* (1753), James Stuart's and Nicholas Revett's *Antiquities of Athens* (1762) and, in 1765, an English translation of Johann Winckelmann's seminal work, originally in German, entitled *Reflections on the Painting and Sculpture of the Greeks*. Hand in hand with this went a switch in the interest of collectors and connoisseurs to the sculpture and artefacts of ancient Greece, a process which culminated in the acquisition of the Elgin Marbles from the Parthenon in the early years of the nineteenth century, subsequently to be bought for the nation in 1816.

Greek influence, though far from all-pervading, made a deep impression on funerary monuments of the early decades of the nineteenth century. Its most obvious effect was the general disappearance of all but black and white marble for the construction of monuments. Colour in any form was conspicuously absent and even black marble was rarely used, save discreetly on borders and backgrounds. The great bulk of monumental output was in white marble, figures almost exclusively so.

In the field of monumental design, the most profound result of Greek influence was the widespread adoption of a characteristic 'stele' form, derived by imitation of ancient Greek memorial slabs set upright in the ground, known as 'stelai', which are still commonly to be seen in Greece and elsewhere in the eastern Mediterranean. It was basically rectangular in outline, topped in most cases by a triangular pediment of shallow pitch and frequently enriched by quadrant-like lobes, called 'acroteria', projecting upward at the ends of the pediment. In essentials it retained this distinctive shape in the nineteenth century, although it was adapted and modified in a myriad of individual ways, several examples opting for the alternative curved or scrolly top, and was employed particularly for hanging and standing wall monuments. Most typically, and again by imitation of antique

119 *Above left* Easton Neston
(Northants): George Fermor,
3rd earl of Pomfret (d. 1830). By
Edward Bailey

120 *Above* Berkswell (Warks):
Mrs Eardley Wilmot (d. 1818).
By Sir Richard Westmacott

121 *Far left* Badger (Salop):
Harriet Cheney (d. 1848). By
John Gibson

122 *Left* Wimpole (Cambs):
John Yorke (d. 1801). By Sir
Richard Westmacott

models, the front of the stele was carved with a figure or group of figures in relief, though many examples were carved with symbolic objects or merely with inscriptions.

Among countless instances in churches throughout the country, very good specimens are provided by the monuments of Bishop George Pelham of Lincoln (d. 1827) at Buckden (Hunts) and the 3rd earl of Pomfret (d. 1830) at Easton Neston (Northants) (*119*), both by Edward Bailey and both standing against a wall. The first is especially simple and austere, depicting a mourning female kneeling in high relief beneath a severely plain pediment without acroteria, while the latter, slightly richer, has a man seated in contemplation of an urn below a carved pediment adorned with ornamental acroteria. By contrast, the hanging monument of Mrs Eardley Wilmot (d. 1818) at Berkswell (Warks) (*120*) exhibits an ornate version which departs markedly from Greek models, having a pediment enriched with leaves and florid acroteria and a front carved with a relief of two embracing angels who look down on two butterflies. It is by Westmacott, who used a simpler version of the same design for the monument of Grace Bagge (d. 1834) at Stradsett (Norfolk). In several cases, such as, for example, the monument of John Yorke (d. 1801) at Wimpole (Cambs) (*122*), the stele is absolutely plain, without articulation of the pediment and acroteria on its face, and serves merely to define the shape of the background for the figures. On some larger-scale standing monuments the stele with relief carving forms part of a composite design, rising as a backplate behind a projecting base which may bear an effigy of the deceased in the round, this being so, for example, in the case of Georgina countess of Bradford (d. 1842) at Weston-under-Lizard (Staffs) (*154*) among others.

The general preference for the 'stele' shape resulted in the fairly general abandonment of the typical eighteenth-century pyramid outline. The latter managed to survive, however, on some nineteenth-century memorials, among them the standing monuments of Anthony Hamond (d. 1822) at West Acre (Norfolk) and Henrietta countess de Grey (d. 1848) at Flitton (Beds) and the hanging monument of Mrs Elizabeth Peel (d. 1865) at Avington (Hants). Nevertheless, even here Greek influence is apparent in the relief carvings of figures on the front of the pyramids.

Classical Greek architecture had much less of an impact, chiefly because monuments continued to be designed without architectural canopies and frames. Having fallen out of fashion in the mid-eighteenth century, canopies were not to be generally revived until the latter half of the nineteenth century, and then in Gothic forms. Consequently, with a few minor exceptions, one does not find impressive Grecian structures over either free-standing or wall monuments. On the other hand, Greek Doric columns and pediments were sometimes incorporated into the designs of wall tablets, including, for example, that of James Bernard (d. 1805) at Crowcombe (Somerset), with its attached Doric colonnettes, and were occasionally employed as surface enrichment in other locations. Similarly, carved decoration was generally in the Grecian neo-classical taste, and Greek influence in many cases determined the forms of such subsidiary items as couches and chairs on which effigies might be depicted as lying or sitting.

In the context of figure sculpture, the Greek revival played a major and highly significant role. The first half of the nineteenth century was supremely the age of relief carvings, many of them on a large scale, showing figures typically (but not exclusively) in profile or semi-profile. In their economy of line and evident concern to indicate the contours of the human body beneath its clothing, they reveal the deeply penetrating influence of classical Greek techniques and ideals, most readily apparent to Englishmen in the Elgin Marbles, which began to arrive here in 1802, though not available for inspection until 1806. However, English reliefs were often flatter and more economical even than these, largely owing to the fact that the arrival of genuine antique pieces in this country was preceded, during the growth of the neo-classical movement, by the dissemination of line engravings, whose two-dimensional character exercised a profound influence on those seeking to recapture the ancient style. Moreover, the powerful Romantic element in nineteenth-century neo-classicism in many cases imposed on relief figure sculpture a degree of sentiment that was not inherently Greek.

Figures in relief were frequently shown in Grecian or semi-Grecian dress, especially where they represented persons other than the deceased. Very common in the early nineteenth century, to the point of being hackneyed and dull, was the depiction of Grecian women leaning in grief over urns, pillars or sarcophagi. On the hanging monument of Mary Sergison (d. 1804) at Cuckfield (Sussex), for example, the woman leans upon an urn, and on that of Sir William and Lady Pitt (d.1819) at Heckfield (Hants) two women lie in mourning across antique sarcophagi. Equally widespread, and persisting far into the Victorian era, was the portrayal of angels in classical dress and sometimes lacking wings. These might be shown without representations of the deceased, engaged in some symbolic act, such as the dropping of flowers on to a sarcophagus or draped urn, which appears, for instance, on the monuments of members of the Denys family (*c*1835) at Easton Neston (Northants) and members of the Gostling family (dated 1857) at Egham (Surrey).

More frequently, however, angels were depicted with the deceased, carrying or conducting them up to Heaven in the form of souls clad in loose night-clothes of a vaguely classical appearance. This theme, symbolic of redemption, will be discussed in more detail in the following chapter. Related to it were other popular scenes involving angels. One was the deathbed scene with attendant angels, used, for example, on the monument of George Crabbe, the poet (d.1832), at Trowbridge (Wilts), where a group of angels hovers in waiting above his recumbent figure lying on a Grecian couch. Another was the equally symbolic portrayal of death itself, in which angels received the deceased in their earthly contexts at the point of death. A superbly Grecian example occurs on the monument of Ellen Legh (d.1831) at Winwick (Lancs), where an angel leads her away, leaving her bereft husband holding their baby child, while on that of Harriet Cheney (d.1848) at Badger (Salop) (*121*) an angel takes the lady by the hand as she sits in a chair reading.

In other cases relief carvings represented the deceased's mourning relatives, these being also often shown in Grecian or semi-Grecian dress. Excellent examples can be seen on the monuments of John Yorke (d.1801) at Wimpole (Cambs), by Westmacott (*122*), and William Selwyn (d.1817) at Chislehurst (Kent), by Chantrey. Both show the deceased's children, in the first case mourning over an urn with a butterfly, in the second grieving beside a stele carved in low relief upon the memorial.

Less commonly reliefs portrayed the deceased in the full vigour of life and in their normal clothes. At Badger (Salop), for example, the monument of Isaac Browne (d.1818) shows him seated in a chair and reading from a book, and in several instances the deceased were portrayed either engaged in their calling or accompanied by symbolic features.

Thus, the well-known and highly successful monument by Flaxman for Joseph Warton, headmaster of Winchester College (d.1800), in Winchester cathedral depicts him seated in his robes, instructing four very attentive-looking boys who stand before him, while at Whitchurch (Bucks) the hanging stele monument of John Westcar (d.1835) (*123*) has a relief of the deceased standing with a group of farm animals, alluding to his agricultural enterprise.

Greek influence is also apparent in figure sculpture in the round, though here chiefly for allegorical figures, angels and the like, rather than for effigies of the deceased. A number of early nineteenth-century monuments of naval and military heroes in St Paul's cathedral include Grecian allegorical figures, but among the most striking examples of the type is the standing personification of Religion which appears on the monument of Sophia Lady Brownlow (d.1814) at Belton (Lincs) (*124*), pointing to Heaven with one hand and draping a medallion portrait of the deceased on a column with the other. This monument was made by the Roman sculptor, Antonio Canova, whose work was much admired and influential in England at that time, even though he produced few monuments for English patrons. Among other examples outside London are the standing figure of Faith with a cross on Westmacott's monument for William Burgh (d.1808) in York Minster and, in more Romantic vein, a similar figure who has put her cross aside to console a mourning woman on the monument of Lady Ellen Astley (d.1848) at Jacobstowe (Devon).

Effigies of the deceased in the round were, on the other hand, less dominated by Greek considerations and imbued rather with what has been aptly called 'Romantic naturalism'. It is true that some monuments, like that of Captain Richard Burgess (dated 1802) in St Paul's cathedral, portrayed the deceased as a pseudo-Greek figure, in this case a virtually nude hero, but this was not typical. For the most part effigies were true-to-life portraits which depicted the deceased in a variety of natural attitudes and dressed in their normal or appropriate clothes. At the same time the portrayals might be idealised and often charged with Romantic feeling and sentiment aimed at moving the viewer and, in the finest examples, revealing the spiritual and intellectual qualities of the deceased. Gone, however, were the affected poses and Roman dress or armour which had characterized much eighteenth-century funerary sculpture and which had already, in the last quarter of the century, given way to the more

123 Whitchurch (Bucks): John Westcar (d. 1835). By John
Gibson

124 Belton (Lincs): Sophia Lady Brownlow (d. 1814). By
Antonio Canova

125 Great Tew (Oxon): Mrs Mary Boulton (d. 1829). By Sir Francis Chantrey

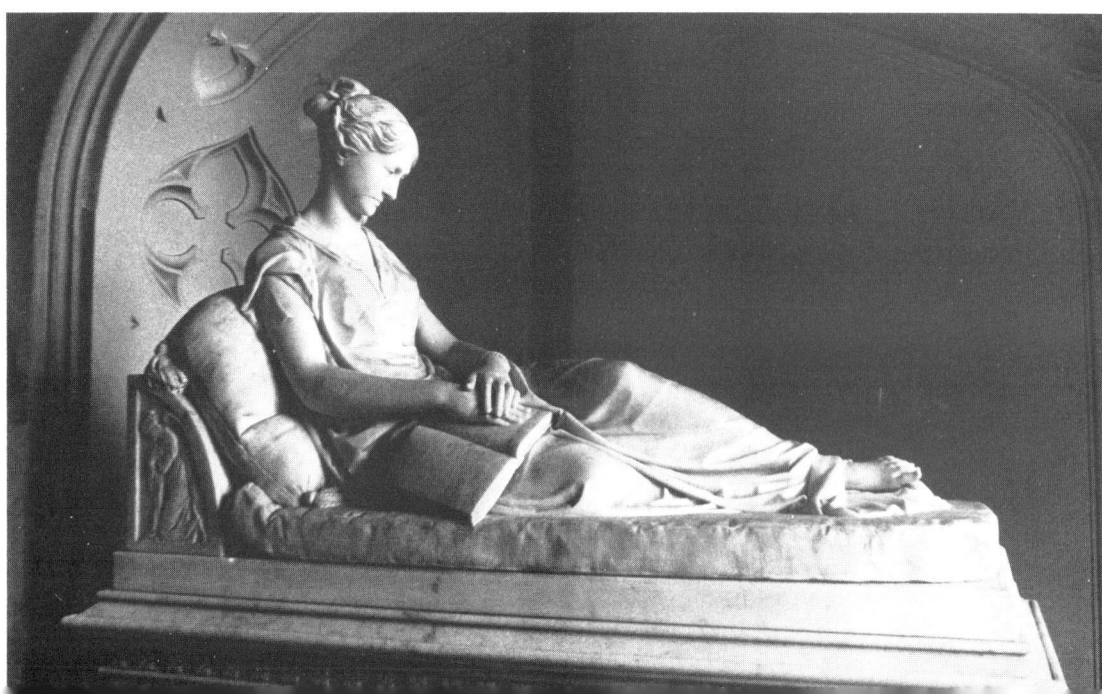

natural treatment.

The postures adopted by effigies in the first half of the nineteenth century covered the entire range from the recumbent to the standing. The most notable aspect was the revival of attitudes which had long been out of fashion, especially the fully recumbent attitude which, after nearly a century's neglect, had begun again to be employed at the end of the eighteenth century. Now it was chosen in particular to portray the deceased asleep in death. As a consequence, the figure was often shown in a relaxed state, lying on a mattress and dressed or wrapped in loose night-clothes with its head resting at an angle on the pillows and its hands placed at ease on or beside the body. Good examples are provided by the effigies of Gen. Christopher Jeaffreson (d. 1824) at Dullingham (Cambs) and Charles Mann, Viscount Brome (d. 1835), at Linton (Kent), the latter's mattress being placed upon a Grecian couch. On occasions, the effigy was half or wholly turned on its side, as in the case of Lady Frederica Stanhope, who died in childbed in 1823, at Chevening (Kent). In this deeply moving work by Chantrey the attitude was especially chosen in order to show the lady suckling her child lying beside her, even though she was not able to perform that rôle in life. Another fine effigy half-turned on its side is that of the 3rd earl of Hardwicke (d. 1834) at Wimpole (Cambs), dressed, however, in Garter robes and with its legs crossed. In two famous instances the posture was employed for monuments of children, namely, those of Penelope Boothby (d. 1791) at Ashbourne (Derbs) and the two Robinson daughters (completed 1817), known as 'The Sleeping Children', in Lichfield cathedral, both pieces being beautifully carved and full of pathos.

The semi-reclining and sitting-up postures similarly implied associations of death, the deceased being depicted on a mattress upon a Grecian couch and, as it were, patiently awaiting the final call. Sir Francis Chantrey was a notable exponent of this form, among his several interpretations being the superbly dignified portrayals of the 2nd marquess of Hertford (d. 1822) at Alcester (Warks) and Mrs Mary Boulton (d. 1829) at Great Tew (Oxon) (*125*), both of whom are caught in a moment of contemplation induced by the book they have been reading. More rarely, and in a manner that was untypical of the age, semi-reclining effigies were charged with suspense or movement, as though suddenly disturbed by some divine or spiritual vision. A notable case is the figure of Mrs Sophia Thompson (d. 1836)

in Great Malvern priory (Worcs), a work of Peter Hollins which is curiously reminiscent of the dramatic portrayals of the Baroque and rococo periods, for the lady appears to start up from her couch in response to the unseen call.

Such scenes were sometimes enlarged to include other figures attending the deathbed of the deceased. In some compositions these were angels receiving the deceased at death or watching over the deathbed, but in others members of the family. Among the most elaborate and effective of the latter is Chantrey's great monument for David Pike Watts (completed 1829) at Ilam (Staffs), which depicts the man semi-reclining on a couch from which he leans forward to bless his kneeling daughter, who has come with her three young children to bid him farewell. It is a masterly and most moving group, carefully distinguishing in its modelling between the father's noble resignation, the daughter's sorrow and the bewilderment of the children, the smallest of whom is so overcome that he takes refuge against his mother's lap. In a sense, though in a quite different idiom, it expresses the ideal of family love and devotion which we have observed in other forms in earlier periods.

The kneeling posture experienced a revival similar to that of the recumbent, although it remained far more frequent for the depiction of mourning women and angels than for effigies of the deceased. For the latter, however, it was employed particularly after 1820 and chiefly at first on monuments of bishops, showing them in a religious attitude and in some cases with their hands closed in prayer. Particularly favoured by Chantrey, it appears on his monuments of Bishops Brownlow North (d. 1820) in Winchester cathedral and Shute Barrington (d. 1826) in Durham cathedral, the former wearing a wig and closing his hands in prayer, the latter bare-headed and placing one hand on his breast. These are both shown in profile against a plain background, but others by Chantrey either kneel frontally, as does Bishop Reginald Heber (dated 1835) in St Paul's cathedral, or can be viewed from all sides, like Bishop Henry Ryder (d. 1836) in Lichfield cathedral. Occasionally the kneeling posture was used for female and other male effigies.

Seated and standing effigies, common in the preceding period, remained in fashion. The characteristic form of seated effigies in the nineteenth century was heralded by Flaxman's monument of the 1st earl of Mansfield (completed 1801) in

Westminster Abbey, which shows the Lord Chief Justice, clad in full-bottomed wig and official robes, seated in a chair upon a high plinth. Despite the presence of large allegorical figures of Wisdom and Justice lower down, the essential and typically nineteenth-century aspect is the naturalism of the principal effigy. In the same manner the attitude was used for, among others, the portrayals of James Northcote (d. 1831) in Exeter cathedral, by Chantrey, and Bishop William Van Mildert (d. 1836) in Durham cathedral, by John Gibson. On a beautiful monument in Christchurch priory (Hants) Flaxman combined a seated effigy with other figures to produce a family group as moving as the Watts monument at Ilam. It is not, however, a deathbed scene, but an idealised picture of motherly care. It depicts Harriet Viscountess FitzHarris (d. 1815) seated on a chair and reading to her three children, the youngest of whom sits on her lap nestling against her breast, while two boys stand close in front of her listening intently. But without doubt the finest seated effigy, and arguably the finest effigy of any kind in the whole of the nineteenth century, is that of James Watt (d. 1819) at Handsworth, Birmingham (*126*). A masterpiece of Sir Francis Chantrey, it is a noble tribute by its creator to the great engineer's memory, and displays in full measure the qualities of Romantic naturalism imbued with moral integrity to which the best work of the period aspired. In a separate chapel specially added to the church to contain it, the monument shows him seated on a chair upon a high free-standing plinth. On his lap is spread the drawing of an engine and in his hand he holds a pair of dividers. Seen through the arch which gives access to the chapel, he appears as a figure alone and somewhat remote, captured in a moment of deep thought and concentration as, looking up from his work, he gazes forward absorbed in the contemplation of some engineering problem, his fine brow revealing the genius and mental power within. No more fitting tribute to a man of the heroic age of the Industrial Revolution could be imagined.

Standing effigies of the deceased in normal dress, mainly commemorating men, had been produced in increasing numbers in the late eighteenth century, but again it was in particular certain works by Flaxman which were to exert a strong influence in the nineteenth century. The most important was his monument in St Paul's cathedral for Horatio Lord Nelson (*127*), the fame of whose exploits and the heroism of whose death in the naval Battle of Trafalgar (1805) gave the piece a certain celebrity. Although the work retains much of the allegorical habit of the eighteenth century, incorporating a lion symbolising British strength and a figure of Britannia who brings two young boys to be instructed by the image of patriotic service and valour, the admiral's effigy itself is a strikingly naturalistic, if slightly idealised, portrait. Standing on a high plinth, he wears naval uniform with decorations and the sash of the Order of the Bath, his stance is easy, with one hand resting upon a rope and anchor beside him, and his finely modelled head is clearly a life-like portrait. Rather less successful is the same sculptor's somewhat similar scheme for Admiral Earl Howe (d. 1799), also in St Paul's and completed a few years before the Nelson monument. Other notable standing figures in contemporary dress, all for men, were produced by Westmacott, Chantrey and others, but the authorship of one of the most remarkable is obscure. It is that of Robert Goodden (d. 1828) at Over Compton (Dorset) (*128*), and deserves to be much better known than it is. Though rather stiff in treatment, it is not only a true and completely unidealised portrait of a man in old age, but is utterly faithful in the depiction of a rural gentleman's everyday clothes. Indeed, standing in his arched niche, slightly stooping and supported by a stick in one hand with the other resting on a tree-stump, he might easily have stepped straight from the pages of a contemporary Romantic novel.

Apart from effigies of the deceased, figure sculpture in the round was much concerned with the depiction of angels, and it was here that the Romantic, not to say sentimental, spirit reached its fullest expression. Portrayed in various symbolic acts or poses on an increasing number of monuments, angels took over in a general way the kinds of function served earlier by allegorical figures, the precise nature of their appearance reflecting nineteenth-century religious attitudes. In particular, they were often shown in the rôle of guardian angels, either on their own, kneeling or sitting in attitudes of prayer and devotion, or with figures of the deceased, watching over them or receiving them at death. So, for example, on the monument of Richard Jodrell (d. 1831) at Lewknor (Oxon) appear two sentimental angels holding floral wreaths, while that of Robert and George Holford (d. 1839) at Westonbirt (Glos) has two kneeling angels facing one another at prayer across an altar on which are placed a bible and cross. The monument of the 5th duke of Dorset (d. 1843) at Lowick (Northants)

126 *Above* Handsworth, Birmingham: James Watt (d.1819). By Sir Francis Chantrey

127 *Above* St Paul's Cathedral: Horatio Lord Nelson (d.1805). By John Flaxman

128 *Far left* Over Compton (Dorset): Robert Goodden (d.1828)

129 *Left* Northington (Hants): members of the Baring family. By Richard Westmacott the Younger (1848)

consists of a great tomb-chest draped at one end with the dead peer's robes, at the other end of which sits a large angel, resting one arm on the chest and holding an open book in the other hand. A particularly pleasing and effective composition was produced by Richard Westmacott the Younger for members of the Baring family (dated 1848) at Northington (Hants) (*129*). Here, above a door representing the entrance to a vault, are depicted two angels, one seated with head erect, holding an open book and a key (symbolic of the passage to heavenly bliss), the other kneeling with head bowed in watchful prayer, awaiting, as it were, the rising of the dead at the Last Day.

These examples lack representations of the deceased. By contrast, the monument of Lady Charlotte Egerton (d.1845) at Rostherne (Cheshire), also by the younger Westmacott, shows her lying on her side asleep, while an angel kneels alongside, bending forward with outstretched hand as though about to wake her to eternal life. Similar or related themes were portrayed throughout the Victorian period, a good example of a generation or so later being provided by the fine monument of the 8th marquess of Lothian (dated 1878) at Blickling (Norfolk), where his recumbent effigy lies upon a tomb-chest watched over by two large standing angels at head and foot. Moreover, by this time the progress of the Gothic Revival led to the reappearance of small angels supporting the pillows under the heads of recumbent effigies after the fashion of the middle ages, although the angels were now treated in a typically Victorian manner. Among numerous examples, an especially charming treatment of the idea can be seen on Frederick Thrupp's monument for Jane Baroness Coleridge (d.1879) at Ottery St Mary (Devon) (*130*), where the angels sit beside the pillow, and a late version on the more sumptuous monument of Robert Stayner Holford (d.1892) at Westonbirt (Glos), where they kneel behind it.

The Gothic Revival

These last examples have taken us far beyond the Neo-classical period and deep into that of the ascendancy of Gothic as the principal influence in the making of monuments. It is, of course, impossible to say precisely when the transition between the two stages occurred, since the process was inevitably gradual, but the balance had certainly swung in favour of Gothic by 1850 and Gothic remained the dominant style for the rest of the century. This is not to say, however, that all traces of Greek influence disappeared or that other stylistic influences did not play a part after 1850, for, as we shall see, Victorian monuments as a whole were characterized by a marked degree of eclecticism in form and style.

The Gothic Revival originated before the mideighteenth century, and it was soon after 1750 that its earliest manifestations began to appear on funerary monuments. Though inspired by a romantic interest in the middle ages, the earliest Gothic (often distinguished by the spelling 'Gothick') was a fanciful, highly decorative and distinctly 'unacademic' form, quite different in its effect from medieval work and likely to deceive no-one as to its real identity. Indeed, like Chinoiserie (which was never employed on monuments), it was at first a development in the rococo vein, as can clearly be seen on one of the earliest monuments to have Gothic details, that of Sir Whitmore and Lady Acton (d.1759) at Acton Round (Salop). This standing wall monument is of a typical eighteenth-century form, comprising a sarcophagus set in an architectural frame, but its details are an extraordinary pastiche of rococo and incipient Gothic. The aperture of the canopy is trefoiled and the side columns, despite their basically Corinthian capitals, are cylindrical shafts with rings, clearly imitated from thirteenth-century architecture. Furthermore, in addition to rococo garlands, burning lamps and other features, the frieze is made up of pseudo-Perpendicular lozenges with foliage surmounted by a line of tiny cinquefoiled Gothic arches.

The number of such pieces was small and, in the face of developing Neo-classicism, Gothic made little headway in funerary contexts for some decades. Nonetheless, the efforts of such prophets of the Gothic Revival in architecture and decoration as Horace Walpole led to the subtle inclusion of Gothick details on monuments which were otherwise un-Gothic. A very instructive case is the monument of Lord and Lady Milton (d.1775) at Milton Abbas (Dorset), where the two effigies, typically late eighteenth-century in character, lie upon a freestanding tomb-chest decorated with arched and gabled Gothick niches and shields set in Gothick cusped circles. At the same time, wall monuments with figured groups, late classical-Baroque or even Neo-classical in style, were beginning on occasions to be outlined with a pointed arch, similar in shape to those of the thirteenth and early fourteenth centuries. John Bacon in particular employed such an arch on, for example, his monuments of James Marwood (dated 1781) at Widworthy (Devon) and Samuel Whitbread (d. 1796) at Cardington (Beds).

In the early decades of the nineteenth century the inclusion of Gothic decorative features on more or less Neo-classical monuments became quite normal, though not used by all sculptors, and serves to warn against any notion that Greek and Gothic elements were felt to be necessarily incompatible or mutually exclusive. By now the fanciful imaginings of Strawberry Hill Gothick had given way to forms deriving more directly from the Perpendicular Gothic of the late middle ages. Applied decoration of this kind is commonly found on tomb-chests, pedestals and bases supporting figures in a Grecian or naturalistic manner, including, for instance, the monuments of Sophia Lady Brownlow (d. 1814) at Belton (Lincs) and James Watt (d. 1819) at Handsworth, Birmingham. Likewise, the semi-recumbent effigy of Mrs Mary Boulton (d. 1829) at Great Tew (Oxon) appears on a Grecian couch-top set upon a tomb-chest enriched with Perpendicular panels, the whole being placed, moreover, in a Perpendicular arched and panelled recess.

As yet, however, apart from the resurgence of the free-standing tomb-chest and the new popularity of the recumbent effigy, monuments were in general wholly un-Gothic in design and certainly in feeling. Nevertheless, even in this respect a remarkably antiquarian experiment was tried out for the monument of Lord George Harcourt (d. 1809) at Stanton Harcourt (Oxon), dated by Dr Penny to before 1826. This comprises a stiffly recumbent effigy placed on a pseudo-Perpendicular tomb-chest set in a corner and backed by Perpendicular panel-work rising to a crested and pinnacled frieze on the walls. To complete the effect the monument is painted and the effigy, though clad in nineteenth-century peer's robes, rests its feet in medieval fashion against an heraldic creature.

Interesting as this piece undoubtedly is as an indicator of trends, it was not only exceptional at so early a date but, more importantly, did not exactly herald the way in which the Gothic Revival was to develop on monuments. This was due far more to men like A. W. Pugin, who in the 1830s passionately advocated a better understanding of Gothic as the only worthwhile style of architecture, and to certain movements of liturgical reform in the Church, such as the Oxford Movement, whose revival of medieval rituals naturally favoured Gothic as the most suitable style for church building. As a result, a new enthusiasm for medieval Gothic was unleashed, especially for that of the thirteenth and fourteenth centuries. Its principles came to be studied more carefully than ever before, and its structural and decorative features were reproduced or imitated with a new degree of accuracy. This inevitably affected funerary monuments along with all other ecclesiastical items, and by about 1850 appreciable numbers of monuments were being produced in a more or less accurate Gothic idiom. The effect can clearly be seen on the monument of Christina Medley (d. 1842) in St Thomas's, Exeter, where her effigy, recumbent and with the hands closed in prayer, lies upon a Gothic tomb-chest recessed under a Gothic canopy in the wall. Although the effigy is rather un-medieval in feeling, the total impression is unquestionably that of a medieval monument, the cusped decoration of the tomb-chest, with the ogee-arch and panel-work of the canopy, being convincing renderings of late fourteenth-century forms. With such pieces as this the more accurate, not to say academic, Gothic monument of the nineteenth century may be said to have arrived.

Aspects of Victorian Gothic Monuments

A number of features were especially typical of the output of Gothic monuments in the Victorian period. Very characteristic was the Gothic tomb-chest with recumbent effigy or effigies, considerable numbers of which were produced in the second half of the century and placed either against a wall or in a free-standing position. A good and fairly early example is provided by the monument of Archbishop Edward Vernon-Harcourt (dated 1855) in York Minster, with its enrichment of arcading in a tolerably accurate thirteenth-century style. Later versions tended, however, to be richer and more individual in their treatment of Gothic details, as can be seen, for example, in the case of Bishop Arthur Hervey (d. 1894) in Wells cathedral (*131*), where, although the constituent motifs can all be individually paralleled in the middle ages, the particular combination cannot. Other chests were still more original, like that, for instance, of Gen. Henry Crealock (d. 1891) at Littleham, near Bideford (Devon), which has a sequence of kneeling angels with shields interspersed by standing figures.

The re-appearance of canopies in the medieval tradition was another notable aspect of the period.

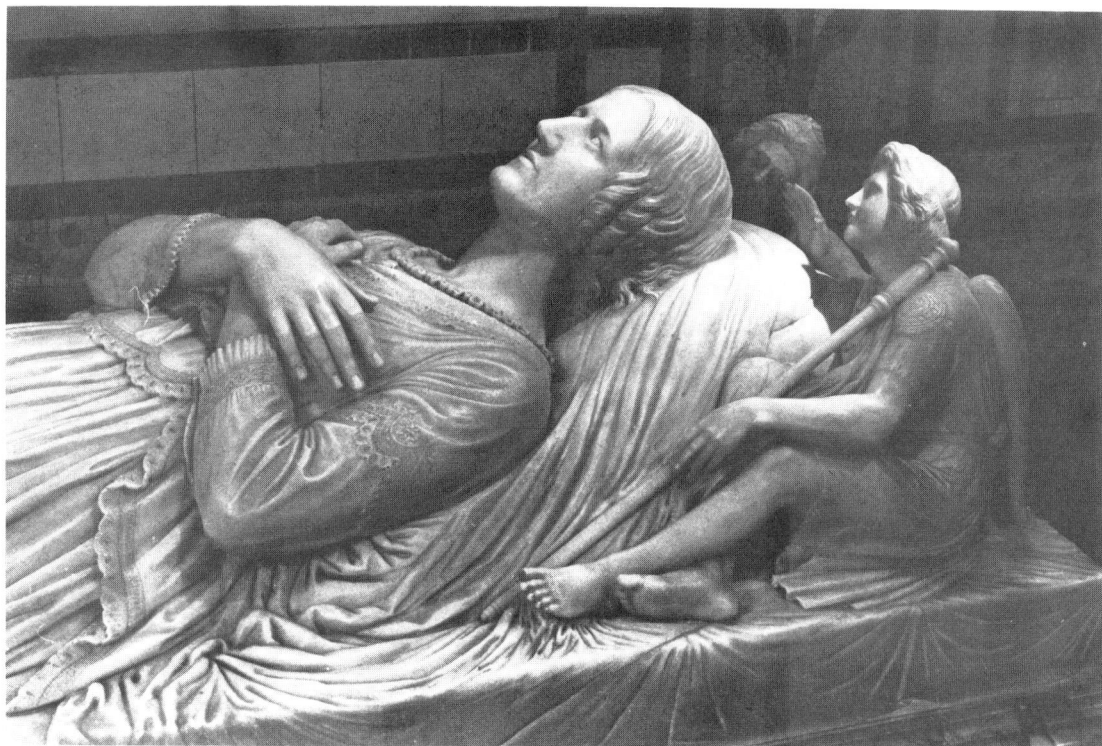

130 Ottery St Mary (Devon): Jane Baroness Coleridge (d. 1879). By Frederick Thrupp

131 Wells cathedral: Bishop Arthur Hervey (d. 1894). By Thomas Brock

132 Winchester cathedral: Bishop Samuel Wilberforce (d.1873). Designed by Sir George Gilbert Scott

133 Buckden (Hunts): Robert Whitworth (d.1831). By Thomas Rickman

134 Englefield (Berks): Richard Benyon (d.1854)

135 Grafton Underwood (Northants): Lady Anne FitzPatrick (d.1841). By Richard Westmacott the Younger

As in the middle ages, Gothic canopies might be placed over recessed wall monuments like the Medley monument at Exeter, later instances of which with varying designs include those of Charles Lefroy (d.1861) at Fleet (Hants), the 14th Viscount Dillon (d.1865) at Spelsbury (Oxon) and Robert Stayner Holford (d.1892) at Westonbirt (Glos). Equally, but appearing somewhat later, canopied monuments might be free-standing, on occasions reaching prodigious proportions, notably, for example, those of Bishop Samuel Wilberforce (d.1873) in Winchester cathedral (*132*), Bishop Christopher Wordsworth (d.1885) in Lincoln cathedral and Dean Augustus Duncombe (d.1880) in York Minster, the last probably inspired by the thirteenth-century monument of Archbishop Gray there.

It is significant, however, in several of these and other instances that the precise forms of the canopy and decorative enrichment were not slavish imitations of medieval work. Indeed, on occasions the zeal for Gothic led to imaginative compositions in which the nineteenth century seemed more medieval than the middle ages. A case in point is the Wilberforce monument at Winchester, where the canopy combines various Gothic features in a rich ensemble not found in the middle ages in England, and the slab with the effigy is borne upon the shoulders of kneeling angels, a device equally unknown. Moreover, the materials from which monuments were made, especially in the later nineteenth century, were not exclusively those employed in the middle ages. Although the typical medieval material of alabaster was brought back into use in the middle of the century, the painting of monuments was not generally revived and colour, when desired, was supplied by the incorporation of coloured marbles. The use of various stones and marbles produced on occasions rich effects, as can be appreciated, among others, on the sumptuous Gothic monument of Robert Holford at Westonbirt. Furthermore, while the earlier ascendancy of white marble was broken, it continued to be employed throughout the century, especially for effigies, even though it had no medieval sanction in this country. In the last quarter of the century bronze came again into fashion, but, unlike medieval monuments which had occasionally used bronze only for effigies and certain other details, monuments were now made wholly of that material.

The relatively free treatment of Gothic forms, combined with a concern for accuracy in detail,

manifested itself also in the application of Gothic to certain types of monument not found in the middle ages. Notably was this true of wall tablets in which the inscription was set in a Gothic frame. The transition from the Grecian to the Gothic taste in wall tablets is nicely illustrated at Sherborne St John (Hants), where there are two for, respectively, William Chute (d.1824) and Elizabeth, his widow (d.1842). Both were made by the London firm of H. Hopper, but, while the earlier takes the form of a draped stele, the latter has a Gothic frame comprising a crocketed and finialed gable over an arch between flanking pinnacled shafts. Countless examples on this simple pattern were produced, but not infrequently more elaborate Gothic tablets are encountered, an especially fine specimen being that of Robert Whitworth (d.1831) (*133*) at Buckden (Hunts) with its rich finials and complex tabernacles at the sides.

Other hanging wall monuments included figures and were equally un-medieval in type. At Blockley (Glos), for example, the monument of Ann Rushout (d.1849) is an interesting tripartite piece which displays the deceased kneeling in profile in a richly cusped Gothic niche, flanked by standing figures in smaller niches, the whole of the 'architecture' being a faithful reproduction of late thirteenth-century forms, with finely crocketed gables and pinnacled shafts. The monument of Richard Benyon (d.1854) at Englefield (Berks) (*134*) is another instructive case of accurate Gothic details, this time basically Early English, used in an unfamiliar context; its centre-piece is a relief of the Three Maries at the empty tomb with the risen Christ above, set under a trefoiled arch beneath a crocketed gable, which rests on shafts with rich stiff-leaf capitals.

In each of these examples, and in numerous others of similar type, the figures are carved in a style of relief which was not that of the middle ages but derived rather from the Grecian style of the early nineteenth century. Indeed, one of the most potent signs of artistic hybridisation in the Victorian period was the persistence of this relief technique on monuments which otherwise had little or no Grecian character, more especially on those which were fundamentally Gothic in conception. For example, the relief scene of Lady Anne FitzPatrick (d.1841) giving food to a poor family at Grendon Underwood (Northants) (*135*) is set in a semi-Gothic context, while many examples of sacred imagery on later, fully Gothic monuments were executed in relief, including that at Englefield and the risen Christ with angels on the monument of Viscount Dillon at Spelsbury.

On the other hand, effigies of the deceased in the round in the Victorian period were profoundly influenced by medieval Gothic precedents. Returning full-circle to the middle ages, the vast majority of effigies were once more depicted lying full-length on their backs. More particularly, although the early nineteenth-century habit of placing the hands in other than prayerful positions endured, as, for example, in the cases of Lady Cope at Eversley and Baroness Coleridge at Ottery St Mary, the medieval Gothic method of showing the hands closed in prayer was revived on a large scale. Among its earliest manifestations is the effigy of Christina Medley (d. 1842) in St Thomas's, Exeter, as we have seen, but after 1850 it rapidly established itself as the standard form, being expressive not only of the Victorian pursuit of medievalism but equally of High Church Victorian religious attitudes. Like many others, for example, Canon Hugh Pearson (d. 1883) at Sonning (Berks), clad in contemporary clergyman's vestments, adopts a pose identical to that of the later middle ages, with two diminutive angels kneeling at his head. Occasionally, however, Victorian originality modified the upward-pointing position of the hands. Bishop Hervey (d. 1894) in Wells cathedral, for instance, clasps his hands together in prayer across his breast (*131*), while, more unusually, the 14th Viscount Dillon (d. 1865) at Spelsbury (Oxon) clutches a Christian cross to his bosom. Again, on the monument of Charles Lefroy (d. 1861) at Fleet (Hants), while his wife closes her hands conventionally in prayer, he holds a model of a church to indicate, in a rare but genuine medieval tradition, that he had founded the church in which he lies (*137*). Moreover, in the last example, and also in many others, the feet of the effigies rest in medieval fashion against animals, but these are often, by a conceit typical of Victorian naturalism and sentiment, not heraldic beasts but domestic pets. Thus, Charles Lefroy and his wife have at their feet two accurately carved dogs of different breeds and, rather later, a similarly realistic dog lies at the feet of Denzil Fox-Strangways (d. 1901) at Melbury Sampford (Dorset).

Furthermore, apart from the re-appearance of the fully recumbent posture with the hands closed in prayer, the treatment of effigies was not in other respects notably medieval. In particular, there was no attempt to portray the deceased as medieval figures in the manner, say, in which the eighteenth century had shown men and women as ancient Romans. Although they might be displayed in Gothic environments, effigies retained by and large something of the Romantic naturalism that characterized the earlier nineteenth century, and were generally realistic portraits clothed in contemporary dress, which marked them out as unquestionably Victorian.

Indeed, dress of all kinds was frequently carved with a degree of meticulous detail reminiscent of the finest work of the seventeenth century and, while the range of clothing depicted was naturally more limited than that actually in use, many Victorian effigies provide interesting and valuable examples of contemporary fashion, especially in female dress. This is admirably illustrated, for instance, by the marvellously detailed costume worn by the effigy of Lady Marianne Cope (d. 1862) at Eversley (Hants) (*136*) and by the beautiful lace-work and ringlet hair-style on that of Jane Baroness Coleridge (d. 1879) at Ottery St Mary (Devon) (*130*). Equally instructive examples of male attire include the figure of Charles Lefroy at Fleet (Hants) (*137*), who appears in long drain-pipe trousers and great coat typical of the period, but more often men were depicted in ceremonial or military dress with the same attention to detail. A case in point is the superbly carved effigy of the 1st Earl Brownlow (d. 1853) at Belton (Lincs) (*138*), who wears the robes and coronet of an earl, subtly different from those of earlier periods and wonderfully evocative of the Victorian age. Another is the military figure of General Henry Crealock (d. 1891) at Littleham (Devon), 'a faithful servant of Her Majesty Queen Victoria', as the inscription relates, who lies in officer's uniform, wearing his medals and the badges of the Orders of the Bath and of St Michael and St George, all carefully detailed, with a soldier's great coat over all.

Despite the universal appeal of the recumbent posture, other postures continued occasionally to be employed, even though they enjoyed little or no medieval precedent. Moreover, most alternative postures were not suitable for the expression of Victorian religious feelings, a circumstance which undoubtedly explains the total disappearance of the semi-reclining attitude in its many variations after being in vogue for two and a half centuries. Standing effigies, too, were very rare after 1850, except in places like Westminster Abbey, where a number of memorial statues to statesmen were erected. From time to time seated effigies were produced, including, for example, that of Sir

136 Eversley (Hants): Lady Marianne Cope (d. 1862)

137 Fleet (Hants): Charles Lefroy (d. 1861) and wife

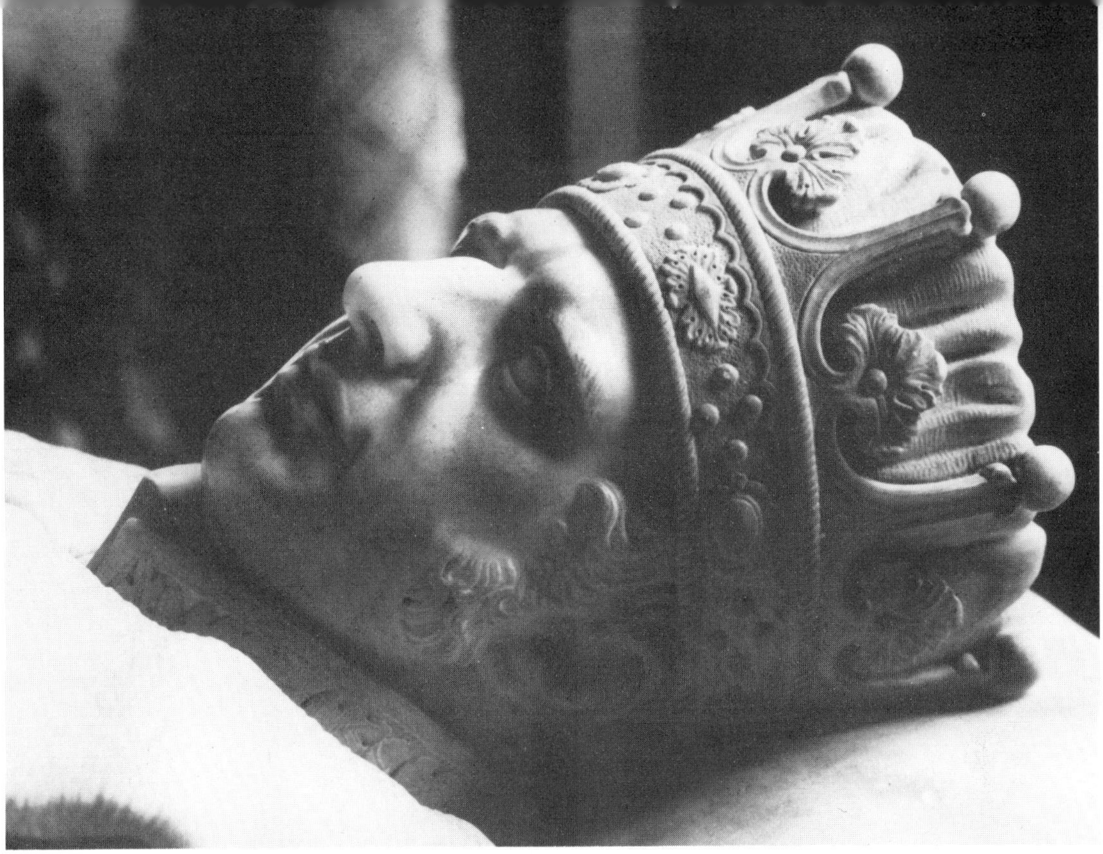

138 Belton (Lincs): John Cust, 1st Earl Brownlow (d.1853). Detail

139 Condover (Salop): Sir Thomas Cholmondeley (d.1864)

Hamilton Seymour (dated 1882) at Alcester (Warks), still much in the Chantrey tradition of the early nineteenth century, but the most frequent alternative to the recumbent posture was that of effigies kneeling at prayer. In a highly Romantic treatment it was used for the monument of Sir Thomas Cholmondeley (d.1864) at Condover (Salop) (*139*), where the deceased kneels on a free-standing pedestal, gazing steadfastly upward and closing his hands over the hilt of a sword placed vertically in front of him, a pose possibly inspired by the dedication vigils of medieval knights. Another rather touching instance occurs after the turn of the century on the monument of George Vansittart (d.1904, aged 14) at Bisham (Berks), in which the boy is depicted kneeling in prayer at a prayer-desk, his pet dog lying asleep in front of it and the whole scene sheltered by an accurate Gothic canopy of early fourteenth-century style. Whatever the posture of effigies, however, animation and display were conspicuously lacking, the portrayals in almost every case being of men and women in the stillness of repose or private devotion. Furthermore, apart from the depiction of husbands and wives together, which itself became rare, the making of family groups died out in the Victorian period.

Conversely, busts and medallion portraits, though in no sense Gothic in type or style, remained as alternatives to the full effigy throughout and beyond the nineteenth century. Both had enjoyed considerable popularity in the first half of the century when, in addition to standard types of bust monument, a new form comprising a bust on a free-standing pedestal appeared. Excellent examples can be seen in the monuments of Thomas Westfaling (d.1817) at Ross-on-Wye (Herefs) and Edward Ward (d.1835) at Iver (Bucks). The bust on the first of these is Grecian in style, but the latter is naturalistic and wears contemporary dress, as was typical of busts throughout the century. Busts and medallions of the Victorian period usually occur on monuments which make no attempt to be Gothic, tending rather to hark back to styles of the seventeenth and eighteenth centuries. A case in point is the wall monument of the 2nd duke of Wellington (d.1884) at Stratfield Saye (Hants), where a bust of the duke appears with symbolic objects in a pedimented frame similar in form to those of the period 1720–50.

In some ways, however, the most striking outcome of the Gothic Revival in the field of funerary works was the re-introduction of the figured monumental brass, in a conscious endeavour to reproduce a characteristically medieval form. Much encouraged by A.W. Pugin, who himself made designs for brasses, these two-dimensional memorials began to re-appear in the 1830s and achieved increasing popularity in the later nineteenth century. As in the middle ages, Victorian brasses, with representations of the deceased, Gothic canopies and other features, were commonly set into a slab placed either in the floor or on a tomb-chest. Westminster Abbey has probably the largest number, but examples are to be found all over the country, including, for instance, the brasses of Sophia Sheppard (d.1848) at Theale (Berks) and the Rev. Jordan Palmer-Palmer (d.1885) in Bristol cathedral. The idiom soon spread also to wall monuments, however, although brasses in this position usually lacked figures. In the great majority of cases they took the form of inscription plates, either set in Gothic frames of stone or alabaster or simply appearing on their own and occasionally reaching quite large dimensions. For these, and for inscriptions on figured brasses, Gothic script was revived and, especially in the treatment of capital letters, new techniques of coloured inlay frequently produced highly decorative results reminiscent of the illuminated pages of medieval manuscripts. Victorian brass wall plates of this type are common in churches up and down the country.

The Victorian period also witnessed the emergence of another form of two dimensional memorial which was not medieval in origin, even though it was usually treated in a Gothic or Pre-Raphaelite manner. This was the multi-coloured mosaic monument, in which a panel depicting a figure and other features was made up of tiny pieces of variously coloured stone and glass, somewhat resembling in effect contemporary stained-glass windows. Indeed, the subject matter was often closely similar to that of individual lights in windows, commonly consisting of an angel or a saint, and the memorials were comparatively small in size and always fixed to the walls of churches. Though less common than brass plates and other types of wall tablet, they can be seen in a surprising number of places.

Other Styles on Victorian Monuments

Despite the overriding importance of the Gothic Revival in the second half of the nineteenth century, it was far from excluding all other stylistic influences. The Victorians were no more tied exclusively to Gothic in funerary monuments than in other spheres, and examples of their drawing on almost every earlier style can be found among the total output of monuments in these years. We have already noted the continuing vitality of neo-classical techniques in relief carving and the use of Baroque or eighteenth-century classical frames for busts and the like. Such phenomena were typical of Victorian eclecticism in this regard, and numerous other instances of similar borrowing from earlier styles can be cited.

Wall tablets provide perhaps the clearest evidence, for, although the dominant style was Gothic, designs based on Grecian models endured throughout the century and experiments in the revival of Baroque were tried out. An example of the latter can be seen at Hambleden (Bucks), where the wall tablet of Edward Marjoribanks (d. 1868) comprises an oval inscription set within a basically rectangular frame decorated with cherubs, cherub-heads and other Baroque motifs. Like others in similar vein, this piece does not deceive the trained eye, but it clearly represents a rejection of Gothic in favour of the earlier style. In other cases wall tablets incorporated elements from more than one antecedent style, producing original effects quite unlike anything that had gone before. At Albrighton (Salop), for instance, that of Richard Yates (d. 1841) consists of a circular inscription plate with Gothic script, surrounded by a border of strapwork containing a serpent biting its tail, the whole placed against a grey background basically eighteenth-century in outline.

Larger-scale monuments reveal similar tendencies. In particular, some tomb-chests were carved with details that were Renaissance or pseudo-classical in style, including that of Lady Marianne Cope at Eversley (Hants) and increasing numbers of others toward the end of the century. Again, the standing wall monument of the 2nd marquis of Hastings (d. 1844) at Ashby-de-la-Zouch (Leics) consists of an inscription panel enclosed in an 'architectural' frame which is fundamentally Jacobean in form, although the details of strapwork

and obelisks are misunderstood. For the important monument of the 1st duke of Wellington (d. 1852) in St Paul's cathedral, Alfred Stevens produced a huge four-poster canopied design with a semi-circular arch, based ultimately on a type of the early seventeenth century, but enriched with Victorian decoration and surmounted by an equestrian statue of the duke.

Moreover, by the end of the nineteenth century the period of greatest devotion to Gothic was over and new artistic influences, such as the Art Nouveau movement, were beginning to affect funerary monuments. Far more importantly, however, the practice of erecting grand monuments in churches was itself in decline by then and was destined virtually to disappear in the course of the twentieth century. For some decades before 1900 people had increasingly chosen to be commemorated by stained glass windows or by church fittings, rather than by monuments of the types we have been considering. Alternatively, if special memorial features were still required, people were turning more frequently to simple wall plaques merely carved or engraved with an inscription and devoid of other adornment. Although larger monuments continued to be produced in decreasing numbers for some decades after 1900, these less ostentatious forms of memorial were to grow steadily in popularity in the twentieth century.

The end of the Victorian era is thus a convenient point at which to conclude our survey. The primary concern of this and preceding chapters has been to examine developments in monumental form and style between 1100 and 1900 and the various means of depicting the deceased in use over that long period. In passing, references have been made to other aspects of church monuments which are no less interesting, but whose detailed consideration is impossible in a work of this size. One aspect, however, symbolism and allegory, is of such importance and is so closely bound up with questions of form and style that it deserves separate treatment. Accordingly, the final chapter of this book is devoted entirely to that complex and fascinating subject.

7 *Symbolism & Allegory*

Taken in their broadest senses, symbolism and allegory were part of the iconography of funerary monuments from the earliest days. Starting with the Christian symbol of the Cross carved on early coffin lids and with the figure of St Michael holding a soul on a twelfth-century slab at Ely, and coming through to the elaborate allegories of the seventeenth and eighteenth centuries and the rather sentimental symbolism of the nineteenth, one can trace a continuous impulse to represent complex beliefs and abstract concepts in concrete visual terms. The importance of symbolism in a predominantly illiterate age is obvious, but that cannot alone explain its popularity, for, even when increasing numbers of people were able to read, its power to convey basic truths and values was not abated. On the contrary, its appeal was more widespread in later centuries than earlier, partly, no doubt, because it continued to make a direct and immediate impact which no amount of expository detail in an inscription could match.

Fashions in the use of symbols and allegory on monuments naturally altered from period to period, in accordance not only with the rise and decline of particular artistic styles, but also with changes in religious and intellectual attitudes. One way of approaching this vast subject would be to consider the typical aspects of each period in succession, but here that method is rejected in favour of a thematic treatment, which will make it possible to bring together various idioms for expressing the same concepts which obtained at different periods. From this point of view, the subject breaks down conveniently into three main sections, each concerned with a basic theme or group of themes, namely, death, resurrection and immortality; the Christian religion; and the secular world.

Death, Resurrection and Immortality

The symbolic or allegorical depiction of death was clearly an appropriate concern of patrons and monument-makers. It did not appear on English monuments, however, before the fifteenth century, when there began what seems at first sight a morbid practice of showing the deceased as a decaying corpse in its burial shroud, the shroud being drawn back to expose the body inside. An effigy depicted in this way is known as a 'cadaver', and occurred most frequently in the fifteenth century as part of a two-fold depiction of the deceased in which a straightforward effigy as in life was placed on a tomb-chest and the sides of the tomb-chest were pierced or cut away to reveal, as it were, the corpse lying within. The earliest surviving example of this arrangement is the monument of Bishop Richard Fleming (d. 1431) in Lincoln cathedral (*140*), followed by others, including those of John earl of Arundel (d. 1435) at Arundel (Sussex), Sir John Golafre (d. 1442) at Fyfield (Berks), Archbishop Henry Chichele (d. 1443) in Canterbury cathedral and Bishop Thomas Beckington (d. 1465) in Wells cathedral. In the case of John Barton (d. 1491) and wife at Holme (Notts) there is a single cadaver, although two life-like effigies lie above, and a similar arrangement obtains on the monument of Richard Willoughby (d. 1471) at Wollaton (Notts), except that here the top effigies are two-dimensional ones in brass. A further variation is provided by that of Alice duchess of Suffolk (d. 1475) at Ewelme (Oxon), for in this case the tomb-chest has un-pierced sides and the cadaver lies beneath it in a low cavity behind short stone bars and arcading. In the later fifteenth and sixteenth centuries the cadaver, if used, was more commonly the sole representation of the deceased and in that case rested like other effigies on top of a tomb-chest with solid sides, as can be seen, for instance, in the monuments of John Baret (d. 1467) in St Mary's, Bury St Edmunds (Suffolk), and an anonymous figure at Feniton (Devon).

Such cadavers were carved with grisly realism

and often shown in an advanced state of emaciation and decay. Especially horrendous are those of Sir John Golafre (*141*), little more than a skeleton with skin stretched tightly across its prominent bones, and Alice duchess of Suffolk, with her wasted breasts and mouth pulled open by her shrinking skin. An extreme case of preoccupation with the gruesome is the late fifteenth-century cadaver on the so-called Wakeman Cenotaph in Tewkesbury abbey (Glos), which shows the body as it might have appeared some time after death, with a total of five creatures, including a worm, a frog and a snail, crawling over the decaying corpse.

The same phenomena occurred on incised slabs and monumental brasses, although in these media the cadaver was always shown alone. Depictions on brasses were very variable. That of John Brigge (d.1454) at Salle (Norfolk), for example, is an emaciated figure in a shroud, while those of William Robert and his wife (d.1486) at Digswell (Herts) are shrouded without noticeable wasting of the body. Others were reduced to bare skeletons, either still in their shrouds, as in the case of an anonymous brass of *c*.1500 at Hildersham (Cambs), or quite free, as in the cases of Richard Notfelde (d.1446) at Margate (Kent) and Thomas Childes (d.1452) in St Laurence's, Norwich. The most horrific version is undoubtedly that of Ralph Hamsterley (*c*.1510) at Oddington (Oxfordshire) (*142*), where the shrouded skeleton is positively infested with worms which are swarming all over and through it, having eaten away the flesh. The visual message is underlined by the tag above the skeleton, which reads in translation, 'Here I am given to worms, and thus I try to show that, as I am laid here, so all honour is laid down.'

Historians have long debated the reasons for the emergence of this practice, but, although prevalence of plague, the approach of the half-millenium and even the 'decline' of the middle ages have been adduced to explain it, no fully satisfactory reason has been found. If plague were the explanation, one may wonder why the cadaver fashion did not arise after the Black Death in the fourteenth century; if the half-millenium, why it continued in the sixteenth century. As for the decline of the middle ages, quite apart from modern historians discrediting the whole concept, it cannot seriously be maintained that men thought in this way in the first half of the fifteenth century. Death was an ever-present reality in the middle ages (and continued to be so until modern times) and plague intensified its

terrors rather than creating them. It may well be, therefore, that the cadaver simply represented a new convention, borrowed in the first instance from France, whose deep psychological roots are lost to us, but which, once it had been introduced, persisted as a powerfully symbolic portrait of death. Certainly in its repellent realism the cadaver served as a *memento mori*, a reminder of death, not only implying the humility of the deceased but also giving salutary reminder to the viewer that, whatever one's status and wealth in life, everyone must come in the end to the same condition. As the inscription on John Brigge's brass at Salle declares (in modern spelling), 'As ye me see in such degree, so shall ye be another day', clearly linking the depiction of an emaciated cadaver with a cautionary admonition to the reader.

The cadaver convention survived in various forms throughout the sixteenth century, though it was at its strongest in the first three decades and became rather rare after about 1550. Even the two-tiered type of monument, which had somewhat declined in popularity by 1500, was occasionally employed. The interesting wooden monument of Roger Rockley (d.1534) at Worsborough (Yorks), for instance, is a very late version of the typical fifteenth-century arrangement with a recumbent effigy of the deceased in life and a cadaver below, but more remarkable is the use of the cadaver with kneeling effigies of the deceased, which occurs in the reign of Elizabeth I. It can be seen, for example, on the monuments of Sir George and Lady Blount (d.1584) at Kinlet (Salop) and George Shirley (d.1588) and family at Breedon-on-the-Hill (Leics), the former having two kneeling effigies, the latter four, above a single recumbent cadaver. A few late sixteenth-century cadavers were treated in an extraordinary way: the shroud was not drawn back in the usual manner and the corpse was shown completely wrapped up, not even the face being visible, exactly as it would have been laid in the coffin. This is the case, for instance, on a Foljambe monument of *c*.1580–90 at Chesterfield (Derbs) (*143*), where the corpse is shown resting on a bier surrounded by a wealth of allegorical carving, and on another to members of the Beresford family (late sixteenth century) at Fenny Bentley in the same county, where two such corpses lie on a tomb-chest whose sides are incised with similarly shrouded bodies of children. The fact that neither monument has inscriptions or heraldry to identify the deceased is clearly deliberate and, in conjunction with the

140 *Above* Lincoln cathedral: Bishop Richard Fleming (d.1431). Note the cadaver on the lower level

141 *Below* Fyfield (Berks): Sir John Golafre (d.1442). Detail of cadaver

142 *Right* Oddington (Oxon): Ralph Hamsterley (*c.*1510). Rubbing of brass

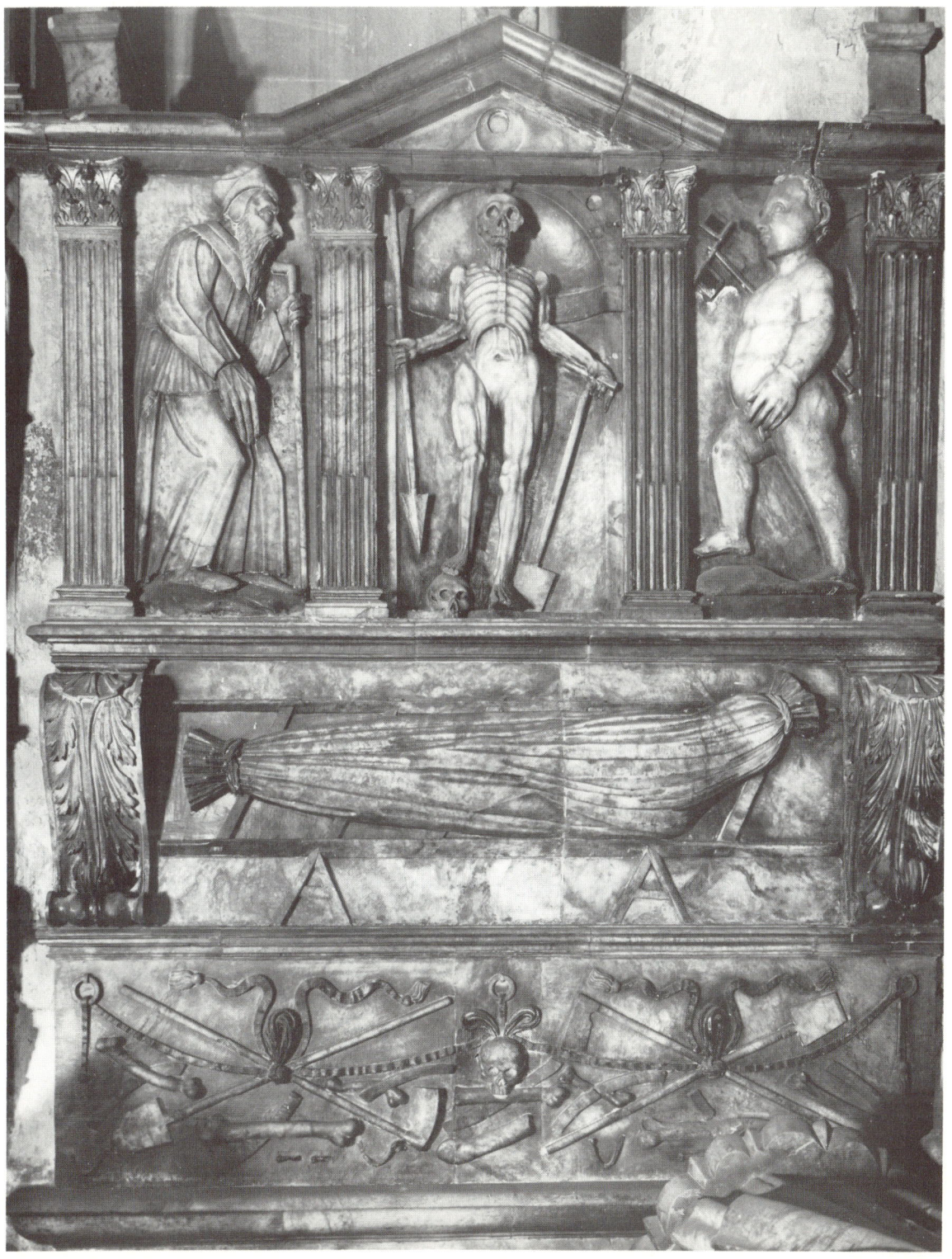

143 Chesterfield (Derbs): Foljambe monument (*c*.1580–90)

144 *Above left* Burton Agnes (Yorks): Sir Henry Griffith (d. 1645)

145 *Left* St Stephen's, Canterbury: Sir Roger Manwood (d. 1592)

146 *Above* St Paul's Cathedral: John Donne (d. 1631). By Nicholas Stone

total anonymity of the corpses, represents an extreme of self-effacement which even the middle ages did not attempt. In this context one should perhaps note also the later monument of Sir Henry Griffith (d. 1645) and his two wives at Burton Agnes (Yorks) (*144*), on which, in place of normal effigies or even shrouded corpses, there appear (amazing though it may seem) three black coffins.

Shrouded corpses in the medieval tradition virtually ceased to occur by 1600, their grim function having been increasingly taken over by skeletons without shrouds lying on straw mattresses and normally displayed with effigies of the deceased as in life. Several examples dating from the later sixteenth and early seventeenth centuries exist, including the monuments of Sir Roger Manwood (d. 1592) in St Stephen's, Canterbury (*145*), where a wooden skeleton lies in front of Sir Roger's demi-figure, and Thomas Parke (d. 1628) at Wisbech (Cambs), with a diminutive skeleton above the kneeling effigies of the deceased and his wife. Moreover, on the monument of the 1st earl of Salisbury (d. 1612) at Hatfield (*58*) we find an up-to-date version of the medieval two-tiered portrayal of the deceased, save that here the lower effigy is not a shrouded cadaver but a naked skeleton.

Then, in the 1630s, the shrouded figure dramatically re-appeared with Nicholas Stone's monument of John Donne (d. 1631) in St Paul's cathedral (*146*), depicting him standing in a shroud upon an urn. In this case the remarkable fact is known that the famous poet and dean of St Paul's chose before his death to pose in grave-clothes for his funerary portrait to be taken. The circumstance that the effigy, though somewhat stiffly erect, is not emaciated and stands upon an urn clearly embodies the notion of resurrection, the urn here serving as a symbol of the grave from which the new body has emerged. Whether the inspiration came originally from John Donne or from Stone, the monument established a fashion which in various forms endured into the Restoration period. This use of the shrouded figure in a resurrection context, to which we shall return shortly, led to the general disappearance of skeletons representing the deceased and to a widespread revival of shrouded effigies, though no longer in the gruesome, emaciated state of the middle ages. A number of monuments of these years depicted the deceased solely in the form of recumbent shrouded effigies, in most cases entirely enveloped except for their faces and one or both hands. They include those of Anne Lady Kinlosse (d. 1628) at Exton (Rutland), William Peck (d. 1635) and wife at Spixworth (Norfolk) and Alice Duchess Dudley (d. 1668) and her daughter at Stoneleigh (Warks). The last of these may contain a clue to the meaning of such portrayals, for it incorporates two cherubs blowing trumpets, suggesting the deceased's lying in their burial clothes awaiting the last trump. However, in at least two peculiar versions, with high-relief shrouded effigies slumped on one side in death, there is no sign of watchful expectancy. They are those of Elizabeth Berkeley (d. 1635) at Cranford (Middx) and Henry Buller (d. 1647) at Bassingbourn (Cambs), the latter figure lying on a black marble slab simply set into the floor of the church. Shrouded effigies fell again out of fashion after the Restoration, although some later examples were produced into the eighteenth century.

Apart from a very few late medieval brasses showing shrouded corpses rising from their coffins, as, for example, William Fettiplace and wife (d. 1517) at Childrey (Berks), the resurrection theme did not appear on monuments before the seventeenth century. However, the closely related theme of the salvation of the soul was present throughout the middle ages. It was always concerned specifically with the soul of the deceased and invariably took the form of a diminutive naked figure standing in a napkin held or borne upwards by one or two angels. The earliest surviving example occurs on the twelfth-century grave slab in Ely cathedral which almost certainly commemorates a bishop, since the carving includes a small crozier, and is most probably that of Bishop Nigel (d. 1169) (*147*). It depicts a tall standing angel, representing St Michael the Archangel, holding the napkin and soul in front of him. The iconography is in no sense blasphemous, since the inscription above the angel, reading (in translation) 'May St Michael pray for me', indicates hope of salvation rather than the certain fact. Such allegorical depictions did not become common until the later thirteenth century, by which time they normally formed part of the carved enrichment of canopies over recumbent effigies. Exceptionally the napkin continued to be held by a single angel, as in the case of an unknown knight of *c.*1425 at Lutterworth (Leics), but normally it was held by two angels, one on each side. A design of this type was formerly at the top of the piscina-monument of *c.*1275 at Long Wittenham (Berks) (*24*), though now only the angels and the soul's head survive. The standard form remains intact on the canopy of Sir Edmund de Mauley (*c.*1340) at Bainton (Yorks), while on that of the contemporary Percy Tomb in Beverley Minster it appears below a seated figure of Christ, to whom the angels present the soul. The device was also employed on monumental brasses, either with a portrayal of the deceased, as in the cases of Sir Hugh Hastings (d.1347) at Elsing (Norfolk) and Laurence de St Maur, rector (d.1337), at Higham Ferrers (Northants), the latter showing the angels presenting the soul to Christ; or as the only depiction of the deceased, as in the beautiful example at Checkendon (Oxon), commemorating Walter Beauchamp (*c.*1430), where two angels with exquisite wings appear in clouds bearing the soul aloft (*148*).

This form of allegory was brought to an end by the Reformation. For nearly a century thereafter it was not prudent to display even angels, let alone souls, and, although the salvation theme returned in later periods, the precise medieval iconography was never revived. In so far as symbolism was permitted on monuments of the Elizabethan and Jacobean periods, it was composed of idioms and motifs which were not overtly Christian or did not offend against the Reformation mentality. However, so strong was the appeal of allegory in general at this time that, after the early seventeenth century, it quickly re-asserted itself and was employed on a scale hitherto unknown. The major theme now was the resurrection of the body, considerable numbers of monuments being designed wholly with this allegorical end in view.

Resurrection monuments took a variety of forms. Two very similar monuments by Nicholas Stone, for example, have no representation of the deceased, but portray the theme of resurrection through the symbolism of the parable of the Sower. They are those of Sir Edward Pinchon (d.1625) at Writtle (Essex) and Lady Joyce Clerke (d.1626) in Southwark cathedral, dating respectively from 1629 and 1633. In each case the allegory is helped on by snippets of inscription distributed over the design. Between pilasters enriched with ribbons and agricultural implements, the Angel of the Resurrection stands upon the Rock of Life, at the base of which sheaves of corn are stacked symbolising redeemed souls; on either side sit two more angels wearing broad-brimmed harvesters' hats, resting tired after their labours (those at Southwark having laid aside their harvesting tools), while, lower down, the inscription panel takes the form of a winnowing pan, under which is the blade of a corn-shovel bearing the arms of the deceased.

These were not typical of resurrection monuments as a whole, however, for the majority included a shrouded effigy of the deceased rising or having risen from the dead. Here the lead was given by Stone's monument of John Donne, discussed earlier, where the standing figure was shown as having already risen. This was followed closely by other artists, notably Edward Marshall and his son, Joshua, who depicted shrouded effigies standing in arched recesses with marble doors open to reveal them in their risen state inside. This is so, for example, on the monuments of Henry Curwen (d.1636) at Amersham (Bucks), where the doors are held open by angels, Edward Noel Viscount Campden and wife (erected 1664) at Chipping Campden (Glos) and Sir Geoffrey Palmer (d.1673) and wife at East Carlton (Northants), the effigies in the last two instances standing on what are clearly meant to be the rims of urns. On the monument of Lady Deane at Great Maplestead (Essex), erected by her son in 1634, there are no doors, for, while her shrouded and risen figure stands eerily at the back of the recess, the reclining effigy of her son in armour faces out to the viewer, apparently unaware of what has happened behind him. It may safely be assumed that other standing effigies in shrouds should be interpreted as having risen from the dead, even though the surrounding iconography does not suggest it. This applies, for instance, to the tall monument of Sir John Astley (d.1639) at Maidstone (Kent), which has four such effigies in tiered pairs of arched recesses.

Another group of resurrection monuments chose not the serenity of the resurrected state, but the more dramatic scene of the resurrection itself, the deceased being depicted as a shrouded figure in the very act of rising out of a coffin, frequently in response to the last trump being blown by a cherub above. Examples of this include the monuments of Mary Salter (d.1631) at Iver (Bucks) (*149*), Sara Colville (d.1631) in All Saints, Chelsea (London), Mary Calthorpe (d.1640) at East Barsham (Norfolk) and George Rodney (d.1651) at Rodney Stoke (Somerset). By contrast, on the monument of Thomas Masham (d.1638) at Stratton Strawless (Norfolk) the deceased is shown not emerging from a coffin, but struggling to throw off his shroud as he rises from his reclining posture. Again, the extraordinary monument of Sir John Denham (d.1638) at Egham (Surrey) (*150*), a piece packed with allegory, has him rising from a mass of bones,

147 Ely cathedral: coffin slab of (?) Bishop Nigel (d. 1169)

148 Checkendon (Oxon): Walter Beauchamp (c. 1430). Rubbing of brass

149 Iver (Bucks): Mary Salter (d. 1631). A resurrection monument

150 Egham (Surrey): Sir John Denham (d. 1638). Resurrection monument

skulls and incomplete skeletons, amongst which another shrouded figure yet awaits its call.

Among other variations the deceased was on occasions depicted emerging from an urn symbolic of the grave. On a tiny wall monument at Ewelme (Oxon), for example, Henry Howard (d.1647) is being veritably pulled from an urn by two angels, but the oddest application of the idea occurs at Great Brington (Northants) on John Stone's monument of Sir Edmund Spencer (d.1655), for he appears as a demi-figure in armour seemingly emerging from an urn and, as he does so, placing his left hand on a bible set upon the pillar of Truth beside him. This curious and unsatisfactory conceit was no doubt devised in response to the patron's wishes. In another unique and more successful piece we know that such was the case. It is the monument of Sir Ralph Bovey (d.1679) at Longstowe (Cambs) (*151*), which depicts the deceased as a naked figure rising from water and clutching at an anchor which is let down by the hand of Christ from clouds above. The inscription records that Sir Ralph left an epitaph for his monument containing the line (in translation), 'I am immersed in the deep, but the anchor of Christ lifts me up again'; it was clearly as an interpretation of this unusual allegory of resurrection that the monument was conceived. Finally, we should note the brass plate of Mrs Dorothy Williams (d.1694) at Pimperne (Dorset), which shows her body (curiously, however, in fashionable clothes) rising phoenix-like from her recumbent skeleton and declaring, 'O Death, where is thy sting; O Grave, where is thy victory?', a familiar biblical tag which is carved also on the coffin of Mary Salter at Iver, mentioned earlier.

This form of resurrection allegory was abandoned early in the Baroque period and, with one or two notable exceptions, was not revived thereafter. One of the exceptions, however, provided the most elaborate and dramatic treatment the theme had ever received. The piece in question is Roubiliac's monument for Gen. William Hargrave (erected 1757) in Westminster Abbey, in which the scene of a shrouded figure rising in response to the last trump is combined with allegorical depictions of the overthrow of Death and the end of Time. At the centre of the composition we see the general throwing off his shroud as he rises from his sarcophagus, while to the right the bearded and winged figure of Time breaks his scythe across his knee and Death, in the form of a shrouded skeleton, falls headlong downward losing his crown in the

process; in the background the pyramid of Time collapses, as a cherub blows the last trump. This monument in turn clearly inspired the less elaborate piece by John Bacon the Younger for Joseph Sykes (dated 1809) at Kirk Ella (Yorks).

Apart from these, allegorical monuments of the later seventeenth and eighteenth centuries turned from the resurrection as such to the symbolism of salvation and immortality. They depicted the deceased in fashionable or antique dress and conveyed their Christian message through imagery which was largely secular or classical in origin. The basic theme was the promise or assurance of eternal bliss represented by a heavenly crown or by a wreath of victory, the latter being taken from classical antiquity and symbolising now triumph over death. In many cases this symbolism was treated in a subdued and rather static manner, the deceased taking no active part in the allegory. The monument of Grace Gethin (d.1697) at Hollingbourne (Kent), for example, shows her kneeling between two standing angels who hold out a heavenly crown and wreath of victory, and that of Richard Welby (dated 1714) at Denton (Lincs) simply has two hovering cherubs holding a crown over his head. In other cases, however, the allegory was more animated, as at Strensham (Worcs), where the semi-reclining figure of Sir Francis Russell (d.1705) turns back to his wife kneeling at his head, who gesticulates upward to the heavenly crown borne by cherubs at the top of the monument. Commonly, too, there were indications that the deceased had laid aside their earthly pomp in preparation for a greater glory. Thus, on a monument of 1675 at Ashburnham (Sussex) (*85*) Lady Ashburnham's coronet lies beside her, as a cherub flies down to place a wreath on her head, and at Elmley Castle (Worcs) the effigy of the 1st earl of Coventry (d.1699) (*91*), though comfortably semi-reclining, points at the coronet which he has laid aside and looks upward in hope of a heavenly crown. Viscount Newhaven (d.1728) at Drayton Beauchamp (Bucks) also looks hopeful of salvation, having discarded his coronet, while his wife sits by, holding what appears to be a wreath of victory (*114*). Among the most allegorical of the group is the monument of the 4th Lord Coventry (d.1687) at Croome D'Abitot (Worcs), but here, since one of its essential features is misplaced and another lost, the meaning is not immediately clear. Reclining on a sarcophagus between the standing figures of Hope and Faith, with his discarded coronet beside him, he turns round seemingly to appeal to Faith at his head, who is apparently gesturing upward. The survivng contract for the monument reveals, however, that the earthly coronet should lie at his feet and that the raised hand of Faith should be presenting a heavenly crown, which he reaches out to catch. Until recently the scene appeared not only puzzling, but ludicrous, for, when the monument was moved to the new church built on a different site in the 1760s, the baron's coronet was placed upon his head, though far too small for it, thereby turning serious Baroque allegory into almost comic pantomime. Fortunately, the coronet has now been removed from his head, though it has not yet found its way back to its original position.

Such allegories were most typical of the Baroque age, but predictably it was in the second half of the eighteenth century that the most elaborate examples were produced, with the significant difference, however, that the allegorical depiction of salvation was then combined with a pictorial scene of the person's death. Two cases in particular are worthy of mention, namely, the monuments of General Wolfe (dated 1772) in Westminster Abbey and Mary duchess of Montagu (d.1775) at Warkton (Northants) (*115*). In both instances the deceased have set aside the symbols of their earthly state, in the former case the general's sword and uniform lying crumpled on the ground, in the latter the duchess's coronet on the floor in front of her, but the rest of the allegory is different. General Wolfe is depicted as a naked hero-figure dying in the arms of a soldier and receiving assurance of immortality from a winged Victory bearing a palm and a wreath. The use of a classical Victory, rather than an angel or a cherub, is clearly appropriate in view of the deceased's military career, but her traditional attributes serve here as symbols of Christian victory and heavenly reward. The duchess of Montagu, on the other hand, expires against an urn and is assured of eternal bliss by an attendant angel who points energetically upward.

More commonly in the eighteenth century immortality was symbolized through the medium of the deceased's medallion portrait. Although not always used in this way, medallion portraits carried implications of immortality which might be made explicit by other elements in the design. Thus, medallions were shown held by cherubs, angels or allegorical figures, as in the case of Charles Sergison (d.1732) at Cuckfield (Sussex) (*109*); or carved on urns draped or garlanded by such figures, as on the monument of John Dalton (dated 1791) at Great

Stanmore (Middx); or tied on to pyramids, symbols of eternity, as in the case of the 4th earl of Gainsborough (dated 1790) at Exton (Rutland) (*108*). Such imagery was made especially forceful on the monument of James Dutton (dated 1791) at Sherborne (Glos), where an angel drapes the medallion portrait and at the same time tramples on the skeletal figure of Death.

In the first half of the nineteenth century quite different fashions in the depiction of salvation and immortality obtained, involving representations of the deceased being carried upward by angels or received by angels at the point of death. The idea of angels taking the deceased with them was not entirely new in English monumental iconography, but examples before the end of the eighteenth century are extremely rare and seem to relate exclusively to children. A remarkably early instance occurs on the monument of Sir William Heveningham (d.1678) and wife at Ketteringham (Norfolk), where, above their kneeling effigies, an angel flies across the inscription plate carrying away their swaddled baby. There is also the well-known monument at Great Barrington (Glos) of the Bray children, Jane (d.1711) and Edward (d.1720), who are shown in everyday clothes being led across the clouds by an angel.

There was no direct link, however, either in form or in style, between these stray examples and the new types of the nineteenth century. Here the scenes were normally carved in relief, a medium which not only reflected the influence of the Greek Revival, but was in many cases deliberately chosen to suggest the spiritual world. Moreover, they were produced in large numbers and in numerous variations of detail, satisfying a widespread religious need for pictorial representations of salvation, and, perhaps because they occurred most commonly on monuments to women, many were imbued with a degree of sentiment, not to say sentimentality, which was characteristic of the period.

Important in this development was the sculptor, John Flaxman, whose late eighteenth-century monuments of Mrs Sarah Morley (d.1784) in Gloucester cathedral and, even more so, Agnes Cromwell (d.1797) in Chichester cathedral (*152*) ushered in a fashion for relief scenes of angels bearing the deceased aloft. On the first they merely receive the deceased rising from the sea, but on the second they visibly carry her upward. In each case it is clearly the soul that is shown rising to Heaven, but, although the scenes may thus smack of blasphemy in appear-

151 *Top left* Longstowe (Cambs): Sir Ralph Bovey (d. 1679)

152 *Above* Chichester cathedral: Agnes Cromwell (d. 1797).
By John Flaxman

153 *Left* Flitton (Beds): Henrietta, countess de Grey (d. 1848).
By Terence Farrell

ing to anticipate the outcome of the Last Judgement, they are probably best regarded, like medieval depictions of souls held by angels, as expressions of hope in a blessed redemption, rather than as assertions of certain fact. These monuments were followed by a host of others, differing only in that a single angel bearing the soul became normal, as in the cases of Elizabeth Stanhope (d. 1816) in Bristol cathedral and Hannah Gostling (d. 1837) at Egham (Surrey)*. On occasions such scenes formed part of more ambitious monuments which also included effigies in the round. On the important monument of Henrietta countess de Grey (d. 1848) at Flitton (Beds) (*153*), for example, a relief of her soul ascending in angelic arms to Heaven is set behind a largely free group showing her husband and children weeping over her draped coffin, the difference between the treatment of the relief and that of the foreground figures signifying different planes of existence in the spiritual and temporal worlds. Sometimes the device was employed to depict a vision of future salvation experienced by the deceased, as at Weston-under-Lizard (Staffs), for instance, where Georgina countess of Bradford (d. 1842) lies asleep and behind there appears a relief of her soul conducted upward by angels (*154*). A more remarkable development occurred, however, when relief scenes showed an angel coming to take a person at the point of death, for in these cases the spiritual and temporal worlds met. At Tittleshall (Norfolk), for example, Mrs Jane Coke (d. 1800) is depicted leaning on a column with an angel descending in clouds to take her aloft; at Burford (Salop) an angel raises Lady Caroline Rushout (d. 1818) from her death-bed; at Badger in the same county Harriet Cheney (d. 1848) (*121*), seated in a chair, is disturbed in her reading by an angel who comes down to take her by the hand; and in Chichester cathedral Eliza Huskisson (d. 1856) receives the angelic visitation on her knees at prayer. A most remarkable case is the monument in Worcester Cathedral of Sir Henry Ellis (killed at Waterloo in 1815), for, as he dies on horseback, an angel takes him straight from the saddle.

These and many other variations on the same theme provide fascinating insights into religious attitudes to death and salvation in the nineteenth century, which it is regrettably not possible to cover adequately here. However, the whole subject has

* In a few exceptional cases the risen body rather than the soul appears to be depicted.

recently been investigated fully by Nicholas Penny in his admirable book, *Church Monuments in Romantic England*, to which the reader may be referred for a more complete account. But we cannot leave the theme of ascending souls without mentioning one extraordinary monument on which the idiom was treated not in relief, but in the round. This is the monument in St George's Chapel, Windsor (Berks), of Princess Charlotte, only child of King George IV, who died in childbirth in 1817. She appears twice on the monument, as a dead figure entirely covered by a pall except for the fingers of one hand, and as an ascending soul flanked by angels, one holding the baby who was the cause of her death.

Mention of a baby in this last piece, together with the earlier references to children in the care of angels, raises the general question of children depicted in conditions of death or immortality on English monuments. By and large their history paralleled that of adult portrayals, although they normally occurred in less complex schemes and possessed some interesting features of their own. From the later fifteenth to about the middle of the seventeenth centuries children who were still-born or who died soon after birth were shown as swaddled babies, known often as 'chrysoms'. They are found either alone, especially on brasses, including that of Elyn Bray (d. 1516) at Stoke D'Abernon (Surrey), or as members of family groups, as, for example, on the monument of Sir Fulke Greville (d. 1559) at Alcester (Warks) (*47*) where the line of children includes a swaddled baby. In these cases the baby's death alone is indicated, but when, as not infrequently happened, the baby was shown in its mother's arms, it signified also the mother's death in childbirth. Sometimes this was made more explicit by showing the mother in bed with the baby either in her arms, like Elizabeth Coke (*c.* 1629) at Bramfield (Suffolk), or lying on the bed-covers, as on the brass of Anne Savage (d. 1605) at Wormington (Glos).

From the late seventeenth century on children who had predeceased their parents were occasionally included on the latters' monuments in a supposedly immortal state. A characteristic, though rather rare, Baroque conceit was the depiction of such children as cherubs, a charming example of which occurs on the monument of Robert Sidney earl of Leicester (d. 1702) at Penshurst (Kent), where nine children are shown in this way, two appearing like youthful angels, the others as named cherubic demi-figures or heads. The same idea, adapted to different stylistic conventions, can be seen on the monument of Cornelia Milbanke (d.1795) at Croft (Yorks), where, as she lies on her death-bed, she sees a vision of her two dead children as cherubic figures above.

Symbols of Death, Resurrection and Immortality

So far we have considered death, resurrection and immortality only as they were portrayed in depictions of the deceased themselves, but in truth these concepts were far more frequently symbolized by objects and other figures incorporated either as central features or as part of the carved enrichment of monuments.

The first and most important of these were skulls and bones, symbols of death and mortality. Both were extremely rare before the late sixteenth century, although odd late medieval instances of their use on brasses survive. For example, the words on a fifteenth-century inscription fragment in Ely cathedral are separated by small skulls, cross-bones and parts of skeletons, and those on the appropriated brass of Walter Curson (d.1527) at Waterperry (Oxon) by skulls and cross-bones. However, after about 1580 bones and skulls were a constantly recurring feature for nearly two centuries.

The skull, or death's-head, was often displayed on its own, quite plain and gruesomely realistic, grinning as though in mockery of the living. On monuments of the Baroque period the effect was commonly heightened by giving the skull bat's wings, like the frightening example on the wall tablet of Robert Cressett (d.1728) at Cound (Salop) (*155*). Winged skulls of this sort were the macabre counterpart of cherub-heads with feathered wings, symbolizing immortality, which also proliferated on monuments at this time. However, in at least one case, to be seen on the tablet of Anne Bridell (d.1725) at Lutterworth (Leics) (*156*), a winged skull was adapted to signify not death, but the passage to immortality through death, for, while its left wing on the traditionally evil side is bat-like, the right wing on the side of salvation is feathered, the skull turning, moreover, from one to the other. It is a nice little Baroque conceit, but in the great majority of instances the skull, winged or otherwise, served as a *memento mori*. If not shown on its own, its most frequent association was with cross-bones, an early instance of which occurs on the monument of Jacob Wheeler (d.1621) at High Wycombe (Bucks). The skull and cross-bones combination was most characteristic, however, of the late seventeenth and early eighteenth centuries, when it is found, for example, on the wall tablets of Mary countess of

Gainsborough (d.1693) at Minterne Magna (Dorset) (*157*), John Shuckburgh (d.1724) at Upper Shuckburgh (Warks) and, in an unusual form with the bones tied together by ribbons, on that of Lady Philadelphia Clerk (d.1698) at Thame (Oxon). The skull might, however, appear in other company, as in the singularly repulsive example on the monument of Hartgill Baron (d.1673) in Windsor parish church (Berks), where it is flanked by serpents whose pointed tails extend into its eye-sockets. Not infrequently, as on some of the above examples, the skull was crowned with a laurel wreath, symbolizing the survival of a person's renown and virtue after death.

In all these cases the skull represented death in general, but, when held or leant upon by an effigy, it particularly signified the death of that person, thus enabling monuments with several effigies, especially those including children, to indicate which of them were dead at the time of erection. The device was much favoured in the seventeenth century, when many monuments incorporating children holding skulls occur, including those of Sir Cope D'Oyley (d.1633) at Hambleden (Bucks) (*80*) and Sir Arthur Heselrige (d.1661) at Noseley (Leics) (*79*). On that of John Rudhall (d.1636) at Ross-on-Wye (Herefs) (*158*) can be seen the moving variation of a swaddled baby lying awkwardly against a skull. Equally, however, the skull may be held or leant upon by the principal effigy, as in the cases of Thomas Sackville (d.1677) at Withyham (Sussex) and Mary duchess of Norfolk (d.1705) at Lowick (Northants), or less commonly it may be placed alongside the effigy or under its foot, as on the monuments of Margaret Watson (d.1713) at Rockingham (Northants) and Elizabeth Russell (d.1601) in Westminster Abbey.

In addition to children holding skulls, others on seventeenth-century monuments were depicted holding roses, as are, for example, some of the children on the monuments at Hambleden and Noseley just mentioned. The precise significance of the device is not clear, but it seems likely that, since the rose was, among other things, a symbol of innocence, it indicated those children who were still young and at an age of innocence at the time when the monument was made.

To return to skulls and bones, however, their *memento mori* potential was exploited to an extraordinary degree in the first half of the seventeenth century. In Canterbury cathedral, for example, the sides of the effigy-less tomb-chest of

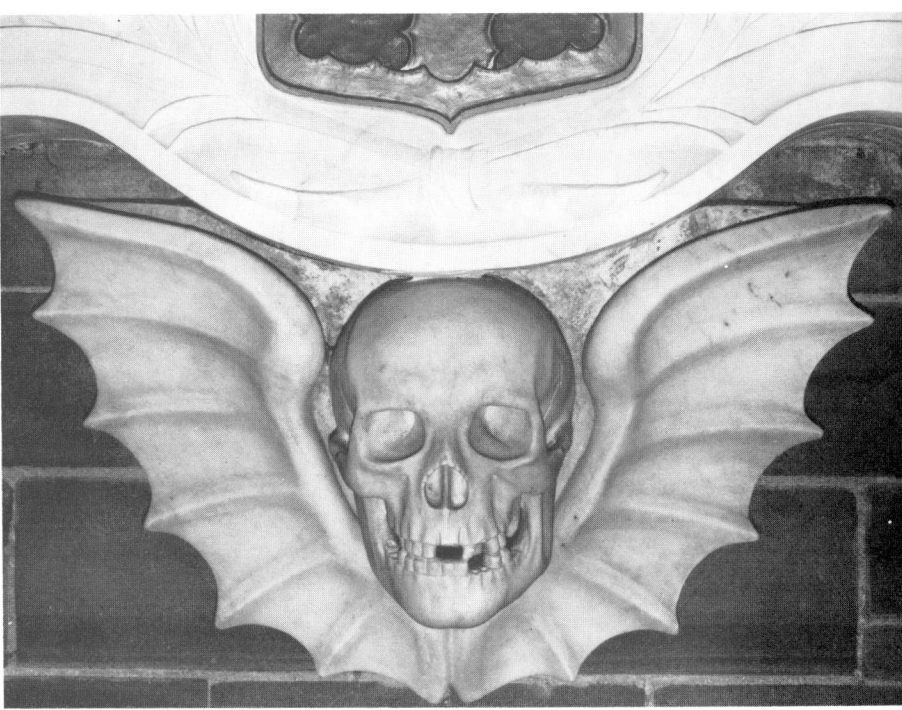

154 *Left* Weston-under-Lizard (Staffs): Georgina, countess of Bradford (d. 1842). By Peter Hollins

155 *Above* Cound (Salop): Robert Cressett (d. 1728). Detail

156 *Below* Lutterworth (Leics): Anne Bridell (d. 1725). Detail

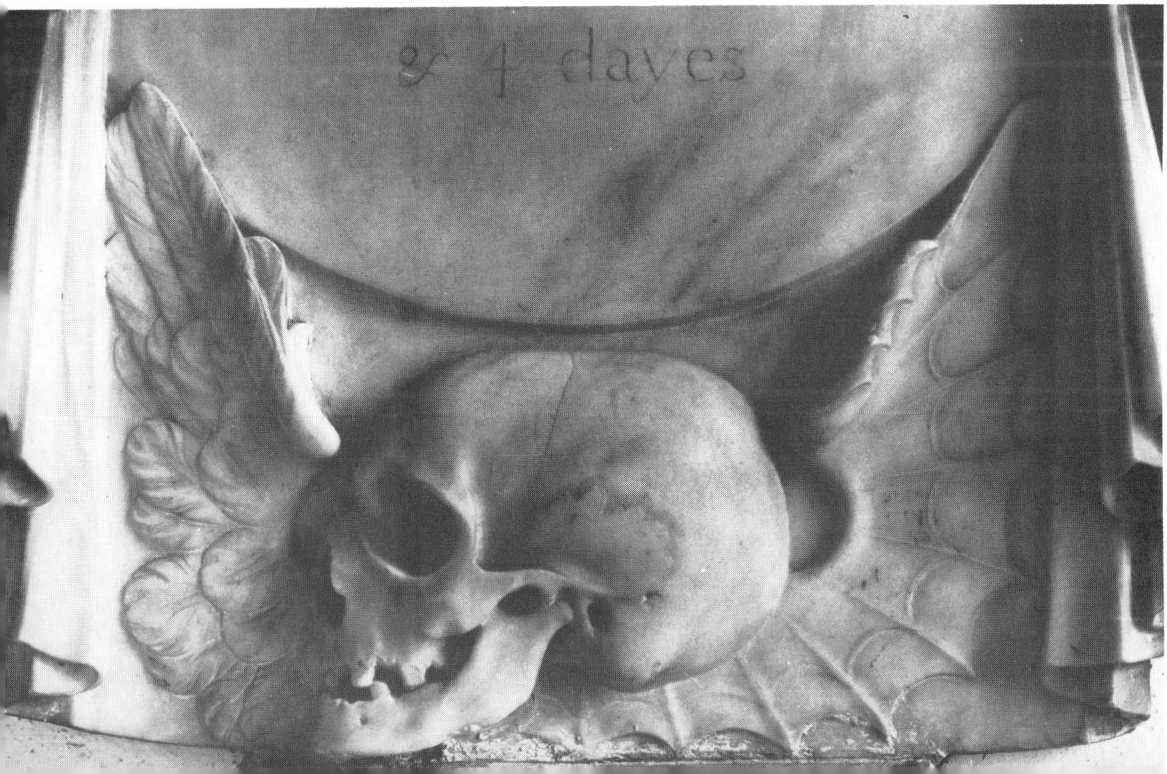

157 Minterne Magna (Dorset): Mary, countess of Gainsborough (d. 1693). Detail

158 Ross-on-Wye (Herefs): John Rudhall (d. 1636). Detail

159 *Above* Spelsbury (Oxon): Sir Henry Lee (d. 1631). Detail of canopy showing Time and Death

160 Westminster Abbey: Lady Elizabeth Nightingale. By Louis François Roubiliac (1761)

Dean Fotherby (d.1619) are encrusted with them, while at Longburton (Dorset) the monument of Sir John FitzJames (d.1625) has the whole of the base below the effigies open to reveal a grim collection inside. A particularly macabre fashion of the period involved the carving of barred openings in the sides of tomb-chests, through which jumbles of bones and skulls carved with grisly realism were visible, the impression being that of looking into a charnel house. It occurs, for instance, on the monuments of Sir Edward Barker (c.1623) at South Acre (Norfolk), the wives of Sir Gervase Clifton (1631) at Clifton (Notts) and Leonora Bennet (d.1638) at Uxbridge (Middx), the last showing bony hands eerily grasping the bars from within.

Complete skeletons, on the other hand, apart from those of the deceased, served as personifications of Death and were almost invariably shrouded. In the seventeenth century Death in this guise was typically shown with Time, both being included as small figures standing at prominent points in the design. Good examples are to be seen at Spelsbury (Oxon) on the monument of Sir Henry Lee (d.1631), where they stand on the canopy (*159*), and at Abbots Langley (Herts) on that of Anne Combe (d.1640), where they flank her kneeling effigy. More dramatically, however, Death was depicted loosing his dart (or arrow) at the effigy of the deceased. This was formerly clear on the monument of Henry Barker (d.1651) at Hurst (Berks), though here the dart has been largely broken away, but is supremely present on that of Lady Elizabeth Nightingale (dated 1761) in Westminster Abbey (*160*), where Roubiliac has imposed his creative genius on the traditional theme. Commemorating the lady's death following a shock induced by lightning, the scene is suitably charged with action and emotion, and constitutes probably the most emphatic statement of the triumph of Death on any English monument. Death, emerging from his grim subterranean stronghold, aims his dart at Lady Nightingale above, as she, despite her husband's desperate efforts to ward off the fatal blow, falls back dead into his bosom. As we have seen, however, Roubiliac's monument of General Hargrave, erected in the Abbey in 1757, portrays by contrast the defeat of Death, as do the monuments of Thomas Freke (d.1769) at King's Sutton (Northants), where the risen Christ tramples on the shrouded skeleton, and James Dutton (dated 1791) at Sherborne (Glos), in which the task is performed by an angel.

Occasionally, and especially in the Baroque age, skeletons were shown without shrouds, that is, not in the standard form for Death, although they clearly did not represent the deceased. In St John's, Chester, for example, the 'reredos-type' monument of Diana Warburton (d.1693) has no effigy, but a large unshrouded skeleton standing frontally and holding up in front of him a marble 'cloth' bearing the inscription, the base of the monument being carved with a fine relief of skulls and branches. Again, the hanging monument of Lady Abigail Stawell (d.1692) at Hartley Wespall (Hants) (*161*) has at the bottom a small unshrouded demi-skeleton which seems endowed with a personality almost human, looking (in Pevsner's happy phrase) 'gruesomely pally' as he leans forward to the viewer.

The numerous other symbols of death and mortality were less macabre and varied much in popularity from period to period. None appeared on monuments before the late sixteenth century. A characteristic group of motifs of the late Elizabethan and Jacobean period is carved on the wall tablet of Anne Lytton (d.1601) at Knebworth (Herts). It includes a spade and mace crossed behind a skull, symbolizing the end of earthly labour and power, an hourglass and scythe crossed, symbolizing mortality, a vase of roses with their stems broken and a coffin, both symbolizing death, and (more unusual) a pair of scissors held by a hand emerging from clouds cutting the thread of life, a symbol of death adapted from classical mythology of the Fates. Most of these occurred very commonly in the first half of the seventeenth century, along with several others. Time, for instance, was frequently symbolized by an hourglass (plain or winged) or personified as a bearded old man with his traditional attributes of hourglass and scythe. Cherubs, too, though basically symbolic of immortality, were often shown in actions which signified death. One form was the cherub leaning on a spade, indicating rest after the labour of life, another was the weeping cherub, but most popular was the cherub extinguishing the torch of life, a device which remained standard for about two hundred years after its first appearance in the early seventeenth century. At first, the torch was usually extinguished by inversion on a skull, as can be seen, for example, on the monument of Giles Reed (d.1611) at Bredon (Worcs), but later the skull was omitted, as on the monument of John Lord Northwick (d.1800) at Blockley (Glos) (*102*). Moreover, in the eighteenth century the torch was on occasions extinguished not by a cherub, but by an angel or by a genius, the ancient Roman guardian spirit, the latter being so, for instance, on the monument of Viscountess Say and Sele (d.1789) at Grendon Underwood (Bucks). Another typical Jacobean conceit involving cherubs did not endure. It showed them in the act of blowing bubbles which in their fragile and ephemeral existence represent the vanity of the world, this imagery being commonly combined with that of mortality symbolized by Time, the universal reaper whose scythe must sooner or later gather all. Both occur, for example, on the monuments of Robert Suckling (d.1589) in St Andrew's, Norwich, George Wylde (d.1616) in St Peter's, Droitwich (Worcs), and Bishop William Cotton (d.1621) in Exeter cathedral (*67*).

The urn and the sarcophagus were both introduced into the repertoire of symbolic objects in the late sixteenth century. At first sight the urn, pagan in origin and associated with cremation and ashes, seems out of place in a Christian context where inhumation was the universal rule, and yet, as a product of the Renaissance interest in antique forms, it remained a persistent feature from the early seventeenth until well into the nineteenth centuries. Its meaning varied, however, according to whether it was shown open and with flames emerging from it or whether it was shown closed. The flaming urn signified eternal life and was the normal form throughout the seventeenth century, while the closed urn signified death and, though it began to occur as early as the 1630s, did not become standard until the eighteenth century, when it was frequently draped as well. It is true that a closed urn might appear with cherubs placing a garland over it, or with a medallion portrait of the deceased carved upon it, but, although the total message might thereby be transformed into one of hope or immortality, the urn itself remained a symbol of death. Urns of both kinds were employed either as the main features of monumental designs or as elements in their embellishment.

The sarcophagus, on the other hand, was almost never reduced to the rôle of subsidiary enrichment and, moreover, served always as a symbol of death. This was particularly underlined by some early seventeenth-century monuments like that of Sir Thomas Russell (d.1632) at Strensham (Worcs), where the base below the effigies is open in front to reveal an ornamental sarcophagus inside. However, its use other than for the support of effigies and the like was exceptional before 1700, and its heyday as an independent feature was undoubtedly the eigh-

teenth century, at which time its popularity was largely due to contemporary pre-occupation with the antique. Like the urn, the sarcophagus differed considerably in appearance from one period to another as style succeeded style, but it can always be recognized and distinguished from coffins by its fundamentally unchanging shape, that of a large oblong casket standing commonly on balls or feet.

Apart from allegorical figures, which will be discussed later, the other important symbols or symbolic depictions which made their appearance in the later sixteenth century were those of faith, resurrection and eternity. The symbol of faith was a burning lamp, antique in design but taking its significance from the Christian parable of the Wise and Foolish Virgins. Never assuming major proportions, it was almost without exception carved as a small independent feature (often in pairs) on the tops of monuments, where it persisted until the early nineteenth century. Resurrection was signified by a cherub blowing a trumpet (or sometimes two trumpets) to raise the dead at the Day of Judgement, a device which was used whether or not the deceased were represented on the monument. Cherubs were frequently shown in this act on canopies or at the tops of wall tablets, and often a trumpeting cherub appeared with another extinguishing a torch, thus balancing the end of earthly life with the resurrection to eternal life. Eternity as such was pre-eminently symbolized by the obelisk, which, deriving ultimately from the religion of ancient Egypt, formed so ubiquitous an element in later Elizabethan and Jacobean monumental designs. As the seventeenth century wore on, it ceased to be employed in a minor, almost ornamental, rôle, but retained its importance as a central feature and, in the eighteenth century, was transformed into the two-dimensional pyramid so familiar as a background for figures and other motifs. Eternity might also be symbolized by a serpent, as, for instance, on the monument of Sir Cope D'Oyley (d.1633) at Hambleden, where the point is elaborated by showing the serpent coiled round an hourglass, thereby representing the triumph of eternity over time. In the second half of the eighteenth century the particular form of a serpent eating its own tail became a feature of monumental designs. A beautiful example, accompanied by crossed torches, is carved in relief on the monument of Lewis Dymoke (d.1760) at Scrivelsby (Lincs) (*162*), and another encircling a recess for urns on that of the 3rd earl of Lichfield (d.1772) at Spelsbury

161 Hartley Wespall (Hants): Lady Abigail Stawell (d.1692). Detail

162 Scrivelsby (Lincs): Lewis Dymoke (d.1760). Detail showing serpent as a symbol of eternity

163 Chilham (Kent): Lady Mary Digges. By Nicholas Stone (1632). A column surrounded by the Four Cardinal Virtues

164 *Above* Westminster Abbey: Vice-Admiral John Baker (d. 1716). By Francis Bird. *A columna rostrata*

165 *Left* Sheringham (Norfolk): Abbot Upcher (d. 1819). By John Bacon the Younger. A fallen column with a weeping woman

166 *Below* Burford (Salop): Elizabeth Rushout (d. 1827). By Sir Richard Westmacott. A cut rose and a butterfly

(Oxon). The symbol continued in use in the nineteenth century, when it occurs, for example, surrounding the inscription on a tablet for Richard Yates (d.1841) at Albrighton, near Shifnal (Salop).

Another symbol of eternity, or rather immortality through fame, was the column, but, although it came into use in the seventeenth century, it was not common before 1700. Among its earliest and most remarkable appearances is the great free-standing column surrounded by the Four Cardinal Virtues which constitutes the monument of Lady Mary Digges at Chilham (Kent) (*163*), completed by Nicholas Stone in 1632. Here the inscription reveals that the inspiration came from the story in Genesis of Jacob erecting a pillar on the grave of his wife, Rachel, with whom Lady Digges is compared, but in other cases the source seems to have been the commemorative columns of ancient Rome, of which the most famous was Trajan's Column. Like the Chilham monument, however, those others which incorporated the column usually displayed it surmounted by an urn, as, for example, in the cases of Judith Dowdeswell (d.1666) at Bushley (Worcs) and Sir William Harvey (d.1719) at Hempstead (Essex). On very rare occasions after 1700 the so-called *columna rostrata* was employed on monuments of naval commanders. It consisted of a column enriched with carved prows of ships projecting at intervals all the way up, and was derived from a free-standing example known to have existed in ancient Rome to commemorate a naval victory. Its revival in England's Augustan Age is hardly, therefore, surprising. Two monuments in Westminster Abbey have it in relief against a black background, namely, those of Vice-Admiral John Baker (d.1716) (*164*), by Bird, and General George Monk duke of Albemarle (d.1670, monument 1730), designed by Kent and executed by Scheemakers. In addition to ships' prows the former has masks on the front of the column, the latter anchors. By contrast, a column decorated with flames forms the main feature on the monument of Henry Plant (d.1784) at Iver (Bucks). By that time, however, the column was beginning most commonly to be shown plain and with a standing female figure leaning on or over it in mourning, as can be seen on the monuments of Thomas Sainsbury (d.1795) at Market Lavington (Wilts), by Flaxman, and Sir Thomas Eyre (d.1799) at Ruscombe (Berks), by Westmacott, among many others. At the same time the rather different motif of the broken column had made its appearance.

This was one of a crop of new fashions, particularly in the symbolism of death and mortality, which were introduced in the later eighteenth century and were to grow enormously in popularity after 1800. Apart from the broken column, the most important were the cut-off rose or lily and the weeping willow. Each had its own overtones of meaning and its own particular uses, but, more significantly, all lent themselves to a sentimental kind of treatment that was fully realised in the nineteenth century. They were almost invariably employed without depictions of the deceased and were most common on hanging wall monuments and tablets.

The broken column first appeared as early as Rysbrack's monument for John Sympson (dated 1752) in Canterbury cathedral, where it occurs with two cherubs. In the 1780s it began to be used as a solitary feature, with its upper part fallen to the ground, and seems initially to have signified that by the death of the deceased an ancient line had become extinct. It was used in this sense on the monument of Robert Walsh (d.1788) in Bath abbey (Somerset). It soon lost this special meaning, however, and could be used in connection with anyone's death, as is the case on the monument of Mary Tratman (d.1826) at Berkeley (Glos). Sometimes the symbolism was elaborated by the presence of a mourning woman, as, for example, on the monument of the 1st Lord Brownlow (d.1807) at Belton (Lincs), where the woman leans against the broken column with its fallen capital beside her, and on that of Abbot Upcher (d.1819) at Sheringham (Norfolk), where she lies in grief across the fallen part of the column and the shattered stump stands alongside (*165*).

The cut-rose motif symbolized the death of a young person 'cut off' in the bloom of youth or early adulthood. A very early instance of its use occurs on the monument at West Horsley (Surrey) commemorating James Kendal, who died in 1750 at the age of 23, which has, below a draped urn, a circular relief showing a rose bush with one bloom and a sickle lying beneath it on the ground (*101*). A similar relief appears on the monument of Willoughby Wood (d.1786, aged 18) at South Thoresby (Lincs), but the idea did not 'take off', as it were, until the early nineteenth century, when it commonly took the simpler form of a rose blossom with a sickle. So it appears, for example, on the touching monument of seven-year old Ernest Udny (d.1808) in Chichester cathedral, where the iconography also incorporates a large arrow representing the dart of Death, the inscription declaring: '. . . Death came with friendly care, the opening bud to Heaven conveyed and bade it blossom there.' The motif was in particular much favoured by Sir Richard Westmacott, who employed it especially on monuments of young women, as can be seen, for instance, in the reliefs of a sickle cutting a rose on that of Mrs Elizabeth Eardley Wilmot, who died in 1818 aged 29, at Berkswell (Warks) (*120*). Westmacott and others made equal use of the cut or broken lily to symbolize the deaths of young persons and children in their years of innocent purity. Both motifs can be seen, for example, on Westmacott's two pathetic little monuments to girls of the Rushout family at Burford (Salop), Caroline (d.1822) and Elizabeth (d.1827). The latter's premature death at the age of 14 is alluded to by a rosebud which has not yet had time to open (*166*), while the death of Caroline at 19 in the purity of maidenhood is symbolized by a sickle cutting a flower from a lily stem.

Weeping willows indicated death through the suggestion of mourning and were often shown in relief drooping their branches over an urn. So they appear, for instance, on the wall monuments of Anne Morley (d.1787) in Winchester cathedral and Mrs Elizabeth Smith (d.1798) at Great Somerford (Wilts). Winchester cathedral has another more elaborate example, for Sir Villiers and Lady Chernocke (d.1779 and 1789), in which an arching willow hangs over an urn flanked by allegorical female figures. The most spectacular occurrence of the motif, however, is on a monument of *c.*1833 at Great Bookham (Surrey), commemorating Elizabeth Andrewes (d.1816) and relatives (*167*), for here the willow has, so to speak, moved off the memorial and grown to prodigious size on its own. The monument comprises a simple inscription tablet set low on the north wall of the chancel below a medieval lancet window, but – and this is the surprise – beside it a large high-relief willow grows from the floor, its trunk clad in ivy, and, reaching to the roof line, droops its great leafy branches over the lancet window.

To these and other rather sentimental symbols was added shortly after 1800 the butterfly, revived from Antiquity and representing now the departing soul of the deceased. Among its earliest appearances is that on the monument of John Yorke (d.1801) at Wimpole (Cambs), where the deceased's children contemplate a butterfly resting on the side of an urn (*122*). Butterflies are depicted also, for example, on Westmacott's monuments of Mrs Eardley Wilmot at Berkswell and Elizabeth Rushout at Burford, mentioned above, on that of Thomas Bridge (dated 1816) at Piddletrenthide (Dorset) and, very interestingly, on the pseudo-Baroque tablet for Edward Marjoribanks (d.1868) at Hambleden (Bucks), which has at the top a minute urn from which a butterfly is escaping.

Symbolism and Imagery of the Christian Religion

Symbols and imagery arising directly from the Christian faith are found on monuments of two periods only: the middle ages and from the late eighteenth century onwards. Their absence in the intervening years and replacement by imagery of non-Christian origin can be explained simply as the effect of the Protestant Reformation and its aversion to Christian images as tainted with idolatry, which persisted unremittingly until the dawn of the Gothic Revival and Romantic movements. The sole exception lay in the depiction of angels, which after a short interlude returned to monumental inconography soon after 1610, but they provoked less hostility, possibly because they were similar in character to the winged spirits of ancient pagan religions and could thus be accommodated without risking popery.

The earliest and most widespread medieval symbol was predictably the Cross, which, as we have seen, was carved on innumerable coffin lids and grave slabs from the early twelfth century onwards and was later engraved freely on brasses, commonly in association with figures. For some reason, however, it was rare as an independent feature on larger monuments in stone and alabaster. After its disappearance in the sixteenth century, it eventually began to creep back on to monuments in the second half of the eighteenth century, at first rather tentatively, as at Acton Burnell (Salop), where the wall tablet of Lady Mary Smythe (d.1764) is surmounted by a small cross keeping company with two burning lamps, also symbolic of faith, but in the nineteenth century more boldly, as at Bramley (Hants), where the stark black and white marble tablet of Bernard Brocas (d.1839) is topped by a tall cross alone and uncompromisingly declaring his Christian faith. Even in the later period, however, the cross never achieved the popularity on interior monuments that it enjoyed on churchyard memorials.

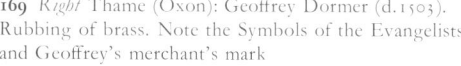

167 Great Bookham (Surrey): Elizabeth Andrewes and relatives (*c.*1833). A weeping willow

168 *Above right* Northleach (Glos): William Lander (d.1530). Detail of brass showing the symbol of the Trinity

169 *Right* Thame (Oxon): Geoffrey Dormer (d.1503). Rubbing of brass. Note the Symbols of the Evangelists and Geoffrey's merchant's mark

The other Christian symbols most commonly found on medieval monuments, especially in the later middle ages, were those of the Holy Trinity and the Four Evangelists. The pseudo-heraldic emblem of the Trinity, as distinct from the figured representation which will be described later, consisted of a shield-like feature with a circle at top left, top right and bottom containing, respectively, the words (in translation) 'Father', 'Son' and 'Holy Ghost', the circles being linked to one another by the words 'is not' and separately linked by the word 'is' to a fourth circle in the centre bearing the word 'God'. The emblem was thus ingeniously devised to make clear the doctrine that, while the Godhead comprises three persons, each person of the Trinity is individually distinct. It was especially popular on brasses and can be seen, among other places, at Cowfold (Sussex) on that of Prior Thomas Nelond of Lewes (d. 1433) and at Northleach (Glos) on that of William Lander (d. 1530) (*168*).

Equally ingenious were the medieval emblems of the Four Evangelists, the writers of the Four Gospels. By a tradition dating back to the fifth century each Evangelist was associated with one of the four winged beasts described in Revelation, IV, verses 6–8, as being perpetually before the throne of God. Soon the practice developed of representing the saints by their respective beasts holding scrolls. Thus, St Matthew came to be represented by a winged man (usually shown resembling an angel), St Mark by a winged lion, St Luke by a winged calf (or ox) and St John by an eagle. These Symbols or Emblems of the Evangelists, as they are called, were most frequently included on monumental brasses, where they were engraved either around the figure of the deceased, as in the case of Roger Campedene (d. 1398) at Stanford-in-the-Vale (Berks), or, more commonly, at the corners of slabs or of marginal inscriptions, as, for instance, on the brasses of Henry Greene (d. 1467) at Lowicke (Northants) and Geoffrey Dormer (d. 1503) at Thame (Oxon) (*169*). They were not unknown, however, on three-dimensional monuments. At Cogges (Oxon) they are exceptionally carved on the sides of a tomb-chest dating from the first half of the fourteenth century, but their most remarkable occurrence is on the mutilated monument of Bishop William of Louth (d. 1298) in Ely cathedral. Here, although the iconography is much damaged and interfered with, the remaining parts of the base on the south side clearly show two seated angels each with one of the Evangelistic beasts, originally balanced on the

north side by similar depictions of the other two Evangelists, which nineteenth-century restoration has now made unrecognizable.

In addition to symbols, later medieval monuments commonly included Christian figures depicted either on their own or in religious scenes. Some earlier monuments ranging in date back to the thirteenth century were carved with such imagery, especially on canopies, but it is probable that many more displayed it in the form of paintings on flat surfaces which have since flaked off or worn away so that hardly anything now survives. For our knowledge of this type of monumental iconography, therefore, we are largely dependent on the more durable carved and engraved versions that predominated especially after 1400. It is true that much of this also was subsequently damaged or destroyed either in periods of religious iconoclasm or simply by carelessness at other times, with the result that what has come down to us is at best an incomplete remnant of the vast amount that once existed. However, it is likely that enough has survived to provide a reasonably accurate picture of the range of subjects most commonly in use.

Sacred imagery was employed in the later middle ages both on three-dimensional monuments in stone and alabaster and on two-dimensional memorials, chiefly brasses. On the former the figures were normally deployed about the structure of the monument and had no contact with the deceased's effigy, other than that of surrounding it with any power or virtue they might be regarded as possessing, but on brasses a more intimate relationship was often portrayed, the most frequent being the depiction of the deceased in an attitude of prayer or devotion to the sacred subject.

Angels and saints were commonly carved on tomb-chests, canopies and chantry chapels, where, however, they have in many cases since been badly mutilated or destroyed, leaving only the empty niches which once contained them. Angels have fared on the whole better in this respect than saints, but still the latter survive in some numbers, notably on tomb-chests, and can be identified by their dress and distinctive attributes. St Christopher, for example, striding through the flood with the Christ-child on his shoulder, is immediately recognizable on the tomb-chests of a Lord Lovell (*c.*1450) at Minster Lovell (Oxon) (*170*) and a fifteenth-century knight of the Constable family at Halsham (Yorks), the latter showing the water swirling realistically round the saint's legs and staff. Equally clear, among others, are the seated Virgin and Child on the chest of Sir Hugh Willoughby (d.1445) at Willoughby-on-the-Wolds (Notts) and four saints in conventional portrayals on that of Sir John Neville (d.1482) at Harewood (Yorks), namely, St Laurence with the gridiron of his martyrdom, St John holding a chalice from which a dragon emerges, St James in the guise of a pilgrim and St Michael weighing a soul. Along with saints, another popular device was the depiction of the Holy Trinity in three persons as a crowned and bearded figure seated frontally on a throne (for God the Father), holding between his knees a cross bearing the crucified Jesus (for God the Son) with, either on the arm of the cross or above the Son's or Father's head, a dove (for God the Holy Ghost), though the last was sometimes omitted. Examples can be seen on the chest of Sir Robert Waterton (d.1425) at Methley (Yorks) and, very beautifully, on that of Sir Hugh Willoughby just mentioned.

Figures of saints and the Trinity were also common on monumental brasses of the period. Sometimes, where the design included an elaborate two-dimensional canopy able to accommodate them, they were set in its side-shafts or in its superstructure, exactly like large-scale stone or alabaster canopies enriched with images in three dimensions. For example, tiers of saints in niches make up the shafts of canopies on two fine brasses of priests, Laurence de St Maur (d.1337) at Higham Ferrers (Northants) and John Blodwell (d.1462) at Balsham (Cambs); while, among brasses with saints in the head of the canopy, good instances occur at Cobham (Kent), including the exceptionally fine specimen for Sir Nicholas Hawberk (d.1407) with the Trinity, Virgin and Child and St George, and at Cowfold (Sussex), where the canopy of Prior Nelond contains the Virgin and Child, St Pancras and St Thomas Becket. On other brasses, by contrast, the deceased were shown in attitudes of prayer or devotion to sacred imagery set, not in canopies but on brackets or in the heads of crosses above. Such brasses have been sadly so ruthlessly destroyed in times of religious iconoclasm that little evidence of their popularity now survives. The destruction was not so total, however, as to deprive us of the exquisite brass of John Mulsho (d.1400) and his wife kneeling before St Faith, now at Geddington (Northants), or that of John Strete, rector (d.1406), kneeling before St Peter and St Paul at Upper Hardres (Kent), among others. A number survive, too, showing the deceased kneeling to the Trinity, including those of Robert Paris and wife (*c.*1400) at Hildersham (Cambs) (*171*), a very attractive piece with the Trinity in a foliated cross, and Thomas Walrond (d.1480) at Childrey (Berks). Very occasionally, an even closer relationship was portrayed between the religious imagery and the deceased, the latter being visibly assisted in their devotions by saintly intercession. So, for example, on the brass of Canon Robert Honywode (d.1523) in St George's Chapel, Windsor, we see him kneeling in prayer before the Virgin and Child, to whom he is being presented by St Catherine of Alexandria.

Religious scenes with sacred figures seem not to have been very common on monuments, and certainly not before the late fifteenth century, although here, it must be said, our knowledge is likely to be particularly curtailed as the result of subsequent destruction, especially with regard to brasses. From what has survived, it would appear that scenes from the Life of the Virgin were among the most popular, reflecting the widespread devotion to her in the medieval Church as the mother of God and queen of Heaven. A particular favourite was the scene of the Annunciation, heralding the incarnation of the Word of God in the person of Jesus Christ, Saviour of mankind; and in such scenes a lily in a pot was always shown beside the Virgin to symbolize her spotless purity. The Annunciation is carved in relief, for example, on the backplate of the canopied monument of Sir Richard Choke (d.1486) at Yatton (Somerset) and on the tomb-chests of (?) Precentor Thomas Boleyn (d.1470) in Wells cathedral and William Rudhall (d.1530) at Ross-on-Wye (Herefs). The last is unusual in depicting the deceased with his family kneeling in prayer before the sacred mystery, but the same convention is also encountered on brasses, like that, for instance, of George Rede (*c.*1500) at Fovant (Wilts). Scenes from the Life of Christ were also portrayed in some numbers and, of course, on occasions included the Virgin, notably in depictions of the Nativity and the Deposition from the Cross. Indeed, the latter was sometimes reduced to a Pietà, that is, a portrayal of the Virgin holding in her arms the dead Christ, as can be seen, for instance, on the brass of Andrew Evyngar (d.1530) in All Hallows, Barking, London. The Nativity of Christ occurs on a brass fragment (*c.*1500) at Cobham (Surrey) and on the altar reredos in the chantry chapel of Bishop Hugh Oldham (d.1519) in Exeter cathedral. The scene from the Life of Christ

170 Minster Lovell (Oxon): a Lord Lovell
(*c.*1450). Detail of tomb-chest: St Christopher

171 *Above right* Hildersham (Cambs): Robert Paris
and wife (*c.*1400). Rubbing of brass

172 *Right* Wells cathedral: Bishop John Harewell
(d.1386). Detail showing the bishop's rebus

most often depicted, however, was the Resurrection, which is carved, for example, on the recess of an Easter Sepulchre monument (*c.*1526) at Woodleigh (Devon) along with the Deposition from the Cross and the Visit of the Three Maries to the sepulchre. Occasionally, scenes from the lives of the saints were included, among them the famous incident in which Pope St Gregory the Great received assurance of Christ's real presence in the Eucharist by the appearance of the Saviour above his altar during Mass. This scene, known as the Mass of St Gregory, enjoyed an appeal on account of its obvious relevance to the doctrine of transubstantiation and the efficacy of the Mass. It appears, among other places, in the carved enrichment of Bishop Oldham's chantry chapel in Exeter cathedral and on the brass of Roger Legh (d.1506) at Macclesfield (Cheshire), the latter showing the deceased and family kneeling in prayer beneath.

All these forms of Christian imagery were effectively brought to an end by the Reformation beginning in the 1530s, since the depiction of angels, saints and religious scenes was anathema to the rising tide of Protestantism. However, although the practice was quickly abandoned over most of the country after the mid-1530s, it could not be eradicated over-night and was for some years astonishingly persistent in one or two areas. In Hampshire and Sussex in particular an interesting group of standing wall monuments combined new Renaissance decoration with a retention of late medieval religious carving into the 1540s and beyond. On one of these at East Tisted (Hants), dating from *c.*1540, Richard Norton and his wife kneel with their children on either side of the Resurrection (*49*), while on another of *c.*1545 at West Wittering (Sussex) members of the Ernley family kneel in prayer to the risen Christ above, with the Annunciation below. Similarly, on a brass plate at Dauntsey (Wilts) Lady Anne Danvers, who died in 1539, continues to kneel in prayer to the Trinity. It is most unlikely that such depictions were produced during Edward VI's reign, but with the return of catholicism under Mary I (1553–58) religious imagery was permitted a general, if short-lived, revival and monument-makers were again free to display it in traditional forms. Thus, the monument of the 6th Lord Delaware (d.1554) at Broadwater (Sussex), a late member of the group mentioned above, includes figures of St George and the Virgin and Child flanking a now empty space formerly occupied by a Christ in Majesty, while the

tomb-chest of the 3rd duke of Norfolk (d.1554) at Framlingham (Suffolk) is adorned with saints differing in style from their medieval antecedents, but serving the same function. Moreover, the brass of Sir John and Lady Spelman (d.1556) at Narborough (Norfolk) shows the deceased kneeling without demur beneath the Resurrection, and that of Humphrey Cheyney (d.1557) at West Hanney (Berks) has the symbols of the Evangelists, which, though less objectionable to reformers, suffered in general the same fate as images. This revival ended, however, with the resumption of Protestantism which followed Mary's death, the rejection of religious imagery on monuments being this time total and unequivocal.

As far as angels were concerned, however, it lasted only until the second decade of the seventeenth century, when angels began to re-appear on monuments, from which they were never again to be banned. At first they were not particularly common, and for much of the seventeenth and eighteenth centuries angelic qualities were more often characterized in the child-like form of cherubs, the great expansion in the depiction of angels coming in the nineteenth century. Numerous examples of their use have been given in previous chapters and there is no need to repeat them here. Suffice it to say, by way of recapitulation, that they returned initially as ancillary figures, often holding curtains open or displaying symbolic objects, but in the course of the seventeenth and eighteenth centuries they tended progressively to take on a more central rôle, commonly of an allegorical nature, culminating in their rather romantic employment on nineteenth-century monuments portraying the salvation and immortality of the deceased. Angels throughout this period, in contrast with those of the middle ages, were depicted in classical or pseudo-classical dress and, as time went by, increasingly assumed a feminine appearance, which became standard in the nineteenth century.

The re-appearance of other religious imagery had to wait much longer. The wall tablet of Robert Plot (d.1671) at Borden (Kent) admittedly shows St Michael overcoming the Devil, but this was highly exceptional at so early a date and it was not before the nineteenth century that the portrayal of divine or saintly figures on monuments again became generally acceptable. The trend was established by such late eighteenth-century monuments as that of Thomas Freke (d.1769) at Kings Sutton (Northants), which in a remarkable way depicts the risen

Christ triumphing over Death, but it came to full development only in the Victorian period in the wake of the medieval revival and the Oxford Movement. The effect, however, was not strictly to copy medieval precedents, for in almost every case the portrayals of Christ and the saints were markedly un-medieval in conception and characteristically Romantic in style. Among many examples, we may cite the monuments of the 2nd Earl Brownlow (d. 1867) at Belton (Lincs), which has the Crucifixion with St Mary and St John; Richard Benyon (d. 1854) at Englefield (Berks), which depicts the Three Maries at the Sepulchre with the risen Christ above; and the 14th Viscount Dillon (d. 1865) at Spelsbury (Oxon), where a relief of the Redeemer flanked by angels appears behind the deceased's recumbent effigy. In Lincoln cathedral the canopied tomb-chest of Bishop Christopher Wordsworth (d. 1885) is enriched all round with standing figures of the twelve apostles, rather after the fashion of saints in the middle ages. But a nice instance of the nineteenth century being more medieval than the middle ages can be seen on the tomb-chest with effigy in Chester cathedral made in 1863 to commemorate Bishop John Pearson, who died in 1686. The sides of the chest are carved with the twelve heads of very Victorian-looking apostles, each accompanied by the statement in the Apostles' Creed traditionally associated with him in the middle ages. Nothing like this was produced in the middle ages, however, and well might the bishop, who died in the High Baroque period, be doubly surprised at the form and iconography of his Gothic and self-consciously medievalist memorial.

The obvious question now arises: What, if anything, took the place of saints and religious imagery on monuments between the mid-sixteenth and nineteenth centuries? The answer is that nothing did so in the fullest sense, since religious attitudes were so different as neither to require nor permit it. And yet society in this period was no less Christian and held fundamentally to the same moral and Christian values, with an equally strong desire to portray them on monuments. This desire found a convenient outlet in allegorical female figures, known as Virtues, which, while being inoffensive to the Protestant mentality, personified the same Christian virtues which the saints in their various ways had exemplified in life. Thus, although the analogy must not be pressed too far, Virtues on post-Reformation monuments performed a rôle which was in part similar to that of saints on

medieval monuments. The emphasis switched, however, from the saving power of virtues external to the deceased, such as those of patron saints, to the moral worth of the deceased's own virtuous life, for, as well as personifying virtues in the abstract, allegorical figures were used to portray in particular the virtues aspired to or possessed by the deceased as a Christian person.

The depiction of Virtues began in the later sixteenth century. Their appearance was undoubtedly a product of the Renaissance, for, although well enough known in non-monumental contexts in the middle ages, they derived ultimately from classical antiquity and were shown typically in loose classical garb, holding the emblems by which they might be identified. At first and in the seventeenth century the virtues most commonly represented were the Four Cardinal Virtues, namely, Fortitude (shown often in a corselet and with a column), Justice (with sword and scales), Prudence (with a serpent and sometimes a mirror) and Temperance (pouring liquid from one jar to another). Often the four were included together, as, for example, on the monuments of Sir William Cordell (d. 1580) at Long Melford (Suffolk), the 1st earl of Salisbury (d. 1612) at Hatfield (Herts), where they support his upper slab (*58*), and Lady Mary Digges (dated 1632) at Chilham (Kent) (*163*), where they surround her commemorative column. Equally, only one or two of the company might be shown. Also personified by allegorical figures were the Three Theological Virtues of Faith (with a cross), Hope (with an anchor) and Charity (with young children). They sit, for example, on the canopy of Sir Anthony Mildmay (d. 1617) at Apethorpe (Northants), but more often appear separately or in pairs. Other virtues, such as Piety, Religion and Truth, were similarly portrayed, and particularly in the eighteenth century the range was much extended to include figures like Benevolence, Innocence, Peace and Sensibility, some of which were not exclusively religious in association but stemmed from the same source. Throughout the period allegorical figures were also used to personify the calling or profession of the deceased, but these will be discussed below in the context of the secular world.

The Secular World

Apart from the symbolism of death and immortality, on the one hand, and of the Christian religion, on the other, monuments of almost every period frequently included symbolic references to people's lives in the world. This 'secular' symbolism was concerned in particular with two main aspects: 1) the deceased's lineage and marriage, and 2) his or her calling or profession.

The first of these involves mainly the enormous subject of heraldry, for, from the early thirteenth century onwards, heraldic shields and devices formed a regular and almost inevitable element of monumental display. Heraldry was (and is) a kind of symbolic shorthand which, to those who understood its principles and were familiar with a sufficient range of armorial bearings, indicated a person's descent and, where appropriate, his marriage connections. The wearing of distinctive coats or shields of arms originated (perhaps in the eleventh century) in the need to be able to recognize armoured knights in battle. At first these arms were personal to the individuals who chose them, but there are signs that in the second half of the twelfth century they were beginning to become hereditary, and clear evidence that this was becoming normal in the early thirteenth century. By about 1225 at the latest, therefore, the situation had arrived in which persons were entitled, by virtue of their birth, to wear and display coats of arms which were exclusive to them. Arms had become, in other words, a mark of birth and individual distinction, the right to which was soon to be closely bound up with titles to lands and honours. Thereafter, the bearing of arms spread from the military classes to ecclesiastics, churches, corporations and, eventually, to a whole range of 'armigerous' (that is, arms-bearing) persons down to the rank of esquire. By the end of the middle ages and in more modern times armorial bearings, having come under centralized control, were granted also to gilds, fraternities, universities, colleges, schools, associations, companies and many other bodies, and are still today a significant aspect of individual and corporate pride.

Heraldic arms were of the greatest importance to those who bore them. It comes as no surprise, therefore, that once arms had become hereditary, they began to appear on monuments. The earliest surviving example in this country occurs, appropriately enough, on the shield worn by a military effigy, William Longsword earl of Salisbury (d. 1226) in Salisbury cathedral, which is carved in relief with six lions deriving ultimately from a shield granted to his grandfather by Henry I in 1127. Arms were carved or painted on the shields of numerous later effigies, though painted versions have since worn away, and were similarly engraved on the shields worn by brass effigies of knights in the first half of the fourteenth century. In the later fourteenth century arms might appear on the jupons of knights, and in the following century on tabards worn over their armour, while effigies of ladies might be clad in heraldic kirtles or mantles. Moreover, in the later thirteenth century shields of arms began commonly to be carved on tomb-chests and, from a little later, to be included in the enrichment of canopies. In the later middle ages heraldic shields, brightly painted and gilded, were extremely common on monuments of all kinds, those on brasses being inlaid with lead to take the necessary colours. The habit reached its height in the later sixteenth and early seventeenth centuries, when monuments were lavishly enriched not only with shields of arms but also with heraldic badges and crests, but, contrary to what is often said about them, these displays were different in degree and not in kind from those of the middle ages. They reflected the same basic desire to set forth the deceased's pride both in his own family descent and in his connections with other families by marriage. In later periods heraldry, though on the whole less obtrusive, remained a constant feature and, even when the deceased was commemorated by a simple wall tablet, his heraldic bearings would be displayed.

In the post-medieval period, and notably in the seventeenth century, monuments often included carvings of full achievements of arms, that is, with shield, helmet, crest, mantling, motto and, in the case of persons of high rank, supporters (usually beasts) at the sides. On the other hand, simple arms, whether of men or women, were typically shown in the seventeenth and eighteenth centuries not on shields, but on oval or roughly oval cartouches. Moreover, in addition to personal arms monuments from the later middle ages onwards might display the arms of a company or other body of which the deceased was a member, thereby referring heraldically to his profession in life.

Before turning to this aspect of secular symbolism, however, it is worth mentioning one charming feature, largely confined to the later middle ages, which, though not heraldic, was equally dependent on the personal identity of the deceased. This was the 'rebus', a carved or painted device which made punning reference to the deceased's name. It is frequently found on church buildings and fittings, where it served to indicate the builders or donors, but occurs occasionally on monuments. Among others, an example can be seen on that of Bishop John Harewell (d.1386) in Wells cathedral (*172*), where, at the feet of the effigy, are carved two hares drinking at a well-head.

The calling or profession of the deceased was, of course, indicated in a general way by the armour or dress in which the effigy, if present, was depicted, but beyond that it was most commonly symbolized by appropriate objects or tools included in the design. As early as the twelfth and thirteenth centuries, carved coffin lids without effigies displayed such things as croziers and mitres (for bishops), swords and shields (for knights), hammers and tongs (for blacksmiths) and so on. This kind of idea recurred on and off throughout the middle ages, notably on brasses of priests which showed merely a chalice and wafer. On other later medieval brasses with figures the deceased was sometimes shown resting his feet against objects indicative of his trade. So, for example, that of Simon Seman, a vintner (d.1433), in St Mary's, Barton-on-Humber (Lincs), has his feet against two wine casks, while several brasses of wool-merchants at Northleach (Glos) have the feet against wool-sacks and sheep. One of the latter has the merchant's personal trade-mark engraved on his wool-sack, exactly as it would have been stamped on real sacks at the time, and so does the brass of John Lyndewode (d.1421) at Linwood (Lincs). In other cases a merchant's mark was commonly engraved on a small plate set separately in the slab, as can be seen on the brasses of Geoffrey Dormer (d.1503) at Thame (Oxon) (*169*) and Thomas Busshe (d.1526) at Northleach.

Symbolism of professions and so on did not, however, become really common until the seventeenth century, from which time it was to be a frequent feature of monumental enrichment down to the twentieth century, whether or not an effigy was included. In the first half of the seventeenth century, for example, it was not uncommon on monuments of scholars and learned gentlemen for upright architectural elements to be carved to resemble piles of books or for 'books' to be displayed on shelves behind effigies. Following the early use of this conceit on the monument of Sir Thomas Bodley (d.1613) in Merton College, Oxford, it is found also, for example, on those of Sir Henry Yelverton (d.1629) at Easton Maudit (Northants) and Sir Thomas Lucy (d.1640) at Charlecote (Warks). The monument of Dean Boys (d.1625) in

Canterbury cathedral (*75*) employs it on so lavish a scale that his recess is visually converted into a study whose walls are lined from top to bottom with books. A delightful variation appears on the monument of a lawyer, Alderman John Jones (d.1630), in Gloucester cathedral, for here the sides consist not of books but of piles of legal deeds, all neatly folded and pigeon-holed, while to the left and right of his demi-figure ink-wells, pens and other clerical paraphernalia are depicted. At High Wycombe (Bucks) the trade of a shoemaker is indicated on the wall tablet of Jacob Wheeler (d.1621) by the whole range of his tools carved in relief. Again, on the front of the monument of George Carew earl of Totnes (d.1629) at Stratford-on-Avon (Warks) an arrangement of cannons, cannon-balls, powder barrels and a flag is displayed, in reference to his having held the office of Master in Ordnance to James I. Nor should one overlook the monument of Lady Dorothy Selby (d.1641) at Ightham (Kent), whose fame as an embroideress is alluded to by the relief carvings of her two most famous pieces of needlework.

Innumerable variations on these themes occurred in subsequent periods. Monuments of military commanders of the later seventeenth and eighteenth centuries commonly displayed elaborate groups of military trophies, usually in relief, including, for example, those of Sir Thomas Wentworth (d.1675) at Silkstone (Yorks) and Gen. Charles Churchill (d.1714) at Minterne Magna (Dorset). Equally, monuments of naval commanders, like that of Rear-Admiral William Caldwell (d.1718) at Birtsmorton (Worcs), depicted ships, nautical instruments and trophies. In the nineteenth century wall tablets of soldiers were frequently carved with weapons and military head-dress, the latter faithfully representing the particular regiments concerned. To take but two examples, they can be seen at Lingfield (Surrey) on the monument of William St Clair, colonel of the Royal Sussex Artillery Militia (d.1879), and at Kinlet (Salop) on that of Charles Childe, captain in the Royal Horse Guards (killed in 1900 in the Boer War) (*173*). By contrast, only a sword and rifle appear on the simple tablet at Aynho (Northants) of Captain Aubrey Cartwright of the Rifle Brigade, killed at Inkermann in 1854 during the Crimean War.

Apart from the military, many other callings, professions and trades were similarly represented. Wall tablets of bishops displayed mitres, croziers and books, such as can be seen, for example, in the cases of Bishops John Pritchett of Gloucester

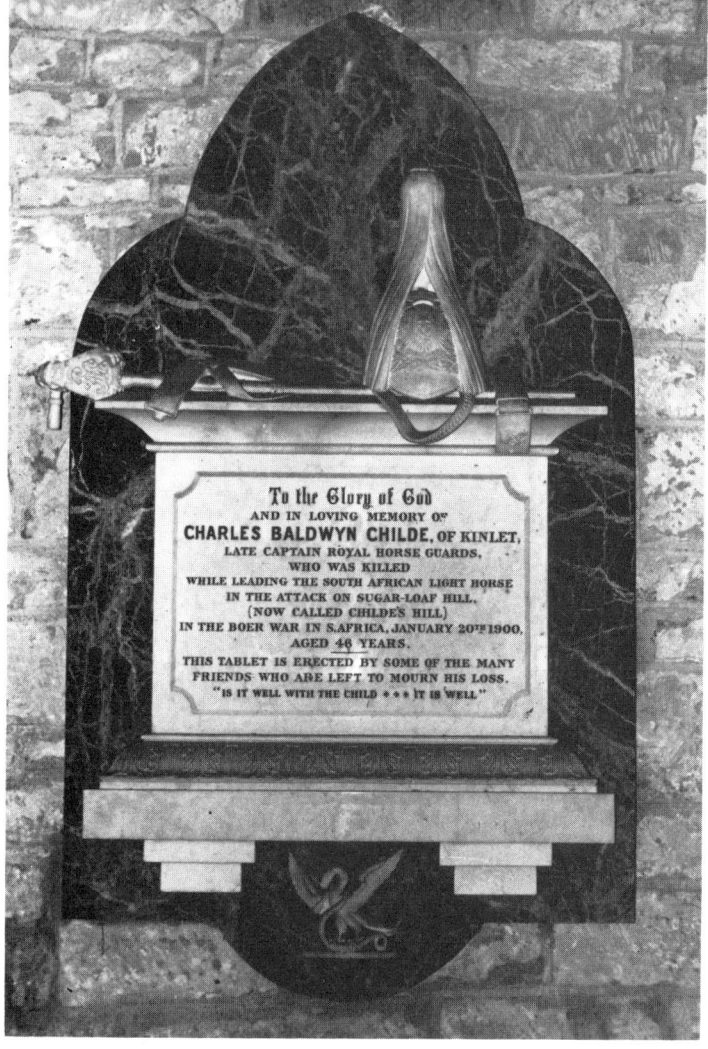

To the Glory of God
AND IN LOVING MEMORY OF
CHARLES BALDWYN CHILDE, OF KINLET,
LATE CAPTAIN ROYAL HORSE GUARDS,
WHO WAS KILLED
WHILE LEADING THE SOUTH AFRICAN LIGHT HORSE
IN THE ATTACK ON SUGAR-LOAF HILL,
(NOW CALLED CHILDE'S HILL)
IN THE BOER WAR IN S.AFRICA, JANUARY 20TH 1900,
AGED 46 YEARS.
THIS TABLET IS ERECTED BY SOME OF THE MANY
FRIENDS WHO ARE LEFT TO MOURN HIS LOSS.
"IS IT WELL WITH THE CHILD *** IT IS WELL"

173 Kinlet (Salop): Charles Childe (d. 1900)

174 Clyffe Pypard (Wilts): Thomas Spackman, carpenter (d. 1786). By John Devall. Detail

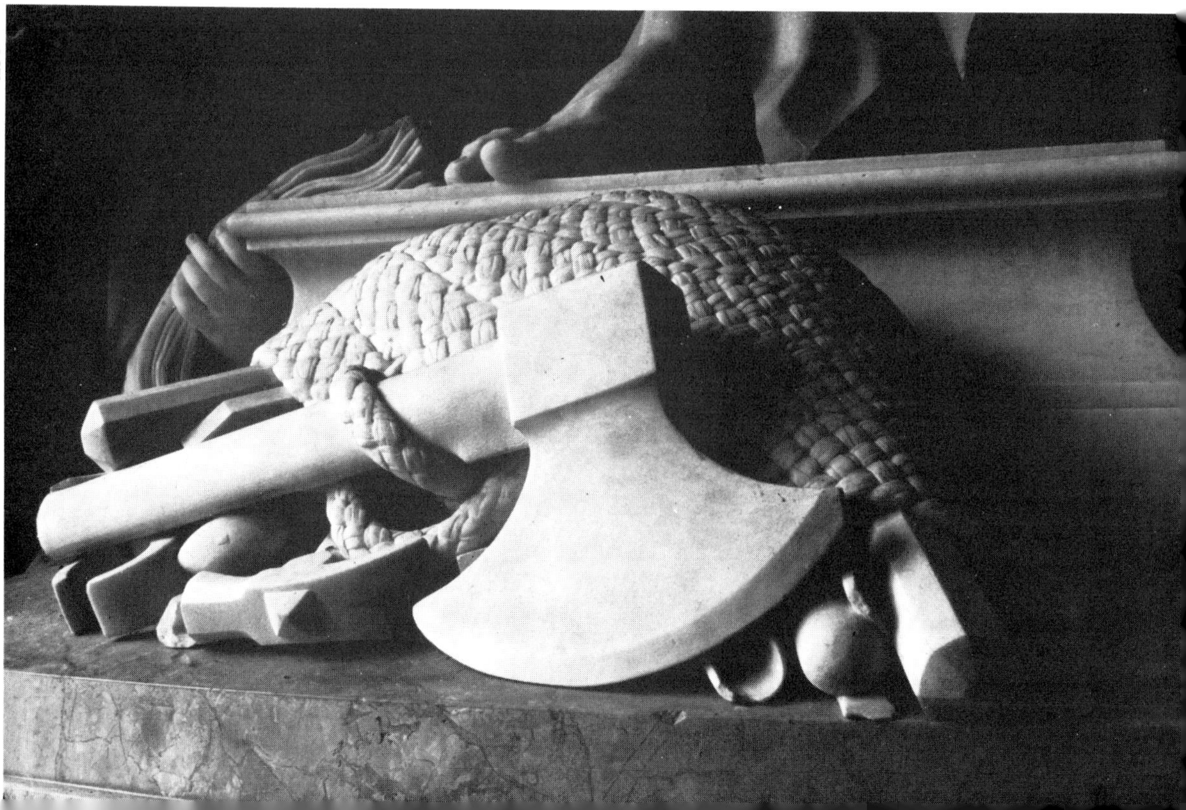

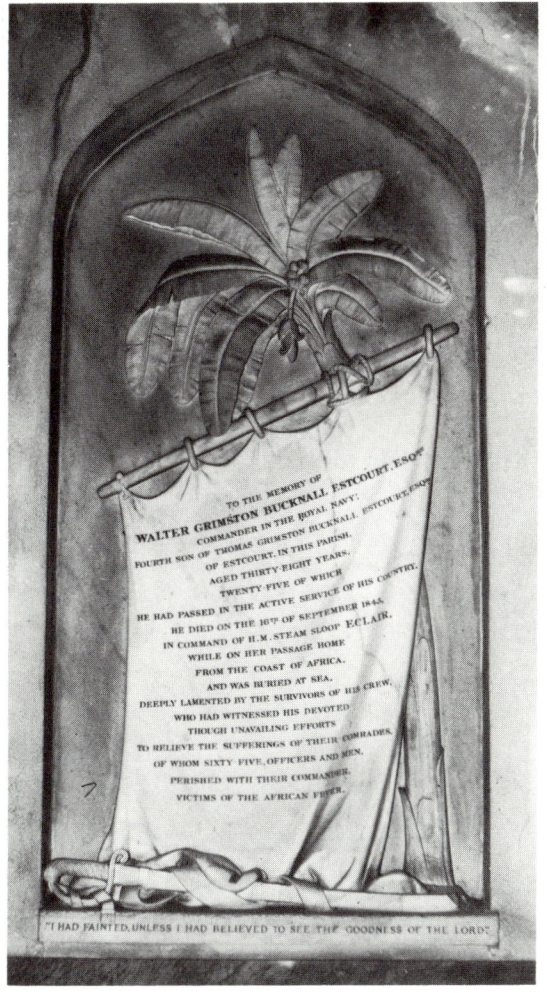

175 Shipton Moyne (Glos): Walter Eastcourt (d.1845)

176 Christ Church, Macclesfield (Cheshire): Charles Roe (d.1781)

(d. 1681) at Harefield (Middx) and Edward Cressett of Llandaff (d. 1755) at Cound (Salop) (*117*). Among the numerous monuments to men of science and the arts in Westminster Abbey, that of William Congreve, the playwright (d. 1728), shows his relief portrait amid books and dramatic masks, while the composer, George Frederick Handel (d. 1759), stands on his monument holding the score of the *Messiah* and surrounded by musical instruments. The monument of a carpenter, Thomas Spackman (d. 1786), at Clyffe Pypard (Wilts) has a beautifully carved basket of tools in front of his standing effigy (*174*); and that of an agricultural improver, John Westcar (d. 1835), at Whitchurch (Bucks) depicts him standing in front of one of his prize cattle with a group of sheep alongside (*123*). So the list goes on.

In the nineteenth century, too, one frequently finds rather involved, though usually quite obvious, symbolism relating to the career of the deceased. Thus, at Bletchingley (Surrey) the hanging monument of Sir William Bensley (d. 1809) displays the kneeling figure of Justice, with her scales, weeping before a draped urn which stands up between reliefs of a ship and an elephant. The inscription makes the references clear, for it records that, after a career in the navy, Sir William went on to serve the East India Company 'in various situations of trust and importance in Bengal'. Again, the modest wall monument of Walter Eastcourt (d. 1845) at Shipton Moyne (Glos) (*175*) shows in relief a palm tree, from the top of whose trunk is suspended, as it were, a sail bearing the inscription, with a sword below. The palm tree suggests Africa, the sail and sword the navy, both being apt in the light of the inscription, which tells of the man's death at sea while in command of H.M. steam sloop, *Eclair*, on her way home from the coast of Africa.

Occasionally in the eighteenth and nineteenth centuries references to the most important event in the deceased's career occur, which, though similar in import to scenes from the life of the deceased common at the time, differed from them in depict-

ing the events symbolically rather than pictorially. A very nice example can be seen at Belton (Lincs), where the monument of Sir John Cust, Speaker of the House of Commons (d. 1770), includes in its design a relief of the Speaker's Chair, the mace and an open book inscribed with the passage from the House of Commons Journal relating to his re-election as Speaker in 1768.

Alternatively, the deceased's calling or profession might be symbolized by allegorical female figures in classical dress, commonly holding appropriate objects or emblems. They first appeared in this rôle in the early seventeenth century, when they occur, for example, on the monument of a mathematician, John Blagrave (d. 1611), in St Laurence's, Reading (Berks) (*57*), and on that of a scholar, Sir Thomas Bodley (d. 1613), in Merton College, Oxford, both of which have been referred to in an earlier chapter. Such figures were most popular, however, in the later eighteenth century. At that time, for instance, the profession of a doctor was indicated on the monument of John Dealtry (d. 1773) in York Minster by a personification of Medicine with her caduceus, and that of an actor on David Garrick's monument (dated 1797) in Westminster Abbey by the Muses of Tragedy and Comedy. Although in these and most other cases the symbolic references were derived from classical antiquity, and indeed sometimes took the form of Greek or Roman goddesses, occasionally allegorical figures were adapted with ease to new and unfamiliar contexts. So, for example, on the monument of an industrialist, Charles Roe (d. 1781), in Christ Church, Macclesfield (Cheshire) (*176*), an allegorical figure holds the unclassical feature of a cog-wheel to symbolize the advancing technology of the Industrial Revolution. Finally, it should be noted that, in addition to these specific allusions, the figure of Fame blowing a trumpet was also employed, especially on monuments of the seventeenth century, to advertise the renown of the deceased's achievements in a general way.

Suggestions for Further Reading

Monuments

Bertram, J., *Lost Brasses*, Newton Abbot, 1976

Burgess, F., *English Churchyard Memorials*, London, 1963; paperback edition 1979

Busby, R.J., *A Companion Guide to Brasses and Brass Rubbing*, London, 1973

Collinson, H., *Country Monuments, their Families and Houses*, Newton Abbot, 1975

Crossley, F.H., *English Church Monuments, AD 1150–1550*, London, 1921

Esdaile, K.A., *English Church Monuments 1510–1840*, London, 1946; *English Monumental Sculpture since the Renaissance*, SPCK, London, 1927

Gardner, A., *Alabaster Tombs of the Pre-Reformation Period in England*, Cambridge, 1940

Greenhill, F.A. *Incised Effigial Slabs*, 2 vols, London, 1976

Macklin, H.W., *Monumental Brasses*, completely revised by J.C. Page-Phillips, London, 1972

Mann, J.G., 'English Church Monuments 1536–1625' *Walpole Society*, vol 21, 1932–3

Norris, M., *Monumental Brasses*, 3 vols, London, 1978

Penny, N., *Church Monuments in Romantic England*, New Haven and London, 1977

Routh, P.E. *Medieval Effigial Alabaster Tombs in Yorkshire*, Ipswich, 1976

Sculpture

Gardner, A., *English Medieval Sculpture*, 2nd edition, Cambridge, 1951

Gunnis, R., *A Dictionary of British Sculptors 1660–1851*, 2nd edition, London, 1968

Mercer, E., *English Art 1553–1625,* Oxford History of English Art, Oxford, 1962

Stone, L., *Sculpture in Britain: the Middle Ages, Pelican History of Art*, London, 1955

Whinney, M., *Sculpture in Britain 1530–1830, Pelican History of Art*, London, 1964

Whinney, M. and Miller, O., *English Art 1625–1714*, Oxford History of English Art, Oxford, 1957

General

Cunnington, C.W., Cunnington, P, and Beard, C., *A Dictionary of English Costume*, 2nd edition, London, 1968

Hall, J., *Dictionary of Subjects and Symbols in Art*, London, 1974

Index

2 Craftsmen, Designers and Sculptors

3 Aspects and Features of Monuments